ENVIRONMENTAL PROTECTION AND JUSTICE

ANDERSON'S
Law School Publications

ADMINISTRATIVE LAW ANTHOLOGY
by Thomas O. Sargentich

ADMINISTRATIVE LAW: CASES AND MATERIALS
by Daniel J. Gifford

ADMIRALTY LAW ANTHOLOGY
by Robert M. Jarvis

APPELLATE ADVOCACY: PRINCIPLES AND PRACTICE (Second Edition)
Cases and Materials
by Ursula Bentele and Eve Cary

A CAPITAL PUNISHMENT ANTHOLOGY
by Victor L. Streib

CASES AND PROBLEMS IN CRIMINAL LAW (Second Edition)
by Myron Moskovitz

THE CITATION WORKBOOK
by Maria L. Ciampi, Rivka Widerman and Vicki Lutz

COMMERCIAL TRANSACTIONS: PROBLEMS AND MATERIALS
Vol. 1: Secured Transactions Under the UCC
Vol. 2: Sales Under the UCC and the CISG
Vol. 3: Negotiable Instruments Under the UCC and the CIBN
by Louis F. Del Duca, Egon Guttman and Alphonse M. Squillante

A CONSTITUTIONAL LAW ANTHOLOGY
by Michael J. Glennon

CONSTITUTIONAL TORTS
by Sheldon H. Nahmod, Michael L. Wells, and Thomas A. Eaton

CONTRACTS
Contemporary Cases, Comments, and Problems
by Michael L. Closen, Richard M. Perlmutter and Jeffrey D. Wittenberg

A CONTRACTS ANTHOLOGY
by Peter Linzer

CORPORATE AND WHITE COLLAR CRIME: AN ANTHOLOGY
by Leonard Orland

A CRIMINAL LAW ANTHOLOGY
by Arnold H. Loewy

CRIMINAL LAW: CASES AND MATERIALS
by Arnold H. Loewy

CRIMINAL PROCEDURE: TRIAL AND SENTENCING
by Arthur B. LaFrance and Arnold H. Loewy

ECONOMIC REGULATION
Cases and Materials
by Richard J. Pierce, Jr.

ELEMENTS OF LAW
by Eva H. Hanks, Michael E. Herz and Steven S. Nemerson

ENDING IT: DISPUTE RESOLUTION IN AMERICA
Descriptions, Examples, Cases and Questions
by Susan M. Leeson and Bryan M. Johnston

ENVIRONMENTAL LAW (Second Edition)
Vol. 1: Environmental Decisionmaking: NEPA and the Endangered Species Act
Vol. 2: Water Pollution; Vol. 3: Air Pollution; Vol. 4: Hazardous Wastes
by Jackson B. Battle, Mark Squillace, Maxine I. Lipeles and Robert L. Fischman

ENVIRONMENTAL PROTECTION AND JUSTICE
Readings and Commentary on Environmental Law and Practice
by Kenneth A. Manaster

Continued

FEDERAL INCOME TAXATION OF PARTNERSHIPS AND OTHER PASS-THRU ENTITIES
by Howard E. Abrams

FEDERAL RULES OF EVIDENCE (Second Edition)
Rules, Legislative History, Commentary and Authority
by Glen Weissenberger

FIRST AMENDMENT ANTHOLOGY
by Donald E. Lively, Dorothy E. Roberts and Russell L. Weaver

INTERNATIONAL HUMAN RIGHTS: LAW, POLICY AND PROCESS
Problems and Materials
by Frank Newman and David Weissbrodt

INTERNATIONAL LAW ANTHOLOGY
by Anthony D'Amato

INTERNATIONAL LAW COURSEBOOK
by Anthony D'Amato

INTRODUCTION TO THE STUDY OF LAW: CASES AND MATERIALS
by John Makdisi

JUDICIAL EXTERNSHIPS: THE CLINIC INSIDE THE COURTHOUSE
by Rebecca A. Cochran

JUSTICE AND THE LEGAL SYSTEM
A Coursebook
by Anthony D'Amato and Arthur J. Jacobson

THE LAW OF DISABILITY DISCRIMINATION
by Ruth Colker

THE LAW OF MODERN PAYMENT SYSTEMS AND NOTES
by Fred H. Miller and Alvin C. Harrell

LAWYERS AND FUNDAMENTAL MORAL RESPONSIBILITY
by Daniel R. Coquillette

PATIENTS, PSYCHIATRISTS AND LAWYERS
Law and the Mental Health System
by Raymond L. Spring, Roy B. Lacoursiere, M.D., and Glen Weissenberger

PROBLEMS AND SIMULATIONS IN EVIDENCE
by Thomas F. Guernsey

A PRODUCTS LIABILITY ANTHOLOGY
by Anita Bernstein

PROFESSIONAL RESPONSIBILITY ANTHOLOGY
by Thomas B. Metzloff

A PROPERTY ANTHOLOGY
by Richard H. Chused

THE REGULATION OF BANKING
Cases and Materials on Depository Institutions and Their Regulators
by Michael P. Malloy

A SECTION 1983 CIVIL RIGHTS ANTHOLOGY
by Sheldon H. Nahmod

SPORTS LAW: CASES AND MATERIALS (Second Edition)
by Raymond L. Yasser, James R. McCurdy and C. Peter Goplerud

A TORTS ANTHOLOGY
by Lawrence C. Levine, Julie A. Davies and Edward J. Kionka

TRIAL PRACTICE
Text by Lawrence A. Dubin and Thomas F. Guernsey
Problems and Case Files with *Video* Presentation
by Edward R. Stein and Lawrence A. Dubin

ENVIRONMENTAL PROTECTION AND JUSTICE

Readings and Commentary
on Environmental Law and Practice

KENNETH A. MANASTER

Professor of Law
Santa Clara University

CINCINNATI
ANDERSON PUBLISHING CO.

MANASTER, ENVIRONMENTAL PROTECTION AND JUSTICE

Copyright © 1995 by Anderson Publishing Co.

Library of Congress Cataloging-in-Publication Data

Environmental protection and justice: readings and commentary on environmental law and practice / Kenneth A. Manaster.
     p.   cm.
   Includes bibliographical references.
   ISBN 0-87084-253-6
   1. Environmental law – United States.   2. Legal ethics – United States.   3. Environmental ethics – United States.   4. Environmental responsibility – United States.   5. Hazardous waste sites – Location – United States.   I. Manaster, Kenneth A.
  KF3775.E546   1995
  344.73'046 – dc20   95-7757
  [347.30446]   CIP

To Ann

Contents

Acknowledgments

I wish to express my appreciation and admiration for the talented research assistance of the following Santa Clara law students who helped greatly in the preparation of this book: Brian Frank, Alexandra McClure, Ted Stevens, and Amy Treadwell. Additionally, the students in the Environmental Law Seminar at Santa Clara in 1993 and 1994 provided invaluable responses to earlier versions of this material.

My thanks go to Barbara Friedrich, Reference Librarian, and to Angeles De Leon and Dorothy Madden, Administrative Assistants, for their generous and hard work. The gracious support of Dean Gerald F. Uelmen, Dean Mack A. Player, and Santa Clara University was indispensable to the completion of this book. The interest and guidance of Dee Dunn and Glen Weissenberger for Anderson Publishing Co. also have meant a great deal to me.

My deepest gratitude is to my family: To my daughter, Jenny, for her enthusiastic interest in this project; my son, Cole, for the extra opportunities he gave me to think about this work (and even this sentence) during nighttime feedings in his first 4½ months; and most especially to my wife, Ann Brandewie, for her unfailing support and so much more for which I am thankful beyond words.

Finally, I gratefully acknowledge the permissions granted by the authors and publishers of the following works to reproduce excerpts in this book:

American Bar Association, Model Code of Professional Responsibility (1969), and Model Rules of Professional Conduct (1983). Copyright © American Bar Association. All rights reserved. Reprinted by permission of the American Bar Association. Copies of this publication are available from Member Services, American Bar Association, 750 North Lake Shore Drive, Chicago, Illinois 60611.

Vicki Been, "What's Fairness Got to Do With It," 78 Cornell Law Review 1001 (1993). Copyright © 1993 by Cornell University. All rights reserved. Excerpts reprinted with permission of the author, the Cornell Law Review, and Fred B. Rothman & Company.

Vicki Been, "Locally Undesirable Land Uses in Minority Neighborhoods: Disproportionate Siting or Market Dynamics?" 103 Yale Law Journal 1383-1422 (1994). Reprinted by permission of the author, the Yale Law Journal Company, and Fred B. Rothman & Company.

Christopher Boerner, Environmental Justice? (1994). Excerpts reprinted by permission of the Center for the Study of American Business, Washington University.

Norman E. Bowie, Towards a New Theory of Distributive Justice, (Amherst: University of Massachusetts Press, 1971). Copyright © 1971 by The University of Massachusetts Press.

Richard O. Brooks, "A New Agenda for Modern Environmental Law," 6 Journal of Environmental Law and Litigation 1 (1991). Copyright © by University of Oregon. Reprinted by permission of the author and University of Oregon.

Bunyan Bryant and Paul Mohai, "Environmental Racism: Reviewing the Evidence." Reprinted from Bunyan Bryant and Paul Mohai, Race and the Incidence of Environmental Hazards (1992), by permission of Westview Press, Boulder, Colorado.

Mary Bryant, "Unequal Justice? Lies, Damn Lies, and Statistics Revisited," Section of Natural Resources, Energy, and Environmental Law News (September-October 1993). Reprinted by permission of the author.

Robert D. Bullard, "Anatomy of Environmental Racism and the Environmental Justice Movement" in Confronting Environmental Racism: Voices from the Grassroots (Robert D. Bullard, ed., 1993). Excerpts reprinted by permission of South End Press.

Robert D. Bullard, Dumping in Dixie: Race, Class and Environmental Quality (1992). Reprinted by permission of Westview Press, Boulder, Colorado.

Robert D. Bullard, "Environmental Equity: Examining the Evidence of Environmental Racism," Land Use Forum, Winter 1993. CEB Land Use Forum, Continuing Education of the Bar, University of California Extension. Reprinted by permission of Continuing Education of the Bar – California.

Celia Campbell-Mohn et al., Environmental Law: From Resources to Recovery (1993). Reprinted with permission of the West Publishing Corporation.

Carnegie Commission on Science, Technology, and Government, Risk and the Environment: Improving Regulatory Decision Making (1993). Reprinted with permission of the Carnegie Commission on Science, Technology, and Government.

Benjamin F. Chavis, Jr., "Foreword" in Confronting Environmental Racism: Voices from the Grassroots (Robert D. Bullard, ed., 1993). Excerpts reprinted by permission of South End Press.

Commission for Racial Justice, United Church of Christ, Toxic Wastes and Race in the United States: A National Report on the Racial and Socio-Economic Characteristics of Communities with Hazardous Waste Sites (1987). Reprinted by permission of the Commission for Racial Justice, United Church of Christ.

John P. Dwyer, "The Pathology of Symbolic Legislation," 17 Ecology Law Quarterly 233 (1990). Copyright © 1990 by Ecology Law Quarterly. Reprinted from Ecology Law Quarterly, Vol. 17, No. 2, by permission of the author and University of California Press Journals Department.

John Hart Ely, Democracy and Distrust: A Theory of Judicial Review (1980). Excerpts reprinted by permission of Harvard University Press.

Monroe H. Freedman and Michael Tigar, Debate on Public Interest Limits on Effective Advocacy (1970). Reprinted by permission of the authors.

Eric T. Freyfogle, Justice and the Earth: Images for Our Planetary Survival (1993). Reprinted with the permission of The Free Press, a Division of Simon & Schuster from Justice and the Earth: Images for Our Planetary Survival by Eric T. Freyfogle. Copyright © 1993 by Eric T. Freyfogle.

J. William Futrell, "Environmental Ethics, Legal Ethics, and Codes of Professional Responsibility," 27 Loyola of Los Angeles Law Review 825 (1994). Reprinted with the permission of the author and the Loyola of Los Angeles Law Review. Copyright © 1994 by the Loyola of Los Angeles Law Review. All rights reserved.

Rachel D. Godsil, "Remedying Environmental Racism," 90 Michigan Law Review 394 (1991). Reprinted by permission of Michigan Law Review.

Benjamin A. Goldman et al., Toxic Wastes and Race Revisited: An Update of the 1987 Report on the Racial and Socioeconomic Characteristics of Communities with Hazardous Waste Sites (1994). Reprinted by permission of the Center for Policy Alternatives.

H.L.A. Hart, The Concept of Law (1961). Copyright © Oxford University Press 1961. Reprinted from The Concept of Law by H.L.A. Hart (1961) by permission of Oxford University Press.

Peter Huber, "Exorcists vs. Gatekeepers in Risk Regulation," Regulation, November 1983. Reprinted with the permission of The American Enterprise Institute for Public Policy Research, Washington, D.C.

W. Thomas Jennings, "California Air Pollution Variances and Federal Enforcement," 1992 California Environmental Law Reporter 111. Reprinted by permission of Matthew Bender & Co., Inc.

Alexandre Kiss and Dinah Shelton, International Environmental Law (1991). Reprinted by permission of Transnational Juris Publications, Inc.

Marianne Lavelle and Marcia Coyle, "Unequal Protection: The Racial Divide in Environmental Law," The National Law Journal, September 21, 1992. Excerpts reprinted with permission of the publisher. These excerpts were originally published in The National Law Journal. Copyright, 1992, The New York Law Publishing Company.

Richard J. Lazarus, "Pursuing 'Environmental Justice': The Distributional Effects of Environmental Protection, 87 Northwestern University Law Review 787 (1993). Reprinted by special permission of Northwestern University School of law, Volume 87, Issue 3, Northwestern University Law Review, pp. 787, 806-08, 810, 816-19, 827-29, 834-36, 839, 842-44, 846, 848-49, 850-52 (1993).

David Luban, Lawyers and Justice: An Ethical Study (1993). Copyright © 1989 by Princeton University Press. Reprinted by permission of Princeton University Press.

Kenneth A. Manaster, "Early Thoughts on Prosecuting Polluters," 2 Ecology Law Quarterly 471 (1971). Copyright © 1971 by Ecology Law Quarterly. Reprinted from Ecology Law Quarterly, Vol. 2, No. 3, by permission of University of California Press Journals Department.

Sheldon M. Novick (ed.), Law of Environmental Protection (1987, 1992). Reprinted with the permission of the copyright holders, Clark Boardman Callaghan and the Environmental Law Institute.

LeRoy C. Paddock, "Environmental Enforcement at the Turn of the Century," 21 Environmental Law 1516 (1991). Reprinted by permission of Environmental Law Journal.

Ellen Frankel Paul, "Set-Asides, Reparations, and Compensatory Justice," in John W. Chapman, Nomos XXXIII: Compensatory Justice(1991). Excerpts reprinted by permission of New York University Press.

Eleanor Randolph, "What Cost a Life? EPA Asks Tacoma," Los Angeles Times, August 13, 1983. Reprinted by permission of the author.

John Rawls, A Theory of Justice (1971), The Belknap Press of Harvard University Press, Copyright © 1971 by the President and Fellows of Harvard College. Reprinted by permission.

Peter L. Reich, "Greening the Ghetto: A Theory of Environmental Race Discrimination," 41 The University of Kansas Law Review 271. Reprinted by permission of the University of Kansas Law Review.

David Richman and Donald B. Bauer, "Responsibilities of Lawyers and Engineers to Report Environmental Hazards and Maintain Client Confidences," Toxics Law Reporter, Vol. 5, No. 45, pp. 1458 *et seq.* (April 17, 1991). Copyright © 1991 by the Bureau of National Affairs, Inc. (800-372-1033). Reprinted by permission of the Bureau of National Affairs, Inc.

Ross Sandler, "Where the Jobs Are," The Environmental Forum (November/December 1993). Copyright © Environmental Law Institute, 1994. Reprinted with permission. All rights reserved.

Santa Clara Center for Occupational Safety and Health, Letter excerpted in Silicon Valley Toxics Action, Vol. 13, No. 1 (Spring 1994). Reprinted by permission of the authors.

Keith Schneider, "Unbending Regulations Incite Move to Alter Pollution Laws," New York Times, January 11, 1993. Copyright © 1993 by the New York Times Company. Reprinted by permission.

David Schoenbrod, "Environmental 'Injustice' Is About Politics, Not Racism," Wall Street Journal, February 23, 1994. Reprinted by permission of the author.

Daniel P. Selmi and Kenneth A. Manaster, State Environmental Law (1989, 1994). Reprinted by permission of Clark Boardman Callaghan.

Philip Shabecoff, A Fierce Green Fire: The American Environmental Movement. Copyright © 1993 by Philip Shabecoff. Reprinted by permission of Hill and Wang, a division of Farrar, Straus & Giroux, Inc.

David Sive, "An Environmentalist's View of 'Environmental Racism'," Environmental Law Newsletter of the Standing Committee on Environmental Law, Volume 12, Number 1 (Fall/Winter 1992-93). Copyright © American Bar Association. All rights reserved. Reprinted by permission of the American Bar Association.

Lawrence J. Straw, Jr., "California Air Pollution Variances," 1991 California Environmental Law Reporter 203. Reprinted by permission of Matthew Bender & Co., Inc.

Roberto Suro, "Pollution Weary Minorities Try Civil Rights Tack," New York Times, November 29, 1993. Copyright © 1993 by the New York Times Company. Reprinted by permission.

Gerald Torres, "Introduction: Understanding Environmental Racism," 63 University of Colorado Law Review 839 (1992). Reprinted by permission of University of Colorado Law Review.

William Tucker, Progress and Privilege: America in the Age of Environmentalism (1982). Reprinted by permission of the author.

Peter S. Wenz, Environmental Justice (1988). Reprinted by permission of the State University of New York Press.

Editorial Note

In the excerpts from other works presented in this book, the editorial omission of words within a sentence is indicated by an ellipsis. Omissions of sentences or paragraphs, however, usually are not indicated.

Similarly, omissions of footnotes and citations from an excerpt are not shown. When a footnote has been retained, the original numbering has not been followed. Lastly, footnotes appearing within an excerpt but added by the author of this book are preceded by "[Ed.]".

Chapter 1
Introduction

A. The Role of the Environmental Lawyer

1. Overview

It is easy to describe the broad purposes of environmental law. Lawyers, judges, legislators, and others working on environmental matters readily speak of the need to protect the quality of the Earth's environment for the benefit of human health and welfare. Similarly, the importance of safeguarding diverse species of plants and animals, and of maintaining a safe and "livable" world for future generations, also is declared in a multitude of statutes, judicial decisions, and other legal pronouncements. The seriousness of these objectives cannot be overstated.

Impressive statutory declarations of these purposes consistently are found in the seminal environmental legislation of the late 1960's and early 1970's, as well as in more recently enacted laws. This repetition reflects more than mere oratorical custom. Instead it highlights the continuing, complex challenge faced by the United States and other nations to take much better care of the global environment.

A large corps of environmental lawyers has developed to work with these environmental protection goals and with the regulatory measures that implement them. These lawyers can be found, of course, in the national environmental law groups that were formed in the halcyon days of the environmental movement beginning in the late 1960's. There are even more environmental lawyers in government agencies and law enforcement offices at the federal, state, regional, and local levels.

Additionally, environmental lawyers are now employed in an infinite variety of regulated entities, including manufacturing corporations, electric utilities, construction companies, food processing firms, waste disposal companies, universities, and mining and other natural resource development ventures. Government agencies that engage in waste disposal, construction, resource development, or other polluting activities also have found it necessary to include environmental lawyers on their staffs. Finally, private law firms now commonly have environmental lawyers within their ranks.

In light of this increasing diversity in the clientele served by environmental lawyers, it becomes increasingly difficult to understand how the work of environmental lawyers links to the broad environmental protection goals our society has declared. In other words, how do we answer the general question often asked by non-lawyers: "What do environmental lawyers do?"

At a very superficial level of discourse, of course, the question is not troublesome: The environmental lawyer responds to environmental protection goals and requirements from the perspective of his or her specific client. This legal work usually places the environmental lawyer in the midst of a process for the resolution of disputes over the standards of conduct that are to govern certain activities that have environmental side-effects.

To describe the attorney's role in this general way is to present a bland description of the environmental lawyer as merely a "hired gun," possessing no personal, environmental values. Clearly that description would not be accepted by the environmental lawyers who represent environmental groups, whether national or local and whether concerned with a broad range of environmental issues or having a single-issue focus. Those lawyers, since the inception of this field, have worked with passion and skill for the strong environmental values they share with their clients.

Beyond this category of environmental lawyers, however, it is less evident that client representation and environmental values are in harmony. Particularly difficult to reconcile is the role of the environmental lawyer who serves a regulated entity – a polluter or developer – on the proverbial "other side of the fence." This is, of course, where most attorneys working in this field are found nowadays. Must we conclude that these modern environmental lawyers, serving these types of clients, either are devoid of concern for environmental protection, or are compelled to set aside their environmental sensibilities if they wish to provide effective representation to a regulated entity? This question is distressing, particularly when pondered by idealistic law students and young lawyers contemplating a career in environmental law.

Before the question can be answered, its implicit premise should be examined. The premise is that any regulated entity by definition is opposed to environmental protection goals and their associated requirements. The good guys – bad guys dichotomy that has characterized much environmental policy debate seems to rest on this premise. In contrast, the experience of environmental lawyers for polluters and developers, and of environmental regulators as well, tends increasingly to undercut the validity of the premise. Few, if any, regulated interests still wish to be free of all, or even most, environmental protection obligations. Whatever vestiges of such an attitude may have been encountered in the early years of environmental law now have largely disappeared,[1] but the rhetoric of our political debates does not usually recognize this.

In this modern context, it is usually both simplistic and erroneous to see the regulated entity's objectives as "anti-environmental," and thus to see its lawyer as just a hired

---

[1] "Recent public opinion polls have shown widespread support for strong environmental protection programs. Increasingly, we also find that the level of environmental sensitivity within the business community mirrors the rising level of public concern for environmental quality. Indeed, we can assume that at least some of the people who express support for environmental protection in opinion surveys are the same people charged with environmental protection duties in industry. . . . [W]e identify good guys and bad guys, yet we know that we distort the truth in doing so." Kenneth A. Manaster, "Ten Paradoxes of Environmental Law," 27 Loyola of Los Angeles Law Review 917, 932-33 (1994).

gun uncritically serving such objectives. In contrast to that view of the environmental lawyer's role, the thesis underlying these readings is quite different. The thesis is that environmental lawyers serving regulated entities, as well as environmental lawyers serving any other type of client, seek to reconcile environmental protection goals with important concepts of justice. That is the distinctive and challenging role lawyers perform in the making and implementation of environmental policy.

This role distinguishes environmental lawyers from the other active participants in environmental processes, most notably the scientific and technical experts who are of increasing importance as environmental laws and regulations become more and more complex. Most of the legal standards environmental lawyers work with nowadays are highly technical in nature. Many environmental managers and consultants are becoming extremely adept at understanding, interpreting, and applying these standards — often without the aid of lawyers. As this trend develops, it might appear that lawyers have less and less to add to environmental regulatory processes,[2] other than their training in the procedures of lawmaking and dispute resolution, and their customary comfort with public speaking in various settings. Surely that training, and that capability of serving as an articulate spokesperson, enable the environmental lawyer to make distinctive contributions of a sort that cannot be made by environmental engineers, chemists, biologists, toxicologists, hydrogeologists, and other such experts. But that is not all the lawyer brings. The lawyer's training and skills, coupled with the lawyer's professional responsibility to work toward a more just society, enable the environmental lawyer to make a unique contribution: To promote environmental quality while at the same time promoting claims for justice — for fair and equitable treatment — in the processes and outcomes the legal system produces. This sensitivity to fundamental values — both environmental and nonenvironmental — and this responsibility to work to reconcile them when conflicts appear, are hallmarks of the environmental lawyer's role.

Although the modern environmental lawyer works almost constantly with technical experts, the lawyer — whether representing a regulatory agency or an industrial polluter, a citizens group or a municipal landfill operator — is not just one more technical expert on the client's team. The environmental lawyer's role ultimately is much more than that: It is to protect the environment and to serve justice. These readings seek to illuminate some of the most important problem areas in which environmental lawyers are called upon to meet this difficult, dual responsibility.

Whether the reader studies all of this book, or only selected chapters, it is the author's

---

[2] A very negative view of environmental lawyers was indicated in a 1993 news report that the Administrator of the U. S. Environmental Protection Agency hoped to reduce litigation under the federal Superfund program "by suggesting, among other solutions, that corporations bypass lawyers by sending their CEOs to negotiate with senior EPA officers. 'This is not to denigrate lawyers,' she says, 'but the CEO can see the company's interest as a whole and will often move when his lawyers are paralyzed.'" "Toxic Dumps: The Lawyers' Money Pit," Time, September 13, 1993, at 64.

A more positive assessment of modern lawyers, including environmental lawyers, is suggested in Robert C. Clark, "Why So Many Lawyers? Are They Good or Bad?" 61 Fordham Law Review 275 (1992).

hope that the reader will gain greater understanding of this responsibility. With such understanding, it also is hoped that the reader will approach both career planning and the actual practice of environmental law with more of the clarity, commitment, and personal integrity that environmental protection and justice deserve.

The last portion of this Chapter 1 explores ethical concerns arising from possible conflicts between the lawyer's own environmental values and the lawyer's duty to the client. In Chapter 2 various concepts of justice are introduced, providing a reference point for later chapters' examination of specific types of legal disputes and their stakes. Chapter 3 addresses the great variety of factors that influence the setting of regulatory priorities in environmental policy, and that thereby allocate the benefits and burdens of environmental protection programs.

Chapters 4, 5, and 6 focus on the types of justice concerns that arise most commonly in the practice of environmental law. These chapters examine fairness issues that arise in three major facets of environmental law, *viz.*, the selection of targets for enforcement or cleanup action, the processes for administering and enforcing environmental standards, and access to decisional processes and data.

Finally, Chapter 7 addresses the extraordinarily complex mixture of environmental protection and justice interests that come into play in controversies over the siting of polluting or risk-creating activities. As will be seen, these siting disputes bring together virtually all of the major environmental concerns and concepts of justice examined in the preceding chapters.

Especially in Chapter 7, as well as in portions of the preceding chapters, the concerns often labeled nowadays as "environmental justice" will be presented, i.e., the impacts of environmental law and regulation on low-income and minority communities. The readings thus address the fundamental claims for fairness and equity that the "environmental justice movement" raises. At the same time, however, and without diminishing the gravity and urgency of those claims, this book is intended to remind us that justice is an essential aspect of the environmental lawyer's responsibility for all types of cases and for all types of clients.

2. The Changing Marketplace

Although environmental law has continued to grow as a practice area, even when demand for other legal specialties has diminished, there are forces at work in the legal marketplace that increasingly will change environmental practice. These changes further compel the attorney to consider carefully his or her role, responsibilities, personal values, and professional objectives.

Ross Sandler, "Where the Jobs Are," The Environmental Forum, Volume 10, Number 6, Nov.-Dec. 1993, at 12.

More industrial firms will turn to in-house personnel to handle regulatory environmental affairs. It is cheaper and the work has [become] and will continue to become more routine. Non-lawyer environmental managers can handle much of the work. Most regulatory work at environmental agencies is performed by non-lawyers. It should be of no surprise that the regulated community also will come to rely on non-lawyers to interact with their counterparts at the agencies.

Engineering firms will hold their own and perhaps even grow at the expense of the law firms. There is substantial overlap between what engineering firms and law firms do in the regulatory area. For many projects, there is no particular reason why a competent engineer cannot handle most regulatory matters, except those involving enforcement proceedings. Environmental lawyers all know horror stories about engineers or other non-lawyers who have caused major problems. But for a large percentage of clients, the risk of a mistake is not large enough to hire both a lawyer and an engineer. With obvious overlap between the professions, cost becomes a major factor, and cost favors the engineer.

Environmental law will not retreat to the world of the 1970's. Regulations and the needs of clients have expanded far too much for that to occur. But it does appear that the pendulum is swinging in favor of firms with regulatory skills rather than litigation skills, in favor of geographical advantage over national practice, in favor of firms with lower fee schedules rather than higher, and in favor of non-lawyers for many routine or regulatory matters. There will, of course, be wide variation from firm to firm and area to area. Nonetheless, these structural forces in the marketplace should have a pronounced impact on the environmental law field for the remainder of [the] 1990s.

B. Ethical Concerns: The Lawyer's Values Versus Duty to the Client

Obviously in environmental law practice, as in all other fields of law, the lawyer works for a client and seeks to further the client's immediate objectives. Thus service to the client provides the context in which the fundamental role of the environmental lawyer is performed. Some environmental lawyers appear to work in a rather different context, for they enjoy the luxury, in effect, of being able to set their client's objectives, or at least to guide them to a very great extent. This is the heady experience of lawyers in public interest, environmental law firms. The firm and the client are essentially one and the same, often with only an advisory board or board of trustees signifying a distinction. Even lawyers in government enforcement offices, such as a state attorney general's office, at times enjoy broad latitude to set the environmental agenda for the client, the people of the jurisdiction.

Ordinarily, however, there is a real client—an individual, a company, a group of citizens, a trade association, an elected or appointed government official, or a governmental board—whose needs and concerns provide the impetus for the environmental lawyer's work. The readings in this book illustrate some of the most basic problem areas in which environmental lawyers seek to serve such clients and at the same time work for environmental protection and justice.

Preliminarily, however, the lawyer-client relationship presents a more personal and worrisome problem for the environmental lawyer: What is the environmental lawyer's ethical, professional responsibility when a present or prospective client proposes to embark on a course of conduct that the environmental lawyer considers repugnant? This repugnance may arise on various bases. The client's intended conduct may be contrary to the lawyer's own environmental values, contrary to legal requirements for environmental protection, or otherwise inconsistent with the lawyer's responsibility to promote a just and efficient legal system. These types of conflicts between the lawyer's values and the client's supposed needs can arise directly as between the lawyer and client. They also can arise indirectly—with equal or greater discomfort coupled with fear of adverse impacts on one's career—whenever a junior lawyer is directed by a senior lawyer in the same office to work on a matter that the junior finds unpalatable on grounds such as these.

1. Problems

Consider the following five hypothetical problems and how you would respond to them on the basis of your own personal values. Consider also what further guidance is offered by the readings on professional responsibility presented after these problems.

a. A chemical company proposes to build a new manufacturing plant adjacent to a river that has long been used for recreational fishing and that thus far has very little industrial activity in its vicinity. The plant design provides for some discharge of water pollutants into the river, although the concentrations of these pollutants will be well within all applicable effluent limitations.

You have been directed, by a senior partner of the law firm that recently hired you, to assist the company in preparation of the permit application for this water discharge and in any ensuing negotiations with the permitting agency over the terms and conditions of the permit. You have long enjoyed recreational fishing on this and other relatively pristine rivers. You would much prefer to see this river continue to be unaffected by any new industrial discharges at all.

b. Your client is a paint manufacturing company some of whose employees recently spilled a small quantity of product on the ground at one of the company facilities. The employees quickly cleaned up the spill, but not before a portion of it had flowed into a nearby creek. Applicable environmental regulations require that a chemical spill on land or into any waterway be promptly reported to regulatory agencies.

The client does not wish to make such reports, because the spill was small, it was quickly cleaned up, the portion in the water was quickly dispersed with no apparent, adverse effects, and the agencies might impose civil or criminal penalties for this minor incident. Your client has told you the details of this incident, but has rejected your advice that the required reports be submitted.

c. You are a lawyer for a state general services agency that is in charge of state buildings. The agency proposes to close one of the state's very large, old office buildings and to demolish it. The site then will be turned into a large public park.

Although the state has a statute that usually requires the preparation of an environmental impact statement before a proposal of this magnitude can be carried out, the top management of the agency wishes to save the expense and delay that would be caused by a full environmental review process. You have been directed by the head of the agency to edit the project description to make sure the proposal would not trigger the statutory environmental review requirements.[3]

d. A well-established, local environmental group is opposed to a new residential subdivision project because of the increased traffic congestion, and decreased open space for parklands, that would result from the project. Although the appropriate government agencies have approved the project on the basis of a thorough environmental impact statement, the group would like you to represent it in filing a lawsuit challenging the adequacy of the statement.

There are a few, minor aspects of the statement that technically may not be in full compliance with statutory requirements. The environmental group hopes that a lawsuit would create enough additional expense and delay to persuade the project developer to give up on this location, and then to kill the project entirely or attempt to build it in another community.

e. A recently-formed, local homeowners association is opposed to a proposed low income housing project to be constructed in the community by the municipal housing authority. The homeowners are opposed to economic and racial diversity in their community, and they also fear adverse effects on their property values.

Although environmental impacts of the project are not their main concern, the homeowners have ascertained that the housing authority's environmental impact statement was very poorly done and probably would not survive judicial scrutiny. The homeowners association wants you to represent it in filing a lawsuit challenging the adequacy of the statement and seeking to enjoin the project for a period of at least one year, the time it would take to prepare a proper environmental impact statement.

2. Professional Responsibility Standards

American Bar Association, Model Code of Professional Responsibility (1969)

Canon 2

A lawyer should assist the legal profession in fulfilling its duty to make legal counsel available.

---

[3] Consider whether your response to management's directive would be different if the proposal were reversed, i.e., if the plan were to destroy a large public park in order to construct a large office building. Should your appraisal of the basic environmental wisdom of the proposal affect your obligations regarding compliance with the statute?

Ethical Consideration 2-26

A lawyer is under no obligation to act as advisor or advocate for every person who may wish to become his client; but in furtherance of the objective of the bar to make legal services fully available, a lawyer should not lightly decline proffered employment. The fulfillment of this objective requires acceptance by a lawyer of his share of tendered employment which may be unattractive both to him and the bar generally.

Ethical Consideration 2-30

Employment should not be accepted by a lawyer when he is unable to render competent service or when he knows or it is obvious that the person seeking to employ him desires to institute or maintain an action merely for the purpose of harassing or maliciously injuring another. Likewise, a lawyer should decline employment if the intensity of his personal feeling, as distinguished from a community attitude, may impair his effective representation of a prospective client.

****

American Bar Association, Model Rules of Professional Conduct (1983)

Preamble

[1] A lawyer is a representative of clients, an officer of the legal system and a public citizen having special responsibility for the quality of justice.

[8] In the nature of law practice, . . . conflicting responsibilities are encountered. Virtually all difficult ethical problems arise from conflict between a lawyer's responsibilities to clients, to the legal system and to the lawyer's own interest in remaining an upright person while earning a satisfactory living. The Rules of Professional Conduct prescribe terms for resolving such conflicts. Within the framework of these Rules many difficult issues of professional discretion can arise. Such issues must be resolved through the exercise of sensitive professional and moral judgment guided by the basic principles underlying the Rules.

Rule 1.2 Scope of Representation

(a) A lawyer shall abide by a client's decisions concerning the objectives of representation, subject to paragraphs (c), (d) and (e) . . .

(b) A lawyer's representation of a client . . . does not constitute an endorsement of the client's political, economic, social or moral views or activities.

. . .

(d) A lawyer shall not counsel a client to engage, or assist a client, in conduct that the lawyer knows is criminal or fraudulent, but a lawyer may discuss the legal consequences of any proposed course of conduct with a client and may counsel or assist a client to make a good faith effort to determine the validity, scope, meaning or application of the law.

Rule 1.16 Declining or Terminating Representation

(a) Except as stated in paragraph (c), a lawyer shall not represent a client or, where representation has commenced, shall withdraw from the representation of a client if:

(1) the representation will result in violation of the rules of professional conduct or other law; . . .

(b) Except as stated in paragraph (c), a lawyer may withdraw from representing a client if withdrawal can be accomplished without material adverse effect on the interests of the client, or if:

(1) the client persists in a course of action involving the lawyer's services that the lawyer reasonably believes is criminal or fraudulent; . . .

(3) a client insists upon pursuing an objective that the lawyer considers repugnant or imprudent; . . . or

(6) other good cause for withdrawal exists.

(c) When ordered to do so by a tribunal, a lawyer shall continue representation notwithstanding good cause for terminating the representation.

Rule 2.1 Advisor

In representing a client, a lawyer shall exercise independent professional judgment and render candid advice. In rendering advice, a lawyer may refer not only to law but to other considerations such as moral, economic, social and political factors, that may be relevant to the client's situation.

Comment: [2] It is proper for a lawyer to refer to relevant moral and ethical considerations in giving advice. Although a lawyer is not a moral advisor as such, moral and ethical considerations impinge upon most legal questions and may decisively influence how the law will be applied.

Rule 3.1 Meritorious Claims and Contentions

A lawyer shall not bring or defend a proceeding, or assert or controvert an issue therein, unless there is a basis for doing so that is not frivolous, which includes a good faith argument for an extension, modification or reversal of existing law.

Comment: The action is frivolous . . . if the client desires to have the action taken primarily for the purpose of harassing or maliciously injuring a person or if the lawyer is unable either to make a good faith argument on the merits of the action taken or to support the action taken by a good faith argument for an extension, modification or reversal of existing law.

Rule 3.2 Expediting Litigation

A lawyer shall make reasonable efforts to expedite litigation consistent with the interests of the client.

Comment: Dilatory practices bring the administration of justice into disrepute. Delay should not be indulged merely for the convenience of the advocates, or for the purpose of frustrating an opposing party's attempt to obtain rightful redress or repose. It is not a justification that similar conduct is often tolerated by the bench and bar. The question is whether a competent lawyer acting in good faith would regard the course of action as having some substantial purpose other than delay. Realizing financial or other benefit from otherwise improper delay in litigation is not a legitimate interest of the client.

****

J. William Futrell, "Environmental Ethics, Legal Ethics, and Codes of Professional Responsibility," 27 Loyola of Los Angeles Law Review 825, 834-40 (1994).

The United States has built up a complex regime of laws and regulations designed to protect public health and the environment. But this system is not self-implementing. Achievement of the environmental protection goals envisioned by these statutes requires not only concerted enforcement efforts on the part of the government, but also the consistent cooperation of the private environmental bar, the lawyers representing the regulated industries.

The key role of the private bar is due to the unique characteristics of environmental law. Environmental law, with its mixture of science and policy, operates through a complex system of regulations that relies for its effectiveness on massive inputs of information and self-reporting by those regulated. The need for more explicit ethical guidance drafted with environmental lawyers in mind becomes greater as environmental regulations proliferate and lawyers take on an increasingly significant role in the administration of the environmental law system—through advising clients on compliance, negotiating with government authorities, and engaging in litigation. These lawyers are essential players in providing the information on which the whole system's performance depends.

Current codes of attorney conduct do not directly address the heightened duties of environmental lawyers to assist their clients in implementing the new self-reporting schemes of the regulatory state. The current codes are based on a tradition of advising the client to offer as little information as possible in order to avoid self-incrimination. Under such codes discreet silence—not open disclosure—is the norm. This approach runs counter to the operation of our environmental laws.

Traditionally, the sources of the rules regulating attorney behavior have been codes of professional conduct drafted by committees of lawyers and administered by state bar associations. Over half the states now have codes patterned after the American Bar Association's Model Rules of Professional Conduct; most of the rest base their codes on the Rules' predecessor, the Model Code of Professional Responsibility. Both the Model Code and the Model Rules implicitly assume that the adversarial system is the lawyer's proper arena. The paradigm case on which most of the rules were modeled is that of the lone criminal defendant, for whom a lawyer is the only means of asserting innocence and who seeks to prevail against the system by stonewalling the government. Although the rules have been supplemented to respond to problems unique to corporate clients, government lawyers, and other specialized practice groups, the underlying premise remains: Lawyers should subsume their personal ethical beliefs and moral stances to the positions that zealous advocacy of their clients' interests require. There is little guidance on how legal ethics meshes with environmental ethics.

The duties of government lawyers also demand scrutiny. The intentional misrepresentation of facts or law is a generic problem in legal ethics, but is especially sensitive in the environmental law field with its law-science mix. The omission, suppression, or willful misinterpretation of facts or law should carry greater penalty in environmental law because of the need to apply uncertain scientific data.[4]

Increasingly, federal agency enforcement officials and others are responding to the critical role of attorneys in promoting or undercutting regulatory compliance by heightening attorney responsibilities under complex regulatory statutes to exceed levels of conduct mandated by state bar rules. Under this approach lawyers who fail to urge their clients to disclose information in doubtful situations may be charged with aiding and abetting – or even causing – any consequent violations. Alternatively, regulatory agencies may argue that the public law aspect of the statutes they administer effectively renders attorneys fiduciaries – not of their clients alone, but of the public interest in implementing federal laws and regulations – thus imposing on the attorneys themselves an independent duty to disclose potential violations.

Most notably, the Federal Office of Thrift Supervision recently applied such an approach to the law firm of Kaye, Scholer, Fierman, Hays & Handler, seeking $275 million in civil penalties against the firm for its alleged failure to disclose to the government the poor lending practices of its client, Lincoln Savings & Loan.[5]

In fact, the practice of environmental law demands even stronger regard for the public interest than does securities or banking practice. Environmental statutes are motivated by a broad need to protect the public, often from harms that may not be immediate but are far-reaching in their ability to disrupt and destroy. Environmental law cannot protect society unless environmental lawyers ensure that it does so. Guidance on how to resolve the conflicting demands of client advocacy and protection of the public interest in environmental protection will benefit not only the legal profession, but society as a whole.

The Model Rules themselves supply a basis for further study of the demands the public interest may make on the environmental attorney in the regulatory world. Rule 2.1 states that "[i]n rendering advice, a lawyer may refer not only to law but to other

---

[4] [Ed.] In a recent case two U.S. Justice Department attorneys were found to have breached their ethical duties by concealing the fact that EPA's on-scene coordinator for a CERCLA cleanup had misrepresented his academic achievements and credentials. *U.S. v. Shaffer Equipment Company*, 11 F.3d 450 (4th Cir. 1993). *See also* "Court Punishes Two Government Attorneys for Concealing Information in CERCLA Case," Environment Reporter (BNA), October 21, 1994, at 1218.

[5] [Ed.] Mr. Futrell's article was written prior to *O'Melveny & Myers v. Federal Deposit Insurance Corp.*, ___ U.S. ___, 114 S.Ct. 2048 (1994), and thus does not address that decision's possible implications for his analysis.

considerations such as moral, economic, social, and political factors, that may be relevant to the client's situation.''

The source of the ethical principles that are needed to guide environmental lawyers may already exist, in the form of the environmental laws those lawyers are charged with interpreting and administering. Aldo Leopold convincingly articulated the idea of an environmental ethic and the vision of how that ethic could guide social development; he called for a land ethic reflecting a conviction of individual responsibility for the health of the land and its self-renewal. [T]his ethical ideal received its strongest and most significant endorsement, and became transmuted into a principle that would shape society, in the environmental protection laws passed by Congress in the late 1960s and early 1970s. Yet these laws are not self-effectuating. Environmental lawyers have a primary role in ensuring that the purposes of these statutes will be fully achieved. The principles of environmental ethics, now endorsed in national statutes, provide the lodestar for the development of an environmentally and socially responsible code of behavior to guide the day-to-day actions of the environmental lawyer.

****

David Richman and Donald B. Bauer, "Responsibilities of Lawyers and Engineers to Report Environmental Hazards and Maintain Client Confidences: Duties in Conflict," *Toxics Law Reporter*, April 17, 1991, at 1458.

Lawyers and engineers are bound by the ethics of their respective professions to keep in confidence information that they learn in the client's service or that the client imparts to them in confidence. At times that confidential information concerns acts of the client or conditions for which the client is responsible that pose a danger to third parties. On these occasions, to keep the client's confidence can mean allowing others to suffer a harm that disclosure could avert.

It is the exceptional case in which the client refuses or fails to act to abate the danger. In those cases, the lawyer and engineer are faced with the vexing dilemma of how to reconcile conflicting obligations. The professional is bound on the one hand by the duty of confidentiality to honor the client's confidences and secrets. Breach of the duty may be actionable under tort law and may subject the lawyer or engineer to professional disciplinary action. In seeming opposition to that duty are three others: the ethical duty to refrain from assisting a client in the commission of acts that are criminal or fraudulent; a possible statutory duty to report unsafe environmental conditions; and the moral duty to protect fellow human beings and the environment from avoidable and possibly irreversible injury. Breach of any of those duties may, in a given set of circumstances, expose the professional adviser to civil or criminal penalties, to tort liability to third parties, or to professional discipline.

[I]t may be legitimately argued that the duty to report [a chemical spill] is the client's[,] not the lawyer's, and therefore the failure to report does not place the lawyer in the position of violating the law. Is the lawyer's position more precarious if the lawyer has been designated by the president of the company as the person responsible for making required reports to government agencies? The case for mandatory withdrawal [under Model Rule 1.16(a)(1)] is clearest if the client directs the lawyer to file a false report. In that circumstance, the lawyer must refuse to follow the client's instructions even at the cost of terminating the employment.

$$**********************$$

Notes

1. One aspect of the lawyer's traditional relationship to the client has been characterized as the "principle of nonaccountability." The idea is that the advocate is "neither legally, professionally, nor morally accountable for the means used or the ends achieved" for the client. David Luban, Lawyers and Justice: An Ethical Study 7 (1988).[6] Luban describes this principle as "a kind of limited liability doctrine of the moral world," consistent with the view of the lawyer as hired gun whose morality is "distinct from, and not implicated in, the client's." *Id.* at 155, 7.

Luban also addresses the psychological implications of nonaccountability and the corresponding sense of the lawyer as a "neutral professional" detached from the substantive interests of the client. His comments would seem to be pertinent to the attorney who encounters discrepancies between his or her own environmental values and those of the client:

> [A] psychologically plausible account of neutrality is this: although I believe in value V when I am out of my lawyerly role, I set that belief aside when I am in the role. Therein lies my neutrality. But nature abhors a vacuum, so it is inevitable that I will replace V with some other belief; the theory of cognitive dissonance suggests that I will replace V with whatever I am devoting my talents to advocating or furthering, namely not-V. More briefly: when I am thinking about those things that I think about when I am playing lawyer, I adopt the attitudes of my client, even though they are in considerable tension with my own nonlawyer attitudes.
>
> On this interpretation, neutrality consists in the initial setting aside of the lawyers' own values. The other interpretation, in which one simultaneously believes V and advocates not-V, is credible only in connection with lawyers who confront moral conflicts of this sort relatively rarely, or (alternatively) have no reason to identify with their clients, because for example the clients are street criminals. Such lawyers will be able to hold onto V and advocate not-V simply because they can confine their advocacy of not-V within narrow boundaries.

---

[6] A companion aspect of the lawyer-client relationship is the "principle of partisanship," meaning that the advocate "must, within the established constraints upon professional behavior, maximize the likelihood that the client will prevail." *Id.* Luban's presentation of these principles is based in part upon Murray L. Schwartz, "The Professionalism and Accountability of Lawyers," 66 California Law Review 669 (1978). That article also examines possible differences in the ethical standards applicable to "the lawyer acting as an *advocate* within the adversary system" as distinguished from "the lawyer acting as *nonadvocate* (*e.g.*, as negotiator or counselor) outside that system." *Id.* at 671.

> The cognitive dissonance interpretation, by contrast, is particularly appropriate for lawyers . . . whose entire work life consists in furthering not-V, and who occupy the same social stratum as their clients, so that it is harder for them to distance themselves from their clients.

Id. at 402-03.

2. Very early in the development of environmental law, controversy arose over the morality of attorneys' representation of large, corporate polluters. The focal point was a consent decree entered into in 1969 between the United States Department of Justice and the major American automobile manufacturers. That decree settled the federal government's civil antitrust claim that the manufacturers had "conspired with other motor vehicle manufacturers, in violation of Section 1 of the Sherman Act, to eliminate competition in the research, development, manufacture and installation of motor vehicle air pollution control equipment, and in the purchase from others of patents and patent rights, covering such equipment." *U.S. v. Automobile Manufacturers Association*, 307 F. Supp. 617, 618 (C.D. Cal. 1969), *aff'd per curiam*, 397 U.S. 248 (1970).

In the controversy ignited by this decree, consumer activist Ralph Nader described the settlement as "feeble" and as "evidence of the resourcefulness of large corporate law firms in overwhelming the opposition on behalf of [their] clients." Ralph Nader, "Law Schools and Law Firms," 75 Case & Comment, No. 3 (May-June 1970) at 30, 36-37. "Through Nader's promptings, a number of law students picketed [Wilmer, Cutler and Pickering, a Washington, D.C. law firm that represented the manufacturers] to draw attention to the settlement, which they felt to be a Justice Department sellout of the public interest. The students felt that the settlement prevented a proper public airing of crucial issues, and noted that the settlement also prevented the possibility of private treble damage actions based on the original judgment, which would have been possible had the government gone to trial and prevailed." Comment, "The New Public Interest Lawyers," 79 Yale Law Journal 1069, 1070 n.3 (1970). The law students charged that the law firm "violated the duty of a lawyer to the public interest by depriving the public of a litigation in which both sides would clash and the public's right to know would be fulfilled." Debate on Public Interest Limits on Effective Advocacy 1 (1970) (unpublished transcript of debate between Monroe H. Freedman and Michael E. Tigar). A few months after the student picketing took place, two law professors reflected on these events in a debate over the following questions: "What is the private attorney's duty regarding the public interest while he represents a client whose interests may clash with those of the public? Is a lawyer's duty to his client limited (outside of fraud and perjury) by a duty to the public?" *Id.* One viewpoint in that debate is capsulized in the following excerpts:

> You are taught in law school, and the adversary system enforces that view, that the law is neutral. I do not believe it is. If it is true that the law is not neutral, then it seems to me that lawyers have an obligation. It is an obligation to understand the mechanisms by which the society in which they live operates to determine what impacts decisions by private decision-makers have over various sectors of

our society, and to decide ultimately where their loyalties are going to be placed.

I am [not] criticizing Wilmer, Cutler & Pickering for going all out on behalf of their clients. I am criticizing them for the choice of their clients that they choose to go all out on behalf of. And that, you see, is an important difference. Nobody is suggesting that a lawyer sacrifice his professional responsibility. The only point is that there are very few public interest law firms operating in the United States today. And what the students at George Washington University were saying is that the lawyers who should be representing the public interest, not compromised by private interest, are the lawyers at Wilmer, Cutler & Pickering. We would like to urge them, with all the means that we know how, to come along with us in this process, secure in the knowledge that General Motors will not be unrepresented.

Id. at 6-7, 17 (statement of Professor Tigar). The opposing position included the following statements:

I have no quarrel with attacking the client. I have no quarrel with putting restrictions on the client. I have no quarrel with limiting the weapons that may be made lawfully available to a lawyer in a particular situation. What I do take issue with is the idea that the lawyer is not to be the advocate for his client, but that he is to be his judge and even his client's own adversary to some ill-defined extent—that he is to say, "This client I do not like as much as some other client. This client is polluting the atmosphere. This client is a corporation. Therefore I must give him less than the limit that the law allows in carrying out my responsibility to protect his interests." I submit to you that it is not all that simple.

The adversary system does not mean just the diligent ferreting out of relevant information, and the persuasive marshaling of data. It means bringing to bear your intellectual capacities in devising arguments that will serve to extend the limits of human rights, of the civil rights of people against the government. And those capacities are an essential part of what the adversary system is about. All those rights that we hold most precious have been advanced and maintained by the adversary system.

There *are* things you can do to protect the public interest. Do *pro bono* work. Work for ACLU or . . . a public interest law firm. See to it that the public interest *is* represented when the government lawyers fail in their job. You're not helpless. If there is a real public interest, it can be represented on the merits. You don't have to do it by attacking *ad hominem* the lawyer on the other side of the case.

Id. at 10-12, 15 (statement of Professor Freedman).

Should the environmental lawyer choose a side consistent with his or her personal values in each and every matter on which he or she works? Is a choice to provide vigorous and honest representation to any client within the adversary process morally sufficient? To the extent that there are more public interest law firms now than there were in 1970, is there greater or lesser justification for an environmental lawyer to be guided by a commitment to the adversary process, rather than by individualized evaluation of each client's environmental *bona fides*?

Professors Freedman and Tigar have revived their debate recently, although they appear to have modified—or perhaps swapped—their positions. *See* Monroe H. Freedman, "Must *You* Be the Devil's Advocate?" Legal Times, August 23, 1993, at 19; Michael E. Tigar, "Setting the Record Straight On the Defense of John Demjanjuk," Legal Times, September 6, 1993, at 22; Monroe H. Freedman, "The Morality of Lawyering," Legal Times, September 20, 1993, at 22.

3. Should the vigor of the private environmental lawyer's representation be moderated when opposing parties are clearly unrepresented or underrepresented? Consider the responsibility of the lawyer for a large manufacturing company that proposes to locate a polluting facility in a poor, minority neighborhood that lacks political organization and environmental lawyers. Consider also the responsibility of an environmental prosecutor pursuing a shutdown order or monetary penalties against a small manufacturing company that lacks the financial resources to hire environmental lawyers and technical consultants to advise it regarding the pollution it is causing.

4. In recent years a number of law schools across the country have developed clinical programs in environmental law for their students. Some of these programs focus on "environmental justice" through the representation of poor and minority communities in environmental disputes. Occasionally, however, community groups have criticized these clinics on various grounds.[7] One group's criticism included the following points:

> [O]ur concern is not only about law school clinics that set the agenda strictly in terms of what is perceived to be best for students, as opposed to the communities the clinics are ostensibly created to serve. We also have a serious concern about students who participate in such a clinic, gain significant insights into (or at least exposure to) environmental justice issues, and then join the "environmental" department of a firm whose business, as usual, is the representation of corporate polluters.
>
> Good environmental justice advocacy work is highly political and strategic. It entails not only sharp legal analyses but also a grasp of the interconnectedness of toxic chemicals, racism, sexism, poverty, power, knowledge, rights and remedies. It is about figuring out how legal and scientific tools relate to community struggles— many of which have been squelched, derailed, or otherwise frustrated by clever and amoral legal and other hired guns. Our experience . . . persuades us, for

---

[7] A coalition of community organizers and poverty lawyers expressed the following concerns in "An Open Letter from Bay Area Environmental Justice Activists to Environmental Law Clinic Proponents at Boalt Hall Law School, Golden Gate Law School & Stanford Law School" (December 20, 1993):

> While environmental justice clinical programs can be presented as a bold new model—a way to bridge academy and community interests—there are risks involved for our communities. What initially appears to be a forum for shared interests and resources primarily results in the benefits being reaped by the academy, while community groups can become marginalized in benefits and acknowledgements. Legal clinics, like any well-intentioned social program, can foster a "dependency mentality"— as opposed to an empowering one—in [their] clients. Extreme caution must be taken to avoid the creation of clinical programs which emphasize communities' deficiencies as a means of creating a role for themselves.

example, that we do not want to be training students in informal discovery techniques and other aspects of proof-building only to run into these students later as our legal adversaries. [W]e view the potential for betrayal to be very real.

Letter from Santa Clara Center for Occupational Safety and Health, excerpted in Silicon Valley Toxics Action, Vol. 12, No. 1 (Spring 1994), at p. 6.

With concerns of this sort in mind, it would seem that ethical issues can confront the student of environmental law even before admission to the bar. If you were a law student considering possible career avenues in environmental law, and considering participation in a clinical program of this sort, what would be your response to this group's criticism? Would the criticism dissuade you from participating? Would it affect the way in which you carried out your duties in the clinic?

Chapter 2
Concepts of Justice

A. Overview

This chapter introduces meanings of the term "justice" that can provide philosophical foundations for important aspects of environmental law. These concepts are relevant both to legal standards governing activities with environmental effects, and also to legal procedures for environmental decision making and conflict resolution. Better understanding of these concepts should illuminate the ways in which environmental lawyers bring justice concerns to bear in environmental disputes.

****

Richard O. Brooks, "A New Agenda for Modern Environmental Law," 6 Journal of Environmental Law and Litigation 1, 26-27, 37-38 (1991)

Most current environmental policy is guided toward the effective achievement of environmental objectives. Yet the proper goal of environmental law is not only effectiveness nor efficiency but also environmental justice – the proper distribution of environmental amenities, the fair correction and retribution of environmental abuses, the fair restoration of nature, and the environmentally fair exchange of resources.[1] The study of specific cases reveals the pursuit of these kinds of environmental justice, but few efforts have been made to assess the more general justice of current environmental protection policies and cases.

---

[1] [Ed.] Professor Brooks's usage of the term "environmental justice" obviously is much broader than current popular usage, which concentrates the phrase on the demands of poor and minority communities for equitable environmental enforcement and facility siting, as discussed in Chapters 4 and 7, *infra. See also* Thomas M. Hoban and Richard O. Brooks, Green Justice: The Environment and the Courts (1987).

Another rather general use of the term is suggested by the following description of the development of modern environmentalism in the late 1960's: "These changes in thought occurred in a time of peak discontent and a restless rising generation. The spectacle of the successful civil rights demonstrations empowered other citizens to seek environmental justice in the streets and the courts just as the despair over the Vietnam War caused them to doubt their government." Celia Campbell-Mohn *et al.*, Environmental Law: From Resources to Recovery 34 (1993).

Given these varied usages, and the innate appeal of a phrase that combines powerful words like "environmental" and "justice," the reader is well-advised to examine closely the intended meaning of "environmental justice" in any particular context in which it is found.

Conflicts between environmental and economic values are inevitable. Any balancing of economics and environmental protection must take into account the different notions of justice – distributive, corrective, retributive, restorative, and exchange – all of which can arguably play a role in environmental protection policy. [T]he balancing of economic and environmental values can be accomplished in principle only within a context of the careful articulation of environmental ideals and their institutional implications, as well as the various concepts of justice.

Finally, we must explore the relationship between specific environmental laws and the broader standards of environmental justice. A considerable philosophical and social science literature on the various forms of justice has been recently published, but few studies of the way in which specific environmental laws advance or fail to advance these forms of justice have been conducted.

****

To recognize that environmental lawyers work for environmental protection and for justice is not to suggest that this recognition automatically will lead to environmental disputes being simplified or resolved in miraculous, new ways. Environmental disputes cannot always be resolved easily, even if the parties are extremely clear – both to themselves and to one another – about exactly what the stakes are for each of them, i.e., exactly what combination of environmental claims and justice claims each party is putting forward. Such clarity, however, can help to facilitate environmental dispute resolution, while promoting better dialogue and mutual respect among the contending parties and their attorneys.

Environmental disputes fundamentally involve disagreements over environmental objectives, standards, and facts. Additionally, there often is an overlay of disagreements over contending claims for just treatment. Those claims may be based upon different concepts of justice urged by different parties, and these competing justice claims create another level of conflict in and of themselves.[2] Finally, there may be conflicts, or at least tensions, between the environmental goals of some parties and the justice-based claims of other parties.

Thus, environmental disputes can be seen as potentially involving three types of conflicts in varying combinations: Competing views of environmental merits; competing claims for justice; and tensions between environmental concerns and justice claims.

---

[2] In a recent study of distributional aspects of environmental policy, the following appears:

> The present book is largely devoted to examining competing principles of distributive justice as they are, or may be used to make environmentally focused decisions. A decision is environmentally focused if environmental considerations become important (though not necessarily the only) factors in the decision-making process. I hope to show that people often differ with one another over questions of environmental policy largely because they are employing different principles of justice and/or accord different weights to some of the same principles.

Peter S. Wenz, Environmental Justice 24 (1988).

With one or more of these levels of conflict active in a given dispute, the complexity of environmental law work obviously is tremendous, and perhaps even greater than is usually assumed. The usual assumption is that the parties to an environmental dispute are at odds simply because of different views and values regarding the environmental aspects of the matter. As succeeding chapters will illustrate, environmental cases are seldom that straightforward.

Indeed a thorough review of the growth of environmental law might well demonstrate an historical pattern in which different concepts of justice have tended to be more important in environmental controversies at different periods in the development of the field. For example, perhaps such a review would show that concerns over corrective justice, especially in debates over whether fault-based or non-fault standards should govern liability for environmental harm, were a dominant aspect of environmental law in its early years. In later periods of regulatory reform, procedural justice may have become a more active aspect of the field. Currently the environmental justice movement is drawing unprecedented attention to the distributional aspects of environmental law in its disparate impacts on various communities. Surely all three types of justice have been implicated in the field since its inception, but the suggested hypothesis is that during some periods one type demands more attention than the others.

Might it also be true that environmental lawyers representing different types of clients tend over time to emphasize certain concepts of justice more frequently than other concepts? Poverty lawyers working on environmental matters in recent years have stressed distributional fairness. Lawyers for regulated entities frequently demand procedural fairness for their clients. Lawyers for government enforcement agencies, and lawyers for environmental groups, often focus on standards of corrective justice for determining liability and punishment for environmental harms. Nonetheless, any of these types of lawyers at any given time may be found urging any of the other types of concerns on behalf of their clients. Furthermore, once a lawyer for one party raises a justice claim, the other parties generally must respond. In short, the full array of justice issues would seem to be of potential concern to all participants in environmental law and regulation.

It also should be remembered that a particular claim for fair treatment may encompass more than one type of justice concern. This is particularly true with respect to procedural fairness claims since procedural justice usually is pursued in order to assist a party in protecting its interests under other justice categories. Thus, for example, a citizens group's demand for access to information in public agency files regarding an environmental controversy would seem to involve procedural justice. At the same time, this demand may be intended to facilitate the development of the group's position on questions of distributional equity, as the information may reveal disparities in environmental burdens affecting the group.

One major purpose of this book is to heighten understanding of these different levels of concern and conflict. This recognition may facilitate better processes and better outcomes, as well as greater self-respect and mutual respect among environmental lawyers representing diverse interests. It is not being suggested here, of course, that the environmental lawyer should shelve his or her personal values and consider all environmental and justice claims as of equal weight in all cases. As addressed in Chapter 1, each of us must make our own choices regarding the values and goals that will guide our careers over time, as well as our approaches to individual cases. Similarly, the ultimate outcome that the legal process reaches in any particular environmental dispute is, in effect, society's collective choice regarding the resolution of the competing environmental and justice claims raised by the parties.

Succeeding chapters will examine some of the most common claims for just treatment that arise in environmental law work. These include, *inter alia*, demands for clarity of standards, distributional equity, and openness of decisional procedures. The concepts introduced in this chapter provide a broader philosophical context within which to analyze these and other justice claims and to understand the environmental lawyer's role in advancing them.

B. Exercise

Assume that you are one of the following:

An executive of a large, diversified company that, among other things, engages in heavy manufacturing and real estate development.

The owner and operator of a small company that manufactures custom-made wooden and metal bookcases.

An officer of a national environmental group with diverse concerns ranging from air quality to endangered species to international ocean pollution.

A resident of a low-income, racial minority neighborhood located in close proximity to both existing and proposed industrial factories and waste disposal sites.

A retail store manager, who lives in a suburban community, has children in public schools, and generally keeps up with news of public issues, including environmental protection developments.

From the perspective of the role you have just assumed, briefly summarize what you believe would constitute justice in the making and implementation of environmental laws and regulations.

Be as specific as possible in identifying the needs or concerns that would have to be accommodated for you to conclude that you are being treated justly. Also, after reading the following philosophical works on justice, consider whether the specific concerns you have identified for your role correspond to one or more of these formulations.

Finally, consider whether there are any areas of tension or conflict between the justice concerns you have identified and the environmental values and goals you would favor in the role you have assumed.

C. Three Types of Justice

Over the centuries philosophers and judges have offered a great many concepts of justice.[3] The readings presented here offer a few such formulations. Although there are various ways in which these ideas could be organized, they are presented here under three broad headings: distributive justice, corrective justice, and procedural justice. There are important links among these categories, and there are important differences as well.

The first two of the categories are normative, i.e., they speak of desired substantive outcomes or conditions to be pursued. Distributive justice can be understood, in a general sense, as addressing the way in which a society should allocate resources, benefits, or burdens among its members. Corrective justice primarily treats the bases on which punishments should be assigned or compensation should be paid for wrongs inflicted on individuals or communities. The third category is different, for it is instrumental in character. Procedural justice addresses the methods by which determinations are made in pursuit of other societal goals, including either of the other types of justice.

1. Distributive Justice

John Rawls, ''Constitutional Liberty and the Concept of Justice,'' in Carl J. Friedrich *et al.*, Nomos VI: Justice 98, 100 (1963)

The concept of justice which I shall use may be stated . . . in the form of two principles: first, each person participating in an institution or affected by it has an equal right to the most extensive liberty compatible with a like liberty for all; and, second, inequalities as defined by the institutional structure or fostered by it are arbitrary unless it is reasonable to expect that they will work out to everyone's advantage and provided that the positions and offices to which they attach or from which they may be gained are open to all. These principles express the concept of justice as relating three ideas: liberty, equality, and reward for services contributing to the common advantage.

****

John Rawls, A Theory of Justice 7 (1971).

Many different kinds of things are said to be just and unjust; not only laws, institutions, and social systems, but also particular actions of many kinds, including decisions, judgments, and imputations. We also call the attitudes and dispositions of persons, and

---

[3] ''In different theories which have been urged justice has been regarded as an individual virtue, or as a moral idea, or as a regime of social control, or as the end or purpose of social control and so of law, or as the ideal relation among men which we seek to promote and maintain in civilized society and toward which we direct social control and law as the most specialized form of social control. Definitions of justice depend upon which of these approaches is taken.'' Roscoe Pound, Justice According to Law 2 (1951).

persons themselves, just and unjust. Our topic, however, is that of social justice. For us the primary subject of justice is the basic structure of society, or more exactly, the way in which the major social institutions distribute fundamental rights and duties and determine the division of advantages from social cooperation. By major institutions I understand the political constitution and the principal economic and social arrangements. Thus the legal protection of freedom of thought and liberty of conscience, competitive markets, private property in the means of production, and the monogamous family are examples of major social institutions. Taken together as one scheme, the major institutions define men's rights and duties and influence their life-prospects, what they can expect to be and how well they can hope to do. The basic structure is the primary subject of justice because its effects are so profound and present from the start. The intuitive notion here is that this structure contains various social positions and that men born into different positions have different expectations of life determined, in part, by the political system as well as by economic and social circumstances. In this way the institutions of society favor certain starting places over others. These are especially deep inequalities. Not only are they pervasive, but they affect men's initial chances in life; yet they cannot possibly be justified by an appeal to the notions of merit or desert. It is these inequalities, presumably inevitable in the basic structure of any society, to which the principles of social justice must in the first instance apply. These principles, then, regulate the choice of a political constitution and the main elements of the economic and social system. The justice of a social scheme depends essentially on how fundamental rights and duties are assigned and on the economic opportunities and social conditions in the various sectors of society.

****

Note

The above statements by Rawls were published before modern environmental awareness had developed pervasively in the American public or had greatly affected regulatory schemes. If you were updating these statements now, what aspects of environmental law and regulation would you include as examples of "major social institutions?" Which of those aspects "favor certain starting places over others?" Consider your answers to these questions both within the United States and on a global scale.

****

Norman E. Bowie, Towards a New Theory of Distributive Justice 4, 9-10, 12-13, 24, 50-51, 77, 102 (1971).

Traditionally, a distinction which goes back to Aristotle exists between distributive justice and retributive (corrective) justice. "Distributive justice" refers to the just distribution of benefits and burdens among a group of people. "Retributive justice" refers to the just administration of punishment.

[T]he basis for a just distribution of benefits and burdens is logically distinct from the basis for just punishment. This line of thought seems reasonable when one realizes that distributive and retributive justice arise from different situations. The need for retributive justice arises because men often break the laws or moral codes of the groups to which they belong. The need for distributive justice arises because men's wants and desires often exceed the means of fulfillment. This gap between desire and satisfaction results either from inadequate resources or from logically contradictory desires between two agents, X and Y, where X desires one thing and Y desires something incompatible with it, and only one person can be satisfied at that time and place. Hence, distributive justice provides the rules for the allocation of scarce resources and for the elimination of conflicting desires. Retributive justice provides the basis for punishment when such rules of distributive justice are violated. The tax policy a community uses may be based on distributive justice. The punishment for tax evasion may be based on retributive justice. It is important to keep these two issues distinct.

[A] list of values must be compiled. It is assumed that these values are elements which one tries to achieve in just distribution. The list is comprehensive in the sense that it represents those values to which appeal is most often made in the literature. They are the basic constituents of the traditional theories. The list includes the following:

1. happiness
2. liberty
3. equality
4. merit
5. optimization or efficiency
6. ability or skill.

. . .

The philosophical utilitarian theory of distributive justice is as follows:

In a set of possible distributions, that distribution which will provide the greatest happiness for the greatest number is the one which is just.

Although an explicit statement of the utilitarian theory of distributive justice is absent in the classical writers, the formulation above is certainly consistent with the view taken by those writers. However, I shall take "happiness" in a somewhat broader sense than Bentham, letting it refer to satisfaction rather than simply to pleasure or the absence of pain. It seems more correct to say that one has maximized satisfaction in winning the race than it is to say that one has maximized pleasure in winning the race. In any attempt to ascertain a just distribution, one must consider the resulting happiness or satisfaction.

In the phrase "greatest happiness," "greatest" is as important as "happiness." Not only are we concerned with happiness but with the greatest balance of happiness over unhappiness. The utilitarian formula is committed to the principle of maxima (efficiency in economic utilitarianism). Both happiness and maximization are factors which should be taken into account in any just distribution.

Philosophical utilitarianism is both too broad and not broad enough. It is too broad because its appeal to the greatest happiness makes it become hopelessly indefinite. It is not broad enough because the problem of distribution is discussed without taking sufficient account of other values. Economic utilitarianism is designed to overcome these difficulties. Moreover, economic utilitarianism has the additional advantage of making reference to the production of goods and services.

Stated briefly, economic utilitarianism asserts that: The principle which should be used for the production and distribution of economic goods and services is to maximize the greatest amount of economic welfare for the greatest number. There is a definite affinity between this principle of distributive justice and economic utility or welfare theory.

. . . .

One of the most influential appeals in disputes concerning distributive justice is the appeal to the value of equality. The emotive force of an appeal to this value has the power to effect revolutions to overthrow the prevailing economic order. Philosophically, however, the concept of equality is one of the vaguest concepts in social philosophy and philosophical discussions of equality are notorious for their ambiguity. Equality functions extremely well as a political slogan; it functions very poorly as a philosophical concept.

The five egalitarian formulas [of distributive justice] are the following:

E_1: For any commodity x, the just method of distribution is to divide x equally.

E_2: Although individual commodities may be distributed unequally, the just distribution of income is the equal distribution.

E_3: Whatever criterion is chosen for distribution, with respect to that criterion equals should be treated equally and unequals should be treated unequally.

E_4: There are certain values to which men have an equal right. If some commodity u is a necessary condition for the achievement of some value y, then it should be distributed so that the equal right is achieved.

E_5: Everyone has an equal right to a minimum standard of living. All commodities should be distributed so that this equal right is achieved.

. . . .

The inadequacies of the utilitarian and egalitarian theories require that we resume our search for an adequate theory of distributive justice. [W]e focus our attention on the so-called socialist formula which can be formulated as follows:

A just distributive system is one in which everyone produces according to his ability and receives according to his need.

This formula is attributed to the French socialist, Louis Blanc. It is . . . apparently accepted as the distributive principle in the final stage of communism by both Marx and Lenin.

In point of fact, the formula above cannot be referred to as the socialist formula without considerable qualification. "Socialism" is given such a wide-ranging application that there is no one formula of distributive justice common to all so-called socialist positions. Moreover, one seldom finds one socialist position that adheres to one formula in all situations. Hence, historically speaking there is no warrant for speaking of *the* socialist position.

****

Ellen Frankel Paul, "Set-Asides, Reparations, and Compensatory Justice," in John W. Chapman, Nomos XXXIII: Compensatory Justice 97, 98-99 (1991)

In book V of the *Nicomachean Ethics*, Aristotle discusses what he terms "partial justice," and he distinguishes between two types of just action that fall within that rubric. The first, what we now call distributive justice, deals with the "distribution of honors, or material goods, or of anything else that can be divided among those who have a share in the political system." Aristotle describes this type of justice as a "geometrical proportion": the individuals stand to each other as the things to be distributed relate[] to each other, that is, "the ratio between the shares will be the same as that between the persons." The root moral concept that Aristotle adduces for this type of justice is desert. As he succinctly puts it, "To each according to his deserts." Those who contribute equally to the common welfare or the society's particular project ought to receive whatever benefits are to be distributed. Correspondingly, those who contribute unequally should receive unequal rewards in the same proportion as their contributions differ. Aristotle wisely observes that people's criteria of desert differ, adding his customary breakdown of criteria by the nature of regimes: democrats favor free birth; oligarchs, wealth or noble birth; and aristocrats name excellence.

****

Notes

1. Some legal scholars and economists view the principal task of environmental law and regulation as distributive in nature, as a response to "conflicting demands placed upon environmental resources." James E. Krier, Environmental Law and Policy 1 (1971).[4] Different allocations of environmental benefits and burdens among different individuals and human communities can be evaluated under concepts such as the versions

---

[4] *See also* James M. McElfish, Jr., "Property Rights, Property Roots: Rediscovering the Basis for Legal Protection of the Environment," 24 Environmental Law Reporter 10231, 10246 (May 1994), where the following appears:

> Environmental regulation promotes fair allocations of property's burdens and benefits, in part, by internalizing to given parcels the externalities that would otherwise be imposed on others. The concept of eliminating the free rider goes far back to the common-law concepts of nuisance and quiet enjoyment. While, in the past, a property owner or user was required to find some unobtrusive place to carry out an activity that affected his neighbors, increases in population and property ownership have limited the availability of such places. Environmental regulation helps rationalize this conflict by preventing manipulations of land that allow one owner to reap benefits while producing detriments to others.

of utilitarianism and egalitarianism Bowie and Paul describe. Which of Bowie's egalitarian formulas corresponds to Aristotle's position?

Further complicating the already difficult allocative task is possible consideration of the interests of non-human species, such as animals and plants, and of the overall natural environment in and of itself. Should the distribution of environmental impacts take such non-human ''needs'' into account, to the extent we humans even can ascertain what they are? Consider the following three commentaries on this question:

> Rawls's highly influential book [A Theory of Justice] was written in the late 1950s and early 1960s, well before American concern for the environment began to 'green' philosophy. He specifically restricted his argument to human interests in equal liberty, justice, and opportunity. But many philosophers who read Rawls in the 1970s seized on his theories to make a case for nature. The more conservative simply contended that Rawls could be understood as supporting a moral obligation to resist environmental degradation in the interests of future generations of humans. Others extended Rawls more radically. In 1974 Laurence H. Tribe, a Harvard law professor, proposed adding nature to the contractual arrangements between people that Rawls presumed occurred at the beginning of any society. Tribe contended that Rawls's principle of maximum liberty (applied equally, Rawls stipulated, to all members of the community) would maximize the benefits for all life as well as for human life.

Roderick F. Nash, The Rights of Nature 131-32 (1989).

> Rawls's Theory has attracted a great deal of attention because it provides a fresh rationale for some of the ideals of Western liberal democracy. It combines considerations of liberty with those of equality, as well as considerations of utility with those of rights. . . . Turning to criticisms of Rawls's Theory, I find that it never escapes the net of utilitarianism, it fails to endorse a duty of justice concerning nonsentient constituents of the environment, and itdoes not provide much support for the principles of justice that we must use when we deal with environmental issues.

Peter S. Wenz, Environmental Justice 232-33 (1988).

> Decades ago, the law's principal tasks were simple: to get resources into the hands of people and determine the relative rights among them. Ownership norms rarely addressed the question of what things we should privately own.

> Today, our natural resources are largely all allocated. Established rules crafted over the centuries protect the rights of the owner over all other people. Today's lawmaking task is much different and much harder: to determine how to reconfigure what it means to own so that we do not exceed the bounds of sustainable-use practices. In this task, lawmakers are just beginning.

> As ecologists have explained, often in delightful detail, the world around us is intricate and intertwined. Each part of nature is attached to each other part, and

what we do to one part has effects that spread widely. If our legal culture is going to reflect this rich reality, if it is going to incorporate the numerous natural links that bind one acre to all others, ownership norms need to be based on a vision of property as community. The person who becomes owner of a tract must be seen, not as some recluse on an isolated island, but as part of a natural as well as social community, with all of the obligations that accompany that status.

We need to resist the legal image of property rights as simply a question of rights among people, because, in fact, far more is at stake than the demands of today's human participants. In coming years, property norms will need to be based on context, on accommodation to the needs of all surrounding life.

In the environmental setting, the equality issue goes more or less like this: should we treat property owners equally when the property parcels that they own are different? If we are going to achieve harmony with the natural world, we are going to need to answer this question in the negative, and decidedly and loudly so. Part of harmonious living involves sensitivity to natural differences. It involves treating each parcel and each resource with respect, which in turn means recognizing its peculiarities.

Eric T. Freyfogle, Justice and the Earth: Images for Our Planetary Survival 52-53, 55, 60 (1993).

2. An additional complicating factor, even if we were to limit our focus solely to the interests of humans, is possible consideration of the interests of future generations. In Section 101(b)(1) of the National Environmental Policy Act, Congress included among our national goals the fulfillment of "the responsibilities of each generation as trustee of the environment for succeeding generations." 42 U.S.C. § 4331(b)(1). Are any of the formulations of distributive justice described by Bowie helpful as principles to govern our environmental obligations to persons not yet born?

This concern for the future has been labeled "intergenerational equity" and described as having two components:

First is preserving natural systems for future generations so that the human species can perpetuate itself at the same quality of life and standard of living as present generations. This objective is different from efficiency and sustainability, because it considers the quality of life in the future, not just the amount of yield. Second is preserving areas of national significance due to their aesthetic appeal, historic attributes, or ecological significance for the use and enjoyment of future generations.

Celia Campbell-Mohn *et al.*, Environmental Law: From Resources to Recovery 122 (1993).

One imaginative commentary on justice touches upon intergenerational equity and includes the argument that "all citizens are at least as good as one another regardless of their date of birth." The argument proceeds to assert that, because of the inherent equality of present and future individuals, the latter "should start out in life with at least as much" in the way of useful resources as their predecessors had. Bruce A. Ackerman, Social Justice in the Liberal State 203 (1980).

2.   Corrective Justice

As will be evident in the following readings on corrective justice, there are a variety of labels in use for this category, and there also are at least two principal subcategories within it. Thus much of what the tort law seeks to accomplish can be understood as a form of corrective justice, also sometimes labeled as compensatory or rectificatory justice. Similarly, much of what the criminal law addresses can be understood under this heading. The criminal law aspect of corrective, or retributive, justice is noted in the commentary by Bowie, *supra*. Much of what is presented in Chapter 4 regarding the selection of enforcement targets, and in Chapter 5 on implementation of enforcement processes, involves corrective justice issues.

****

James Gould Cozzens, The Just and the Unjust 431 (1942)

[W]hen a man said he was seeking justice, what he meant, if he was plaintiff, was that he aimed to do someone dirt and the Court ought to help him; and if he was the defendant, that he already had done someone dirt, and the Court ought to protect him.

****

Ellen Frankel Paul, "Set-Asides, Reparations, and Compensatory Justice," in John W. Chapman, Nomos XXXIII: Compensatory Justice 97, 100-01, 103 (1991)

Aristotle's second component of "particular justice" [is] rectificatory justice. Rectificatory justice, as distinguished from distributive justice, does not look to the goodness or badness of the person, but to the damage: "it treats the parties as equals and asks only whether one has done and the other has suffered wrong, and whether one has done and the other has suffered damage."
Aristotle continues:

As the unjust in this sense is inequality, the judge tries to restore the equilibrium. When one man had inflicted and another received a wound, or when one man has killed and the other has been killed, the doing and suffering are unequally divided; by inflicting a loss on the offender, the judge tries to take away his gain and restore the equilibrium.

In involuntary transactions of this sort, Aristotle says, the just occupies a median between a gain and a loss: each ought to have an equal amount before and after the event.
The essential features of rectificatory justice (or, interchangeably for us, compensatory

justice) are these: (1) it treats the parties as equal; (2) it looks to the damage suffered by one party and inflicted by the other; (3) it is restorative, that is, it attempts to restore the victim to the condition he was in before the unjust activity occurred.

A more complete set of criteria for compensatory justice . . . is the following: (1) it is backward-looking, in the sense that what is relevant is an act or acts in the past that transpired between the contesting parties (i.e., the victim and the perpetrator) that violated the victim's right(s); (2) it looks to the injury suffered by the victim and inflicted by the perpetrator; (3) in effecting a remedy it treats the parties as equals in the sense intended by the idea of "equality before the law," that is, that the rights of each party must be respected; (4) it attempts, through compensation of one sort or another, to bring the victim to the condition he would have been in, or its equivalent, had the injurious event never occurred.

****

H. L. A. Hart, The Concept of Law 154-55, 160-62 (1961)

The distinctive features of justice and their special connexion with law begin to emerge if it is observed that most of the criticisms made in terms of just and unjust could almost equally well be conveyed by the words "fair" and "unfair." Fairness is plainly not coextensive with morality in general; references to it are mainly relevant in two situations in social life. One is when we are concerned not with a single individual's conduct but with the way in which *classes* of individuals are treated, when some burden or benefit falls to be distributed among them. Hence what is typically fair or unfair is a "share." The second situation is when some injury has been done and compensation or redress is claimed.

The general principle latent in these diverse applications of the idea of justice is that individuals are entitled in respect of each other to a certain relative position of equality or inequality. This is something to be respected in the vicissitudes of social life when burdens or benefits fall to be distributed; it is also something to be restored when it is disturbed. Hence justice is traditionally thought of as maintaining or restoring a *balance* or *proportion*, and its leading precept is often formulated as "Treat like cases alike"; though we need to add to the latter "and treat different cases differently."

The connexion between the justice and injustice of the compensation for injury, and the principle "Treat like cases alike and different cases differently," lies in the fact that outside the law there is a moral conviction that those with whom the law is concerned have a right to mutual forbearance from certain kinds of harmful conduct. Such a structure of reciprocal rights and obligations proscribing at least the grosser sorts of harm, constitutes the basis, though not the whole, of the morality of every social group. Its effect is to create among individuals a moral and, in a sense, an artificial equality to offset the inequalities of nature. For when the moral code forbids one man to rob or use violence on another even when superior strength or cunning would enable him to do so with impunity, the strong and cunning are put on a level with the weak and simple. Their cases are made morally alike. Hence the strong man who disregards morality and takes advantage of his strength to injure another is conceived as upsetting this equilibrium, or order of equality, established by morals; justice then requires that this moral *status quo* should as far as possible be restored by the wrongdoer. In simple cases of theft this would simply involve giving back the thing taken; and compensation for other injuries is an extension of this primitive notion. One who has physically injured another either intentionally or through negligence is thought of as having taken something from his victim; and though he has not literally done this, the figure is not too far fetched: for he has profited at his victim's expense, even if it is only by indulging his wish to injure him or not sacrificing his ease to the duty of taking adequate precautions. Thus when laws provide compensation where justice demands it, they recognize indirectly the principle "Treat like cases alike" by providing for the restoration, after disturbance, of the moral *status quo* in which victim and wrongdoer are on a footing of equality and so alike.

[S]ometimes the demands of justice may conflict with other values. This may occur, when a court, in sentencing a particular offender for a crime which has become prevalent, passes a severer sentence than that passed in other similar cases, and avowedly does this "as a warning." There is here a sacrifice of the principle "Treat like cases alike" to the general security or welfare of society. In civil cases, a similar conflict between justice and the general good is resolved in favour of the latter, when the law provides no remedy for some moral wrong because to enforce compensation in such cases might involve great difficulties of proof, or overburden the courts, or unduly hamper enterprise. There is a limit to the amount of law enforcement which any society can afford, even when moral wrong has been done. Conversely the law, in the name of the general welfare of society, may enforce compensation from one who has injured another, even where morally, as a matter of justice, it might not be thought due. This is often said to be the case when liability in tort is strict, i.e., independent of the intention to injure or failure to take care. This form of liability is sometimes defended on the ground that it is in the interest of "society" that those accidentally injured should be compensated; and it is claimed that the easiest way of doing this is to place the burden on those whose activities, however carefully controlled, result in such accidents. They commonly have deep pockets and opportunities to insure. When this defence is made, there is in it an implicit appeal to the general welfare of society which, though it may be morally acceptable and sometimes even called "*social* justice," differs from the primary forms of justice which are concerned simply to redress, as far as possible, the *status quo* as between two individuals.

****

Note

Liability under many environmental statutes (e.g., the Clean Water Act and the Comprehensive Environmental Response, Compensation, and Liability Act) is often strict liability for various forms of compensation, corrective action, and penalty. Does Hart's view of strict liability provide a sufficient explanation for the heavy reliance on strict liability in some or all of these statutory schemes?

3. Procedural Justice

H. L. A. Hart, The Concept of Law 162-63 (1961)

An important juncture point between ideas of justice and social good or welfare should be noticed. Very few social changes or laws are agreeable to or advance the welfare of all individuals alike. Only laws which provide for the most elementary needs, such as police protection or roads, come near to this. In most cases the law provides benefits for one class of the population only at the cost of depriving others of what they prefer. Provision for the poor can be made only out of the goods of others; compulsory school education for all may mean not only loss of liberty for those who wish to educate their children privately, but may be financed only at the cost of reducing or sacrificing capital investment in industry or old-age pensions or free medical services. When a choice has been made between such competing alternatives, it may be defended as proper on the ground that it was for the "public good" or the "common good." It is not clear what these phrases mean, since there seems to be no scale by which contributions of the various alternatives to the common good can be measured and the greater identified. It is, however, clear that a choice, made without prior consideration of the interests of all sections of the community would be open to criticism as merely partisan and unjust. It would, however, be rescued from *this* imputation if the claims of all had been impartially considered before legislation, even though in the result the claims of one section were subordinated to those of others.

Some might indeed argue that all that in fact could be meant by the claim that a choice between the competing claims of different classes or interests was made "for the common good," was that the claims of all had been thus impartially surveyed before decision. Whether this is true or not, it seems clear that justice in this sense is at least a necessary condition to be satisfied by any legislative choice which purports to be for the common good. We have here a further aspect of distributive justice, differing from those simple forms which we have discussed. For here what is justly "distributed" is not some specific benefit among a class of claimants to it, but impartial attention to and consideration of competing claims to different benefits.

****

Notes

1. Hart describes "prior consideration of the interests of all sections of the community," before a policy decision is made, as an aspect of distributive justice. Under the three-part categorization of justice presented here, such consideration is probably better understood as an aspect of procedural justice. Chapter 6, *infra*, explores this aspect as

an issue of access to decisional processes. As will be seen there, open and equal access for "the interests of all sections of the community" is of great importance in the making and implementation of environmental policy.

2. The recent emergence of the "environmental justice movement," as discussed especially in Chapter 7, *infra*, has focused attention on the extent to which environmental laws of various types discriminate in effect, if not in intent, against various poor or minority communities. Perhaps one reason it has taken so long for this type of discrimination to receive much attention is a widely held assumption that environmental laws fall into Hart's category of social changes or laws that "are agreeable to or advance the welfare of all individuals alike." Which environmental laws would you say clearly do belong within that estimable category? Which environmental laws might you suspect "provide[] benefits for one class of the population only at the cost of depriving others of what they prefer?"

****

John Rawls, A Theory of Justice 85-86 (1971)

The notion of pure procedural justice is best understood by a comparison with perfect and imperfect procedural justice. To illustrate the former, consider the simplest case of fair division. A number of men are to divide a cake: assuming that the fair division is an equal one, which procedure, if any, will give this outcome? Technicalities aside, the obvious solution is to have one man divide the cake and get the last piece, the others being allowed their pick before him. He will divide the cake equally, since in this way he assures for himself the largest share possible. This example illustrates the two characteristic features of perfect procedural justice. First, there is an independent criterion for what is a fair division, a criterion defined separately from and prior to the procedure which is to be followed. And second, it is possible to devise a procedure that is sure to give the desired outcome. Of course, certain assumptions are made here, such as that the man selected can divide the cake equally, wants as large a piece as he can get, and so on. But we can ignore these details. The essential thing is that there is an independent standard for deciding which outcome is just and a procedure guaranteed to lead to it. Pretty clearly, perfect procedural justice is rare, if not impossible, in cases of much practical interest.

Imperfect procedural justice is exemplified by a criminal trial. The desired outcome is that the defendant should be declared guilty if and only if he has committed the offense with which he is charged. The trial procedure is framed to search for and to establish the truth in this regard. But it seems impossible to design the legal rules so that they always lead to the correct result. The theory of trials examines which procedures and rules of evidence, and the like, are best calculated to advance this purpose consistent with the other ends of the law. Different arrangements for hearing cases may reasonably be expected in different circumstances to yield the right results, not always but at least most of the time. A trial, then, is an instance of imperfect procedural justice. Even though the law is carefully followed, and the proceedings fairly and properly conducted, it may reach the wrong outcome. An innocent man may be found guilty, a guilty man may be set free. In such cases we speak of a miscarriage of justice: the injustice springs from no human fault but from a fortuitous combination of circumstances which defeats the purpose of the legal rules. The characteristic mark of imperfect procedural justice is that while there is an independent criterion for the correct outcome, there is no feasible procedure which is sure to lead to it.

By contrast, pure procedural justice obtains when there is no independent criterion for the right result: instead there is a correct or fair procedure such that the outcome is likewise correct or fair, whatever it is, provided that the procedure has been properly followed. This situation is illustrated by gambling. If a number of persons engage in a series of fair bets, the distribution of cash after the last bet is fair, or at least not unfair, whatever this distribution is. I assume here that fair bets are those having a zero expectation of gain, that the bets are made voluntarily, that no one cheats, and so on. The betting procedure is fair and freely entered into under conditions that are fair. Thus the background circumstances define a fair procedure. Now any distribution of cash summing to the initial stock held by all individuals could result from a series of fair bets. A distinctive feature of pure procedural justice is that the procedure for determining the just result must actually be carried out; for in these cases there is no independent criterion by reference to which a definite outcome can be known to be just. Clearly we cannot say that a particular state of affairs is just because it could have been reached by following a fair procedure. This would permit far too much and would lead to absurdly unjust consequences. It would allow one to say that almost any distribution of goods is just, or fair, since it could have come about as a result of fair gambles. What makes the final outcome of betting fair, or not unfair, is that it is the one which has arisen after a series of fair gambles. A fair procedure translates its fairness to the outcome only when it is actually carried out.

****

Note

The fairness of procedures used in environmental law is a frequent focus of environmental lawyers' work. Throughout the remaining chapters of this book, examples will be found of legal disputes in which one or more parties are concerned about procedural justice. In studying these examples, consider whether the decisional processes in question approximate Rawls's formulations of perfect, imperfect, or pure procedural justice. Do any of those formulations correspond to Hart's emphasis on decisional processes that allow input from all interested sectors of the affected community?

Chapter 3
Setting Regulatory Agendas

A. Overview

In the development of environmental law and regulation, many different factors have influenced the determination of which areas of environmental concern are placed on our regulatory agendas, i.e., become subjects of regulation and are given greater or lesser priority in the allocation of regulatory resources. This chapter explores these factors and their significance in placing different environmental problems on regulatory agendas at the federal, state, regional, and local levels. This exploration should further illuminate the role of the environmental lawyer in the regulatory process either as regulator, as advocate for a potentially regulated entity, or as advocate for broader environmental interests. More generally, these evolving regulatory priorities are the context in which most environmental lawyers ply their trade. The assumption being made here is that lawyers' fuller understanding of that context will facilitate more effective and responsible performance of their functions.

To state this chapter's focus somewhat differently, the questions being asked here include the following: Who are the intended beneficiaries of environmental protection efforts? By what criteria are these beneficiaries selected? Who are the ultimate clients of the environmental lawyer acting as regulator or prosecutor? How are priorities set in the selection of environmental problems for regulation and other legal action?

The answers to these questions collectively identify the types of environmental problems our society considers most serious and in need of attention. The answers also raise considerations of distributive justice, for different regulatory emphases and influences ultimately allocate the benefits of environmental protection in different ways. Thus, in studying the various factors presented here that shape environmental law and policy, the reader may wish to consider the relevance of the distributive justice formulations presented in Chapter 2, particularly those expressed by Rawls and Bowie. Do any of those formulations help us to assess how our environmental priorities, as shaped by the factors discussed here, do or do not contribute to a more just society?

B. Social, Political, and Economic Factors

The introductory language of most environmental statutes declares the environmental concerns that have prompted the legislature to take action. If one were to read this language and nothing more, in order to identify the motivating factors behind environmental statutes and regulatory actions, one would have a very incomplete understanding of those factors. Certainly it is true that relatively pure concern about environmental degradation is the most important element behind most environmental enactments. Thus, for example, the Clean Water Act generally was intended "to restore and maintain the chemical, physical, and biological integrity of the Nation's waters," 33 U.S.C. § 1251(a); the Clean Air Act undoubtedly was based on recognition "that the growth in the amount and complexity of air pollution brought about by urbanization, industrial development, and the increasing use of motor vehicles, has resulted in mounting dangers to the public health and welfare," 42 U.S.C. § 7401(a)(2); the Toxic Substances Control Act reflected sound findings that "human beings and the environment are being exposed each year to a large number of chemical substances and mixtures [some of which] may present an unreasonable risk of injury to health or the environment," 15 U.S.C. § 2601 (a)(1)-(2); and the California legislature evinced deeply felt public concerns when it stated that:

> the people of the State of California have a primary interest in the quality of the physical environment in which they live, and that this physical environment is being degraded by the waste and refuse of civilization polluting the atmosphere, thereby creating a situation which is detrimental to the health, safety, welfare, and sense of well-being of the people of California."

California Health and Safety Code § 39000.

Beyond these types of straightforward worries about environmental damage, non-environmental concerns also figure prominently in the mixture of considerations that ultimately shapes the priorities and forms of regulatory action. The readings that follow introduce some of the more dominant social, political, and economic ingredients of this mixture.

****

William Tucker, Progress and Privilege: America in the Age of Environmentalism 34-38 (1982)

In the early days of the crusade, there was a great deal of hope that environmentalism could be characterized as "everybody's issue." After all, who could be in favor of pollution, or against saving the earth? This early hope was vastly encouraged by the speed with which the pro-business Nixon Administration picked up the environmental banner and made it a major issue. In his 1970 State of the Union address President Nixon announced that the deterioration of the environment was a national crisis, and that new environmental legislation would be a major priority of his administration. Although there has been much criticism that Nixon was only "co-opting" the issue and was not sincere, there is no question from the record that the Nixon Administration was remarkably sincere in its commitment to environmental legislation.

At the time of Nixon's speech, the National Environmental Policy Act of 1969 (which inaugurated the "environmental impact statement") was the only major piece of legislation that had resulted from the new movement. Over the next two years, the Clean Air Act and the Federal Water Pollution Control Act—both major departures from previous legislation—were pushed through Congress with broad bipartisan support. Memoirs from the inner circles of the Nixon Administration show clearly that the executive branch pushed ahead on the environmental program with very few misgivings about what some of the limitations might be.

Throughout the period, environmentalism has attracted a broad variety of conservative and liberal support. On Earth Day, 1970, the inaugural moment when the academically based environmental movement "went public," the featured speaker at one very liberal Long Island university was Barry Goldwater, who reminisced about his love of Arizona's natural landscape. "[I]f Richard Nixon and Edmund Muskie, Barry Goldwater and Edward Kennedy, Arthur Godfrey and Robert Redford, Republicans and Democrats, liberals and conservatives could all be in favor of environmentalism, who could conceivably be against it?" The answer did not emerge clearly for many years, until the true implications of environmentalism began to make themselves felt.

What environmental enthusiasts unfortunately failed to recognize is that, if environmentalism was indeed "everybody's issue," that only held true as long as "everybody" included people whose status was at least upper-middle class. What environmentalism did was to cut society *laterally*. Environmentalism, because it is oriented toward the status quo, had an inevitable appeal to people toward the top of the social ladder, and a negative appeal to those nearer the bottom. When environmentalists said "we already have enough," and "it's time to stop all this growth-for-growth's-sake," they were very accurately representing their *own* position of economic security. But anyone who was further down the scale and was depending on future growth and progress to improve their lot would be instinctively opposed to the environmental doctrine. The basic flaw of environmentalism—and indeed of all the previous "environmental movements" in history—was beginning to emerge. At heart, environmentalism favors the affluent over the poor, the haves over the have-nots.

But this was not entirely obvious in 1970. What was most surprising at that point was the alacrity with which this supposedly "liberal" cause was adopted by "conservative" business leaders. Even environmentalists seemed somewhat surprised by this pattern, and were inevitably suspicious that the business establishment was only *pretending* to embrace environmentalism in order to subvert it. In fact, these fears were unfounded.

What emerged instead was a notable split personality among many business people— the executive who worried at the office all day about the costs of curbing pollution but found when he returned to his suburban home at night that environmentalism expressed his interests almost perfectly. Often it was the husband of the family who remained business-oriented while the wife became the strong environmentalist. Perhaps the classic example of this ambivalence is Walter Hickel, President Nixon's Secretary of the Interior and a self-made millionaire who almost wasn't confirmed by the Senate because of his views about the need to proceed with development in Alaska. After less than two years in Washington, Hickel made a complete conversion to environmentalism, and wrote a book worrying about how "growth" and "prosperity" were destroying the country. Few college radicals who had begun to swing the banner of "ecology" could have anticipated the tremendous fervor with which suburban America suddenly embraced environmentalism in the early 1970s. What had been assumed to be a rather "radical" cause suddenly had all the markings of a middle-of-the-road issue.

Who was against environmentalism then? Initially, blacks were one of the few groups heard expressing some reservations about the sudden turn in liberal thought. On Earth Day, 1970, when a group of California college students buried an automobile in order to symbolize their renunciation of materialism, the event was picketed by a group of black students, who said that resources, rather than being wasted in such a conspicuous fashion, should be put to work in improving the lot of the poor. (The event did indeed come perilously close to Veblen's description of "conspicuous waste.")

This constant dissent of articulate blacks from the environmental agenda has been a running source of embarrassment to a movement that has tried desperately for over a decade to preserve the idea that it is a liberal crusade. As late as 1979, for example, Vernon Jordan, Director of the Urban League, was asked to attend a joint conference on urban and environmental affairs, intended to heal the breach in the liberal ranks. He responded with these remarks:

> Walk down Twelfth Street [in Washington, D.C.] and ask the proverbial man on the street what he thinks about the snail darter and you are likely to get the blankest look you ever experienced. Ask him what he thinks the basic urban environmental problem is, and he'll tell you jobs. I don't intend to raise the simple-minded equation of snail darters and jobs, but that does symbolize an implicit divergence of interests between some segments of the environmental movement and the bulk of black and urban people . . .
> [Environmentalists] will find in the black community absolute hostility to anything smacking of no-growth or limits-to-growth. Some people have been too cavalier in proposing policies to preserve the physical environment for themselves while other, poorer people pay the costs.

Bayard Rustin, the veteran civil-rights and labor leader, has called environmentalists "self-righteous, elitist, neo-Malthusians who call for slow growth or no growth. . . [and who] would condemn the black underclass, the slum proletariat, and rural blacks, to permanent poverty." Thomas Sowell, the prominent California economist, has said: "Regulatory rules have impeded people who are climbing rather than people who are already at the top. There is a fundamental conflict between the affluent people, who can afford to engage in environmental struggles, and the poor . . . . You don't see many black faces in the Sierra Club." It is probably some measure of the way in which black opinion tends to get submerged in the political arena when it does not support the liberal agenda that so little of this black opposition to environmentalism is ever visible in the press.

Labor unions have also been in the forefront of opposition to the environmental movement. By the early '70s, labor columnist Victor Reisel was repeating the joke about God telling Moses that before He parts the Red Sea he is first going to have to get permission from the Environmental Protection Agency. The bumper sticker "If You're Hungry and Out of Work, Eat an Environmentalist!" was originated by labor unions. Considering that many, many environmental campaigns have involved opposition to large-scale construction projects, power plants, highways, and factories that involve blue-collar jobs, this is not surprising. Whenever enthusiastic college students go out to picket a nuclear plant, they always find a group of hard-hat construction workers ready to throw bricks at them. As one union official put it: "These environmentalists are a bunch of bloody elitists . . . . [I]f it's 'no growth' they're advocating, then what they're really saying is: 'We've got enough for ourselves, but you stay down there.' "

****

Notes

1. At least one labor union went on record quite early not only in expressing its support for the environmental movement, but even in recognizing the significance of environmental deterioration for minority communities. In a pamphlet published in March 1973, entitled "Pollution is Not a White Thing," the United Auto Workers presented statements such as the following by the union, African-American union officials, and other political leaders:

> "Some black leaders are telling those who listen to them that the issue of pollution is 'a white thing.' Facts show, however, that air, water, sewage and food pollution threaten Black people most because of where we live and under what conditions." (Mayor Richard Hatcher of Gary, Indiana.)

> "The critical environmental problems of the inner-city compound the evils of poverty and deprivation that must be eliminated through the combined efforts of all Americans." (UAW President Leonard Woodcock)

> America's inner cities present the worst concentration of nearly every kind of environmental problem. Polluted air, garbage-littered streets and alleys, rats, roaches, the lead paint peeling from tenement walls, overcrowding are all environmental problems that plague the inner city. Blacks in the ghetto and workers in the factory suffer more acutely from this blight for the simple reason that they cannot escape. Government studies on life in the inner cities give lie to the claim that the pollution problem is purely a middle-class issue.

For a recent description of the interests of some labor unions that have been active in promoting enforcement of environmental laws, see Michael Belliveau and Richard Toshi-yuki Drury, "Blue Collar Greens: Why Labor Unions Care about the Environment," San Francisco Daily Journal, August 2, 1994, at 4 ("No one who raises legitimate environmental concerns should receive second class justice because of a perceived lack of the requisite degree of purity in pursuit of environmental protection.")

For early recognition of the danger that environmental law's responsiveness to "majoritarian, middle-class, white concerns" would distract attention "from the pressing problems of the black and poor people of America," *see* Edgar S. Cahn *et al.*, "Power to the People or the Profession? — The Public Interest in Public Interest Law," 79 Yale Law Journal 1005, 1043-44 (1970) ("Under the banner of pollution, we are asked to postpone expenditures for and to avert our eyes from the greater waste and pollution of our nearly bankrupt and poverty-ridden cities, our migrant camps, our Indian reservations, and the poverty-blighted mountain hollows of Appalachia.").

2. Not surprisingly, the views expressed by Tucker are not universally shared.[1] The next reading is a later response that takes a decidedly different view. It also identifies some recent changes in attitudes and alliances. Does it persuasively refute Tucker's analysis?

****

Philip Shabecoff, A Fierce Green Fire: The American Environmental Movement 145, 281-83 (1993)

. . . While the law treats corporations as persons, they bear no resemblance to human beings. They have no soul, no conscience, no ethics, no long-term vision of where society or the economy should be headed, no purpose other than the generation of profits through the production of goods and services. This does not mean that corporate executives are soulless and evil. No doubt they are just as good or bad, wise or stupid, generous or mean as the rest of us. But the structure and tradition of American business and industry and the fierce competitive pressures of the market impose ironbound imperatives on those who would climb the corporate ladder. Annual profits must be maximized. Costs must be kept to a minimum. Interference with the corporate decision-making process, by law, by regulation, and by the public, must be resisted. Long-term planning is unrewarding to the manager seeking promotion or intent on retaining his top-floor executive suite; he or she must show results on the year-end balance sheet.

But change is taking place, however slowly. Environmental management is now well established in the curriculum of many business schools. Economic incentives are gradually making environmental standards and performance a legitimate line item on year-end balance sheets. Establishing environmental performance standards for business executives may sound like training tigers to be vegetarians, but new economic incentives, management training, and the widening environmental ethic may eventually do the trick.

---

[1] A detailed criticism of Tucker's book can be found at Zach Willey, Book Review, 11 Ecology Law Quarterly 95 (1983).

The great failure of much of the national [environmental] movement in recent years, in my ópinion, has been its unwillingness or inability to take up the causes of social justice in the United States. This failure is all the more dismaying because one of the deepest roots of contemporary environmentalism lies . . . in the activist civil rights/peace/women's tradition of the 1960s.

Opponents of the environmental movement often brand it as "elitist." For example, William Tucker's book *Progress and Privilege*, published in 1982, called environmentalism "the politics of aristocracy." Tucker described the environmental movement as "essentially a suburban agrarianism" espoused by those who have achieved a high level of comfort and security and want to preserve their privileged position by blocking further economic and technological progress. Such arguments, deliberately or out of ignorance, overlook the fact that almost all Americans, particularly the poor and underprivileged, are the victims of environmental degradation. It is a point of view that fails to recognize that pollution is a serious public health concern and that misuse of resources is a threat to our national security. It is a perspective that is out of touch with reality.

Unfortunately, it is true that the leadership of national environmental groups *is* largely white, male, and well educated, with incomes above the national average. This description, however, would fit activists in virtually every social movement. As one study concluded, "people who are politically active, whether in environmental or any other issues, tend to be uniformly drawn from the upper middle class." While relatively well-to-do, few of today's national environmental activists could be considered rich. The tradition of wealthy, highborn amateurs of the early conservation years is long since gone. Sociologists Denton Morrison and Riley Dunlap point out, moreover, that "the *opponents* of environmentalism come much closer to being an elite than do core environmentalists. Most of the most vocal, coordinated opposition comes from top levels of corporate management. Such objections to environmental reform are hardly above suspicion as representing upper-class interests, even if frequently couched in a rationale of concern for general, including underclass, welfare."

The imbalances in the social composition of the leadership and staffs of the national environmental organizations cannot, however, be simply dismissed. One of the reasons that there are not more representatives of minority groups is that the leaders of the groups have not, until very recently, taken the trouble to reach out to those communities. I am not sure of the reasons for this, but I doubt that they reflect conscious racism. I suspect that many of the environmentalists are so confident that they are doing the Lord's work that it did not occur to them that they have other obligations to society.

Most of the environmental organizations have recently started to take steps to change "the whiteness of the green movement," but one senses they are doing so basically out ofa sense of obligation or in response to criticism. . . .

****

Notes

1. Can you identify any areas of environmental regulation that appear to be principally directed at benefitting poor and racial minority individuals, either in their work environments or in their residential neighborhoods? If any can be identified, do these regulatory efforts appear to be as aggressive and effective as necessary?

With regard to the efficacy of occupational health and safety programs for protection of workers of color and low wage workers, see George Friedman-Jimenez, "Achieving Environmental Justice: The Role of Occupational Health," 21 Fordham Urban Law Journal 605 (1994).

2. Shabecoff notes in passing the dominance of males in the leadership of national environmental groups. In recent years the development of ecofeminism offers some new perspectives by women on environmental needs and priorities, and also reiterates some of the philosophical starting points of modern environmentalism. *See generally*, Reweaving the World: The Emergency of Ecofeminism (Irene Diamond *et al.*, eds. 1990). Dominant themes of ecofeminist writings include the interconnectedness of all life, and the need to restore values associated with "ancient prepatriarcal and contemporary tribal cultures," such as images of nature as a nurturing mother, rather than a wild force to be controlled and dominated. *Id.* at xiii, 157. For ecofeminists, "overcoming the division between humanity and nature . . . promises release from a complex set of exploitations based on patriarchal identification of femaleness with the order of nature." Ariel Salleh, "Class, Race, and Gender Discourse in the Ecofeminism/Deep Ecology Debate," 15 Environmental Ethics 225 (1993).

Ecofeminism also calls attention to the distinctive role of women's reproductive capacities as "biological markers," the "sites upon which local, regional, or even planetary stress is often played out" and studied. Reweaving the World: The Emergency of Ecofeminism (Irene Diamond *et al.*, eds. 1990) at x, 180. Ecofeminism, in short, is "a diverse movement" with "a common thread [in] recognition that solutions to ecological problems must be tied to social and gender transformations." Carolyn Sachs, "Reconsidering Diversity in Agriculture and Food Systems: An Ecofeminist Approach," Agriculture and Human Values, Volume 9, Number 3, at 4, 6 (1992).[2] For a critique of ecofeminism, *see* Janet Biehl, Rethinking Ecofeminist Politics (1991).

An additional point of ecofeminist emphasis is the increasing involvement of women in organizing and leading community efforts to alleviate environmental burdens and hazards in many parts of the world. Reweaving the World: The Emergency

---

[2] *See also* Myra H. Strober, "Rethinking Economics Through A Feminist Lens," The American Economic Review, Volume 84, Number 2, at 143 (1994) ("Feminist economics argues that many of economics' core beliefs and policy recommendations are out of date, products of the peculiarities and politics of the periods in which they were developed and products of sexism in the Western world during the past two centuries.").

of Ecofeminism (Irene Diamond *et al.*, eds. 1990) at x, 181-87. This type of involvement in recent disputes in the United States is noted in Chapter 7(B), *infra*.

****

John P. Dwyer, "The Pathology of Symbolic Legislation," 17 Ecology Law Quarterly 233, 233-34, 245-47, 250-51, 302 (1990)

Most regulatory statutes instruct agencies to balance competing concerns in setting standards. Some regulatory statutes, however, impose short deadlines and stringent standard-setting criteria that are designed to address a single, overriding concern to the exclusion of other factors. Typically addressed to exotic and particularly dreaded health threats, this type of legislation reflects the public's urgent desire to avoid such risks. Well known examples include the Delaney Clause in the Food, Drug and Cosmetic Act (food additives, color additives, and animal drug residues), the original section 307 of the Clean Water Act (toxic pollutants), and section 112 of the Clean Air Act (hazardous air pollutants).

The programs mandated by such legislation are more symbolic than functional. Frequently, the legislature has failed to address the administrative and political constraints that will block implementation of the statute. By enacting this type of statute, legislators reap the political benefits of voting for "health and the environment" and against "trading lives for dollars," and successfully sidestep the difficult policy choices that must be made in regulating public health and the environment. Thus, while the statute, literally read, promises a risk-free environment, the hard issues involved in defining acceptable risk are passed on to the regulatory agency or to the courts. The actual regulatory program takes shape only after additional legislative, administrative, or judicial developments that transform symbolic guarantees into enforceable standards.

The enactment of symbolic legislation reflects a breakdown of the legislative policy making machinery, a system that all too frequently addresses real social problems in an unrealistic fashion. It also creates a dilemma for regulators and judges. While they generally are reluctant to usurp the legislature's policy making prerogatives by substituting their own version of appropriate public policy, they also are loath to implement and enforce a statute whose costs are grossly disproportionate to its benefits. The critical issue, then, is whether and how the agency or court should take the initiative to transform symbolic legislation into a functional regulatory program.

Believing that it would be irresponsible and politically mad to interpret and implement symbolic statutory provisions literally, the agency's usual response is to resist implementation. Although an agency may experiment with interpretations that moderate the stringent statutory standard-setting criteria, it will implement its reformulation slowly in order to delay judicial review. As a result, the agency adopts very few standards.

The most significant problem with symbolic legislation, however, is not delay; it is the resulting distortions in the regulatory process. Symbolic legislation hobbles the regulatory process by polarizing public discussion in agency proceedings and legislative hearings. Environmental groups take the legislation's promise of a risk-free environment at face value and tend to refuse to compromise the "rights" inherent in such promises. Industry fears that regulators will implement the statute literally and, consequently, vigorously opposes the regulatory process at every stage. By making promises that cannot be kept, and by leaving no middle ground for accommodation, the legislature makes it more difficult to reach a political compromise (either in the agency or the legislature) that would produce a functional regulatory program.

Charges about the insensitivity of "big business" and corporate greed have long been part of the American political fabric, but such rhetoric is especially prevalent in debates about proposed environmental legislation. As James Q. Wilson points out, legislation conferring diffuse benefits and concentrated costs, which describes most environmental legislation, can be enacted only if large constituencies are mobilized. So,

> in order to ensure vital publicity and develop political momentum in the competition for attention in and around Congress, the bills will focus attention on an "evil," personified if possible in a corporation, industry, or victim. [In addition], the proposal will be "strong" – that is, there will be little incentive in the developmental process to accommodate conflicting interests and thus little incentive to find a politically acceptable formula which all affected parties can live with. (To compromise the proposal would be to sacrifice the capacity of the bill to mobilize support by its moralistic appeal).

The political risks and benefits associated with taking a position on environmental issues are magnified when hazardous chemicals are involved because the regulation of hazardous chemicals raises "deeply disturbing questions about national attitudes toward life and death [and] about the appropriate claims which proponents of environmentally secure surroundings can make against other socially advantageous goals and norms." With so much potentially at stake in the regulation of hazardous pollutants, there is a tendency for interest groups to be strongly polarized on basic policy issues. Public consensus is not easily achieved.

In such a volatile policy area, even legislators who understand that complete safety is unattainable avoid positions that can be characterized as trading lives for dollars. It is safer politically to vote "for" safety – or better yet, an "ample margin of safety" – and to let the agency or the courts deal with the unresolved legal, ethical, and political questions. Requiring health-based standards allows legislators to assert that society can have a virtually risk-free environment without significant social or economic costs, while avoiding difficult choices and the accompanying political costs.

Legislating in this fashion may not be responsible, but neither is it unusual or surprising. Legislators want to enact sound public policies, but they also have personal goals, which may include acquiring wealth, gaining prestige or power within the legislature, being reelected, or being elected to another office. Viewing congressional behavior as fundamentally strategic reveals a deeper pathology of lawmaking in a representative democracy. Rational behavior by individual legislators may produce irrational public policy. Thus, in anticipating the next election, some legislators will propose or support symbolic legislation, such as section 112, because it minimizes political costs and maximizes political credit.

Supporting symbolic legislation is not necessarily the most efficient election strategy. Truly self-interested legislators concentrate their resources on relatively risk-free constituent services and pork-barrel legislation and try to avoid controversial positions on legislation. When legislators must take a position on a substantive statute, they often prefer to support statutes that explicitly or implicitly (through ambiguous statutory language) delegate policy making authority to regulatory agencies. However, legislators are less likely to prefer delegation when they view regulatory agencies as slothful, captured, or jointly responsible with polluting industries for environmental problems. In these cases, legislators prefer statutory language that ostensibly limits agency discretion in setting standards and forces agency action by imposing short deadlines. Where, in addition, the threatened risks are unfamiliar and the injuries are especially dreaded—and latent cancer risks from hazardous chemicals are particularly feared in American society—legislators are more likely to favor a symbolic statute that expresses their firm commitment to eliminate such threats, even if the legislation does not promote their own vision of sound public policy.

Symbolic legislation does not suppress the conflicts that arise in designing and implementing a regulatory scheme; instead, it transfers those conflicts to agencies, and at times to courts, for resolution. Not only must the agency resolve the policy and technical disputes that the legislature so deftly avoided, it also must frame its resolution in terms of statutory interpretation. Confronted with this challenge, an agency has three options. It can implement and enforce the legislation literally. Alternatively, it can use the rule-making process to "rewrite" the legislation to a form more compatible with the agency's policy goals or its notions of practicability. This rewrite may be done openly with the agency announcing its intentions and consulting with Congress, or it may be done silently if the political costs or the risk of judicial reversal are too high. Finally, the agency can use the time-honored bureaucratic tactic of delay in the hope that either Congress or the courts will rescue it.

Agencies view literal implementation of symbolic legislation as politically and professionally unsound. They do not want to bear the political consequences that inevitably flow from adopting excessively stringent standards, and they do not believe that regulatory consequences should be ignored. Moreover, the professional values of regulators generally demand that regulatory decisions be made in light of costs.

Rewriting the statute and delaying implementation are not exclusive of each other. In practice, agencies resist by degrees—rewriting a little here, delaying a little there—to achieve their goals. An agency's response to the legislative mandate will reflect its evaluation of two factors: the intensity and durability of political support for the statute, and the risks of judicial reversal or legislative revision. Delay, for example, could be a politically costly strategy if Congress becomes sufficiently irritated with the agency.

But delay may be a more practical approach than revision if the agency believes the courts would reject its construction of the statute.

Courts obviously can play a critical role in shaping legislative and administrative responses to symbolic legislation. By monitoring sublegislative arrangements, for example, courts protect the integrity of the legislative process. However, it is unclear how or when a court should deal with symbolic legislation. Outright reversal could damage both agency morale and EPA's credibility with interest groups. Potentially the most important political cost to the Agency would be its loss of bargaining power in the legislature. By striking down the Agency's reformulation of a symbolic provision . . . , courts would give environmental groups great leverage in negotiating subsequent legislation.

At the extremes, the court can either interpret literally or nullify symbolic legislation in an effort to force Congress to deal concretely with the underlying policy issues. Alternatively, a court can engage in or tolerate a certain amount of instrumental interpretation either by interpreting the statute itself to remove the symbolic conditions or limitations, or by deferring to the agency's reformulation. None of these approaches is ideal. But, given the relative capacities of courts and agencies to compel congressional reform or to produce a functional regulatory program, deference is the best approach.

****

Notes

1. Dwyer's observations on symbolic legislation suggest further questions about the functions of lawyers in the creation of such laws, and in the confusion and conflict such laws engender. Are there any justifications for the lawyer as lobbyist—whether for a regulated entity, an environmental group, or a government agency—to promote the adoption of the type of overambitious, unrealistic, yet noble-sounding provisions Professor Dwyer criticizes? What types of strategic advantages for various types of clients might such laws offer in the subsequent working out of regulatory details before the regulatory agency, or in subsequent litigation testing the validity of the laws themselves?

2. Dwyer expresses concerns regarding symbolic legislation that imposes "short deadlines and stringent standard-setting criteria." Similar concerns earlier were expressed with regard to overly general and vague, yet noble-sounding, laws. *See* John Hart Ely, Democracy and Distrust: A Theory of Judicial Review 131-134 (1980). Ely voiced his criticism as an objection to the legislative practice of delegating the lawmaking function to "the legions of unelected administrators whose duty it becomes to give operative meaning to the broad delegations the statutes contain." He invited resuscitation of the generally moribund nondelegation doctrine and observed:

> That legislators often find it convenient to escape accountability is precisely the reason *for* a nondelegation doctrine. Were it to turn out that legislators forced to govern wouldn't have the courage to do so energetically, that would often be too

bad – though administrators with formless delegations often and understandably don't turn out to be so active themselves – but at least it would be our system.

The problem . . . may lie not in a propensity to make politically controversial decisions without telling us why, but rather in a propensity not to make politically controversial decisions – to leave them instead to others, most often others who are not elected or effectively controlled by those who are. If we can just get our legislators to legislate we'll be able to understand their goals well enough. I'm not saying we may not still end up with a fair number of clowns as representatives, but at least then it will be because clowns are what we deserve.

Id. at 133-34.

Can both Dwyer and Ely be correct, i.e., do both overly specific and overly general environmental laws represent an inadequate discharge of legislative responsibilities?[3] Can we realistically expect – or demand – that legislators provide enough guidance so that administrative agencies are not allowed to engage in basic lawmaking, yet leave enough statutory flexibility to allow agencies to fill in gaps and adjust implementation to meet society's needs in the post-legislative phase?

3. The above readings by Tucker, Shabecoff, and Dwyer address the subtle yet undeniable influence of social attitudes and political perceptions in the development of environmental policy. The next excerpt reminds us of a much less subtle factor: money, or the lack thereof.

****

U.S. General Accounting Office, Environmental Protection Issues 4-7 (1992)

As a result of the legislation enacted over the last 20 years, American industry and government are currently spending about $115 billion a year to meet environmental goals. The amount is expected to increase to $160 billion a year by the end of the decade. State and local governments, which will have to bear a particularly large share of this increase, face over $80 billion in investment costs for wastewater alone, and the federal government will have to spend about $200 billion simply to clean up contaminated Department of Defense and Department of Energy installations.

Under current economic conditions, meeting these financing challenges will be an important concern of all levels of government. In the next few years, the Congress and the new administration will have to deal with these difficult issues as anumber of major

---

[3] *Compare* R. Shep Melnick, "Pollution Deadlines and the Coalition for Failure," in Environmental Politics: Public Costs, Private Rewards (Michael S. Greve *et al.*, eds. 1992) 89, 95 ("Today both liberals and conservatives proclaim that Congress should set policy directly rather than delegating such responsibility to agencies, and that it should write detailed legislation rather than trying to exert post hoc control through such means as the legislative veto. What these advocates of legislative specificity generally ignore is the institutional capacity of Congress.")

environmental statutes — including those that govern pesticides, toxic chemicals, hazardous and solid waste disposal, surface water pollution, drinking water safety, and the cleanup of abandoned hazardous waste sites — are scheduled for reauthorization. In addition, the Congress may again consider proposals to elevate the Environmental Protection Agency (EPA) to a Cabinet department. In the international arena, the Congress and the administration will have to consider how to implement the environmental agreements reached during the United Nations Conference on Environment and Development and weigh the environmental implications of the North American Free Trade Agreement.

Given high public expectations for environmental protection, one of the most important issues the Congress and the administration will have to contend with is the limited resources available to meet environmental requirements. Altogether, the nation has invested about $1 trillion in environmental protection over the last 20 years. Despite the current economic downturn, opinion polls show that Americans support continued and even additional spending on environmental protection. Nevertheless, the federal budget deficit limits the federal government's ability to respond. State and local governments are also confronting fiscal crises, and industry's capacity to invest further is similarly constrained.

Resource limitations have particularly strained EPA. The Congress has substantially increased the agency's responsibilities for regulating hazardous waste, drinking water, and water and air pollution, among other things. However, the agency's fiscal year 1992 operating budget, in constant dollars, was roughly the same as it was in fiscal year 1979.

With the widening gulf between EPA's responsibilities and the resources available to carry them out, EPA has often been unable to meet statutory mandates and to implement plans for addressing pollution, as the following example illustrates. The agency believes that most of the nation's remaining water quality problems stem from nonpoint, or diffuse, sources of water pollution resulting from agricultural and urban runoff. EPA has developed an ambitious plan to deal with nonpoint pollution. However, for lack of resources, the agency has hardly acted on key elements of the plan, including the development of monitoring techniques to help states determine the extent of their nonpoint source pollution problems and the effectiveness of corrective actions.

****

Note

Economic constraints on the setting of regulatory priorities are found at the national level addressed by the GAO's comments on the federal budget's impact on the EPA. Toward the other end of the spectrum, the economic factor is introduced with even greater drama when we consider the impact of environmental protection measures on individuals' jobs and local communities' welfare. The intense controversy about the Northern Spotted Owl, and the economic effect of protecting it and its habitat, is a recent illustration of this factor.[4]

The following article provides another, earlier illustration and addresses the difficulty of ascertaining public preferences with regard to competing economic and environmental interests. This excerpt also introduces the techniques of risk analysis that are discussed more fully in sections 3(D)-(E), *infra*.

****

Eleanor Randolph, ''What Cost a Life? EPA Asks Tacoma,'' Los Angeles Times (August 13, 1983)

[P]eople in Tacoma [Washington] are tormented by pressure to take a public position on a grim question, a life-and-death issue that may never have been presented quite so bluntly to any community in the nation. On the one hand, they can sacrifice the jobs of 570 local residents, banish a $30-million-a-year payroll from a community that has known hard times and weaken the tax base that supports the police, the fire department and other vital services. Or they can decide to keep all those material benefits – and let one more Tacoma citizen die of lung cancer every year.

At the center of the controversy is a 90-year-old copper smelter, a battered hodgepodge of buildings that the Environmental Protection Agency says is spewing more than 310 tons of arsenic into Tacoma's air every year, spreading the known carcinogen over a circle 12-1/2 miles wide. EPA has designed a plan for cutting the airborne arsenic emissions almost in half, but this half-a-loaf plan still would leave enough arsenic pouring into the air to cause one more lung-cancer death each year than would occur normally. Yet tougher action to curb the arsenic pollution probably would force the smelter to close, EPA specialists calculate.

The question for Tacoma is whether it would rather cut the pollution in half, keep the plant open – and suffer one more cancer death each year – or demand further pollution controls and risk losing the smelter's payroll.

Trade-offs between economic benefits and greater health or safety are made all the time in everyday life, of course; automobiles could be made virtually crash-proof, for instance, but they would be prohibitively expensive. But the decisions on such questions usually are made indirectly – implicitly instead of explicitly.

What sets the Tacoma situation apart is that the federal government has called upon the people most immediately affected to state explicitly and publicly how safe they want to be. William D. Ruckelshaus, the new administrator of the Environmental Protection Agency, deliberately created the confrontation as a way of focusing national attention

---

[4] *See, e.g.*, Michael C. Blumm, ''Ancient Forests, Spotted Owls, and Modern Public Land Law,'' 18 Boston College Environmental Affairs Law Review 605, 620 (1991) (''[T]he era in which the public's interest in forest management is a mirror reflection of local economic concerns is clearly over. The stakes are now much broader.'').

on the interplay between costs and benefits that is involved in cleaning up the environment. And he is not surprised that many in Tacoma are confused, even angry at being asked to state a preference.

"Listen, I know people don't like these kinds of decisions," Ruckelshaus said in an interview with The Times. "Welcome to the world of regulation. People have demanded to be involved and now I have involved them and they say: 'Don't ask that question.' What's the alternative? Don't involve them? Then you're accused of doing something nefarious. My view is that these are the kinds of tough, balancing questions that we're involved in here in this country in trying to regulate all kinds of hazardous substances. I don't like these questions either, but the societal issue is what risks are we willing to take and for what benefits?"

Legally, Ruckelshaus himself must make the final decision by early next year on how much abatement to demand from Tacoma's smelter, which is run by ASARCO Inc., a major national smelting firm. But he is presenting the issue directly to the community through four workshops in the weeks ahead, followed by a hearing.

Beside the difficulties of explaining this issue, EPA officials are faced with an even tougher task of taking the community's pulse. Do you poll the community, counting on a random sample? Do you count the pros and cons at the massive hearing that could run to two days or more? One EPA official has suggested a postcard vote.

Already the debate has stirred strong feelings. Some critics of Ruckelshaus' approach challenge EPA's analysis and statistics. Others recoil at the thought of putting a price on a neighbor's job, or worse, a friend's life. Still others bridle at being asked to consider such a difficult, anguishing philosophical question at all; that's the government's job, they say.

And on the central question, there so far is no consensus on what to do about the airborne arsenic, which spreads in a circle that extends from a scorched, desertlike area near the smelter's smokestack to the lush forests of Vashon and Maury islands across the bay, overland to golf courses dampened to a blue-green by the eternal rainfall, and, ironically, even over a new, multimillion-dollar downtown development financed by a subsidiary of Ruckelshaus' old employer, Weyerhaeuser Inc.

"Some of us don't understand why EPA is doing this," said Linda Tanz, who is active on environmental issues for the Tacoma League of Women Voters. "EPA came in recently and found that our drinking water was contaminated and just cleaned it up, saying they'd find out why later. Now, why aren't they just cleaning this mess up instead of asking people how much cancer they would like to have? It's a very confusing, difficult issue."

Charlie Davis, a 49-year-old contractor from the small community of Fife, downwind from the smelter, said he and his wife are tired of not raising vegetables because of the arsenic fallout and they are unhappy about the metallic taste in their mouths some days when the wind shifts in their direction. But Davis has a hard time understanding why his community is deciding something that engineers and government officials are appointed and elected to decide. "They're the experts, aren't they? We don't want extra cancer, but I also hate to see those people lose their jobs. It looks to me like they should be able to catch some of that arsenic and use it."

Some Tacomans simply deny that arsenic poses any hazard at all. "I don't feel there's an arsenic problem. It's all mass hysteria," said Loretta Prettyman, the town clerk in Ruston, the half-mile square community where the ASARCO smelter provides the most jobs and a hefty tax base. "Arsenic doesn't cause cancer. Nothing about it causes cancer. We've had so much flak over the years about the big, bad smelter that we just turn it off."

The balancing of risks and benefits is a controversial political issue when it involves health matters, but experts in the fledgling field of "risk assessment" say that some Americans are beginning to understand that there is no such thing as a risk-free world. In a recent discussion of the subject, the Journal of the American Medical Assn. noted that people voluntarily assume risks all the time—ranging from the risk of smoking 20 cigarette a day, which causes one death per 200 smokers a year, to the risk of driving a car, which brings one death per 5,900 drivers a year, to the risk of riding motorcycles, a much more dangerous activity that causes one death per 50 riders a year. But the same people feel differently about community risks, especially risks that can be fixed— such as hazardous wastes that can be removed with enough money and time or a bridge that should be shored up with community taxes.

As Walter R. Lynn, director of the Program on Science, Technology and Society at Cornell University said, "People don't mind being accountable for the safety of decisions that they make themselves, but they may want absolute safety in situations where they feel that someone else is imposing a risk on them that they don't want to bear."

"In the past, politicians and some judges have said that human life is beyond all price and that sounds fine," said William H. Lowrance, author of a 1976 book on the subject called "Of Acceptable Risk." "Vaccines and auto safety devices, medical procedures and airplane landing systems do have a price. It's not that we're paying for life—you could make autos with incredibly low risks that cost $100,000 each," Lowrance said. "In the end, we compare protection measures. We argue whether it's worth putting more money into an airport for even lower risks or whether to spend that same money on a new vaccine or reduction of acid rain."

Lowrance argued at the Royal College of Physicians in London last spring that science has now progressed to the point that often "we know enough to 'worry' but not enough to know how much to worry . . . . Scientific knowledge has progressed enormously and we even have the luxury of going around searching for possible trouble."

In Tacoma, specifically, the smelter as it is now operating—without any new equipment to cut down arsenic emissions—is causing about four more lung cancer deaths each year than would be normal in a population of the area's size, according to EPA statisticians. What is proposed is the installation of massive hoods to reduce the amount of arsenic escaping from the smelters' two huge vats of molten metal. If the $4.5 million hoods are installed, EPA estimates, an average of one additional person over the normal annual death rate still would die from lung cancer in this area. Seventy-one to 94 people died here annually in the 1970s from the disease. The risk of lung-cancer death in Tacoma is 20% higher than the national rate.

By shifting much of the psychological burden to the community for what is legally his own decision under the Clean Air Act, Ruckelshaus is acknowledging that scientists do not have the final answers on many environmental questions.

There is almost always an argument, even about the science of an issue. For one thing, there is the "threshold" question. That is, with any particular toxic chemical or substance, is there an exposure level below which *no* damage will be done? Or is the substance so toxic – and the factors determining how individuals react so complex – that *any* level of exposure, no matter how small, always will produce some damage.

In the Tacoma case, EPA, the National Cancer Institute and other health organizations say there is no threshold for arsenic; even the smallest amount of arsenic in the air would cause cancers if exposed to enough different kinds of people – all of them reacting in different ways over the years to the poison, scientists at these organizations say.

Lawrence W. Lindquist, Manager of the ASARCO plant, takes the other side of this almost-classic environmental argument. He says there is a threshold – an exposure point below which arsenic no longer causes health problems. He argues that "toxicity depends on concentration" – a lot of arsenic, like a lot of alcohol, is dangerous. A little bit may not hurt, may even be beneficial.

"It's hard for us to understand how we can make an informed decision and inform the people when they've got so many bad numbers," Lindquist said as he was interviewed in his stark offices near the gates of the smelting plant. "We have yet to see any scientific evidence that arsenic causes cancer. We don't see a risk-benefit problem (because) we see no discernible risk here."

Dr. Samuel Milham Jr., head of the epidemiology section of the Washington State Department of Social and Health Services, said that arsenic is indeed carcinogenic, but he contends the EPA projections of possible lung cancers in the area are "baloney." "I don't believe any of it," said Milham, who added that he has done a "ton of studies" on the Tacoma community and has found no evidence of any increase in lung cancers because of the smelter.

Milham said that studies very clearly show that workers can get cancer from exposure to high levels of arsenic on the job and a study of ASARCO retirees showed that eight times as many died of lung cancer as the normal rate for such deaths in any community. But we have been looking for extra lung cancers in the community (among those who do not work at the smelter) and we haven't found them. Nothing," he said.

After the residents of the Tacoma area hear Milham at the Nov. 2 hearing, they will then hear the other side from Dana Davoli, an environmental scientist with EPA in Seattle.

"We haven't shown which people are dying in the community, but that doesn't mean they aren't," Davoli said. "This is a projection based on the best health information we know; we can't wait for dead bodies. If we could document the increase in lung cancers, it would already be too late. It would be an epidemic."

Indeed, even complete objectivity may not be enough for a community that is becoming increasingly involved in the question. The Bellevue Washington Journal demanded in an editorial, "Who speaks for the guy with lung cancer? Who will teach his children to fish or buy funeral bouquets in gratitude for his sacrifice on behalf of 'all of us here in the smelter?'"

As the argument in the community becomes more complex and people begin to understand what is being weighed in the balance, many feel more and more strongly that the decision should not be theirs. It belongs to the experts, but to experts people can trust.

"The most natural first reaction from people would be—why do I have to decide?" said Lester B. Lave, professor of economics and public policy at Carnegie Mellon University in Pittsburgh. "Until fairly recently, we had this impulse as a society to trust such matters to the experts. We would believe them by and large—the experts on nuclear power, chemical industry, who told us things were safe. But in this last generation, experts say it is safe and we say 'I don't believe you.' In the end, we may have to come back to trust the experts, because for most people these hard choices are too painful. If somebody close by got lung cancer, we would wonder if we caused it. Nobody likes to have on their conscience that they allowed two or three more lung-cancer deaths in their community."

As Lave puts it: "Ultimately, if we don't trust the experts, then we have to make the decision. That's what is happening here."

****

Note

Following the EPA's initial proposal for cutting arsenic emissions at the Tacoma copper smelter, further study indicated that the Agency's original risk estimates were overly high and that two, rather than four, excess cancer deaths per year could be linked to smelter operations. "Arsenic Standards for Tacoma Smelter Said to be Tighter Than Those Proposed," Environment Reporter (BNA), June 22, 1984, at 297.

EPA's proposal would have been part of a National Emission Standard for Hazardous Air Pollutant (NESHAP) for inorganic arsenic under Section 112 of the Clean Air Act, but by the time the NESHAP was finally adopted, ASARCO had ceased copper smelting operations at Tacoma. "Proposed Regulations on Arsenic Smelters to be Combined into One Rulemaking, EPA Says," Environment Reporter (BNA), August 31, 1984, at 692 ("The agency was in the final stages of review of proposed standards to regulate the ASARCO smelter when the company announced July 2 that it would shut down the smelter within a year . . . ."). Upon adoption of the NESHAP, EPA noted that the ASARCO smelter was the only one to which the original proposal would have applied. EPA stated, "Because of ASARCO's action, EPA is withholding further action on the proposed standard for existing high-arsenic primary copper smelters. The EPA will continue to monitor ASARCO's actions and will reconsider the need for a separate standard applicable to existing high-arsenic smelters if there is evidence that ASARCO-Tacoma will resume copper smelting operations." 51 Federal Register 27956 (August 4, 1986). It appears, in short, that ultimately Tacoma was not called upon to answer the unusual question EPA had intended to ask.

****

A more commonly suggested method of letting the public express its preferences as between economic interests and environmental pollution is through greater operation of free market forces and the pricing system. "Economic theory suggests that the cost of pollution is either what individuals would be prepared to pay to eliminate pollution or what they would demand as compensation for exposure to pollution." Marc J. Roberts *et al.*, Book Review, 88 Harvard Law Review 1644, 1647 (1975). This approach, of course, is reflective of the economic utilitarianism approach to distributive justice discussed in Chapter 2.

Since early in the development of environmental regulation, there has been considerable debate over the relative merits of standard command-and-control regulation versus market incentives for environmental protection purposes. *See generally*, Harold Wolozin, ed., The Economics of Air Pollution (1966); Larry E. Ruff, "The Economic Common Sense of Pollution," 19 The Public Interest 69 (Spring 1970); William F. Baxter, People or Penguins: The Case for Optimal Pollution (1974); and Allen V. Kneese *et al.*, Pollution, Prices and Public Policy (1975). *See also* Daniel R. Mandelker, Environment and Equity: A Regulatory Challenge 153 (1981) ("Protective environmental controls preserve the public interest in the diffused benefits of environmental quality. These environmental benefits cannot be monetized for consideration in bargaining.").

Only now in the 1990s, does there appear to be substantial acceptance of the economists' invitation to try these alternative economic strategies.[5] As the following commentary suggests, however, the distributional impacts of these strategies remain controversial. *See also* "EPA Staff Warn of Equity Concerns in Emissions Trading Programs,"

---

[5] *See* 42 U.S.C. § 7651b (auction and trading system for allocated allowances of sulfur dioxide emissions under Clean Air Act acid deposition control provisions). In October 1993 the South Coast Air Quality Management district in the Los Angeles area adopted an ambitious emissions trading program, the Regional Clean Air Incentives Market (RECLAIM). Initially RECLAIM will address emissions of nitrogen oxides and sulfur oxides, and later it is to be expanded to cover organic compounds as well. For further discussion of RECLAIM and the trend toward greater use of economic incentives, *see* Daniel P. Selmi, "Experimentation and the 'New' Environmental Law," 27 Loyola of Los Angeles Law Review 1061 (1994).

See also Michael Kellogg, "After Environmentalism: Three Approaches to Managing Environmental Regulation," Regulation, Volume 17, Number 1, at 25, 34 (1994) ("Command-and-control style regulation is a relic of an earlier age (the '60s and '70s) when primitive information technologies seemed to require large bureaucracies to deal with complex problems. Today, market-based solutions to our environmental problems seem clearly preferable on any number of grounds."). *But cf.* Environmental Risk, Environmental Values, and Political Choices: Beyond Efficiency Trade-offs in Public Policy Analysis 1 (John M. Gillroy, ed. 1993) ("[W]e argue that environmental risk, as a policy problem, requires moving beyond the market principle of efficiency as the basis of decision making and toward the articulation and use of environmental

Inside EPA, July 2, 1993, at 16 (''EPA staff are suggesting that the agency hold off on developing new emissions trading programs until it can address emerging concerns that such market-based incentives may be encouraging companies to increase health risks to poor and minority neighborhoods.'').

****

Richard J. Lazarus, ''Pursuing 'Environmental Justice': The Distributional Effects of Environmental Protection,'' 87 Northwestern University Law Review 787, 848-49 (1993)

[B]ecause EPA is currently contemplating greater utilization of decentralized approaches, such as market incentives, for the accomplishment of environmental quality objectives, the need for overt distributional inquiry may be all the more pressing. Reliance on market incentives reduces the distributional inequities that result because of the enhanced political access that some enjoy to centralized decisionmakers under a command-and-control regulatory regime. But, rather than eliminate inequities, this approach more likely just shifts the cause for such distributional inequity away from a relative absence of political power at the national level to the relative absence of market power at home. For instance, the distribution of pollution under a market system of transferable pollution rights will tend to replicate existing income and property distributions that, to the extent that such distributions are themselves the product of racial discrimination, will only continue to produce and exacerbate inequitable results. The likely outcome is the further occurrence of pollution ''hot spots'' in racial minority communities and low income neighborhoods.

This problem could be addressed in a number of ways. One approach would be to impose certain substantive limitations on the market system to guard against the likelihood of inequitable distributions. For instance, there could be fixed limits on the amount of pollution that would be permitted within any one geographic community. Another approach would be to work within the market system by leveling the playing field. Communities identified as lacking in resources might, for example, be allocated vouchers that would allow them to bargain more effectively within the pollution rights market.

C. Global Factors

The readings in this chapter thus far have concentrated on the making of environmental policy in and for the United States, taking into consideration factors arising only within our borders. Increasingly we know, however, that it is ultimately inescapable – for economic and security reasons and perhaps on moral grounds as well – that we take account

---

values to produce good public choices.''); Mark Sagoff, ''At the Shrine of Our Lady of Fatima, or Why Political Questions Are Not all Economic,'' in Ethics and the Environment 221, 227 (Donald Scherer *et al.*, eds. 1983) (''When efficiency is the criterion of public safety and health one tends to conceive of social relations on the model of a market, ignoring competing visions of what we as a society should be like. Yet it is obvious that there are competing conceptions of how we should relate to one another.'').

of environmental conditions and economic needs elsewhere on the planet as we formulate American environmental policy and legal requirements.

The clearest example of American environmental law explicitly recognizing global environmental concerns arose in the 1990 Clean Air Act Amendments.[6] There Congress incorporated detailed provisions for stratospheric ozone protection on the basis of an earlier international agreement, the Montreal Protocol on Substances that Deplete the Ozone Layer. 42 U.S.C. §§ 7671-7671q. Requirements such as these, linking international needs to national law, involve environmental lawyers in work that has global implications.

Lawmaking of this type will increase in future years. Greater global economic interdependence, and greater scientific understanding of worldwide environmental conditions, will combine to require much greater attention to international factors in the setting of American regulatory agendas. Although at present this trend does not yet appear to have affected the work of most environmental lawyers, the forces behind the trend and the principles that will guide it are becoming clear, as the following readings suggest.

****

U.S. General Accounting Office, Environmental Protection Issues 20-23 (1992)

Resolving today's environmental problems — including global climate change, depletion of the stratospheric ozone layer, and deforestation, among others — will require an unprecedented level of international cooperation. At the United Nations Conference on Environment and Development in Rio de Janeiro in June 1992, participating nations drew up an action program for environmentally sustainable development as well as conventions to address climate change and threats to biological diversity. But while reaching these agreements is, in itself, a noteworthy accomplishment, their effectiveness in correcting problems ultimately depends on how well the agreements are implemented. Moreover, because the costs of compliance are high, uneven implementation may place the countries that carry out the agreements at a competitive disadvantage with those that do not.

Since 1972, the number of international environmental agreements in which the United States participates, or in which it has a significant interest, has grown from fewer than 50 to about 170. Yet little is known about how well environmental agreements are being implemented. In a review of eight major international agreements, we found that the reports that parties are supposed to provide on their compliance with agreements are often late, incomplete, or not submitted at all, and the secretariats responsible for overseeing the agreements lack the authority or resources to monitor implementation independently. In addition, many parties, particularly developing countries, lack the technical and financial capability to comply.

---

[6] Another example is Executive Order 12114 issued by President Carter to require federal government agencies to consider their actions' environmental effects outside the United States. 44 Fed. Reg. 1957 (Jan. 9, 1979).

The environment has also become a critical element in trade agreements and will have to be addressed directly in future negotiations. As the United States and its trading partners seek to phase out tariffs and traditional barriers to free trade, incompatible environmental standards can themselves be perceived as trade barriers and can stand in the way of trade liberalization. This, in turn, generates concern about the potential for trade agreements to encourage the adoption of "lowest common denominator" environmental standards that would be weaker than existing U.S. standards.

Moreover, existing trade agreements do not fully address environmental issues. The General Agreement on Tariffs and Trade (GATT) – the major international trade agreement – was developed long before countries had many environmental laws and international environmental agreements. And when the North American Free Trade Agreement (NAFTA) was created, the administration promised to deal with environmental issues in a separate process, outside of the agreement itself.

****

Declaration of the United Nations Conference on the Human Environment (1972)

In the developing countries most of the environmental problems are caused by underdevelopment. Millions continue to live far below the minimum levels required for a decent human existence, deprived of adequate food and clothing, shelter and education, health and sanitation. Therefore, the developing countries must direct their efforts to development, bearing in mind their priorities and the need to safeguard and improve the environment. For the same purpose, the industrialized countries should make efforts to reduce the gap between themselves and the developing countries. In the industrialized countries, environmental problems are generally related to industrialization and technological development.

Principle 1: Man has the fundamental right to freedom, equality and adequate conditions of life, in an environment of a quality that permits a life of dignity and well-being, and he bears a solemn responsibility to protect and improve the environment for present and future generations.

Principle 11: The environmental policies of all States should enhance and not adversely affect the present or future development potential of developing countries, nor should they hamper the attainment of better living conditions for all, and appropriate steps should be taken by States and international organizations with a view to reaching agreement on meeting the possible national and international economic consequences resulting from the application of environmental measures.

Principle 21: States have, in accordance with the Charter of the United Nations and the principles of international law, the sovereign right to exploit their own resources pursuant to their own environmental policies, and the responsibility to ensure that activities within their jurisdiction or control do not cause damage to the environment of other States or of areas beyond the limits of national jurisdiction.

Principle 22: States shall co-operate to develop further the international law regarding liability and compensation for the victims of pollution and other environmental damage caused by activities within the jurisdiction or control of such States to areas beyond their jurisdiction.

****

United Nations Conference on Environment and Development, Rio Declaration on Environment and Development (1992)

Principle 1: Human beings are at the centre of concerns for sustainable development. They are entitled to a healthy and productive life in harmony with nature.

Principle 3: The right to development must be fulfilled so as to equitably meet developmental and environmental needs of present and future generations.

Principle 4: In order to achieve sustainable development, environmental protection shall constitute an integral part of the development process and cannot be considered in isolation from it.

Principle 5: All States and all people shall cooperate in the essential task of eradicating poverty as an indispensable requirement for sustainable development, in order to decrease the disparities in standards of living and better meet the needs of the majority of the people of the world.

Principle 6: The special situation and needs of developing countries, particularly the least developed and those most environmentally vulnerable, shall be given special priority. International actions in the field of environment and development should also address the interests and needs of all countries.

Principle 11: States shall enact effective environmental legislation. Environmental standards, management objectives and priorities should reflect the environmental and developmental context to which they apply. Standards applied by some countries may be inappropriate and of unwarranted economic and social cost to other countries, in particular developing countries.

****

Alexandre Kiss and Dinah Shelton, International Environmental Law 381 (1991)

There is urgent need to draft and adopt a general covenant of environmental law, which would oblige states to protect the planetary biosphere, outside as well as inside the limits of their jurisdiction. This instrument would be similar to, but more far-reaching than, the international covenants for the protection of human rights, which oblige all states to respect and ensure the enunciated rights and freedoms to all human beings within their territory and subject to their jurisdiction.

A comprehensive environmental covenant should begin by proclaiming the general obligation of states to ensure the sustainable use of natural resources for the benefit of present and future generations and thus their obligation to protect and preserve the environment. Other elements would elaborate both the general principles and the means of implementation. The former category could include provisions requiring national conservation strategies in order to sustain and rehabilitate natural systems and prevent environmental harm. It also should recognize the fundamental right of individuals to an ecologically sound environment. This right includes the right to public information and participation in the decision-making process, as well as access to means of prevention and redress for environmental damage. This right should be afforded on an equal basis to both residents and nonresidents.

To adequately detail the obligations of states in a comprehensive fashion, an international covenant should establish the duties and obligations for specific resources and environmental sectors. These may provide for land use allocation; the conservation of biological diversity; sustainable use of wildlife; the conservation, rehabilitation and enhancement of vegetation, including forests, wetlands, and other flora; soil conservation; protection of the marine environment; management of fresh water resources; and pollution control.

Notes

1. Can you envision not only the adoption of a general, international covenant of environmental law, but its actual integration into United States environmental law in specific and enforceable features? What types of events or developments would it take to stimulate greater recognition of the value of such integration?

2. Are increases in population growth rates, poverty, and public health crises in many other parts of the world likely to have impact on American environmental policy? One commentator on the development of environmental law recently lamented the relatively low level of publicity in Western nations about the large numbers of Third World people, principally children, who "are indubitably dying *each day now*" from treatable diseases. He contrasted that inattention with the relatively high level of publicity given to the specter of global climate change, even though there is great uncertainty in forecasts of adverse climate change and even though some of the most dire predictions still do not approach the magnitude of current suffering. He asked, "What forces motivate the Western press and determine so much of the human agenda?" Christopher D. Stone, "Bringing Environmentalists Back Down to Earth," U.S.C. Trojan Family, Winter 1994, at 44, 49.

3. In what areas of environmental law would you consider it most likely that United States lawyers will find their practices affected by international considerations?

D. Risk Analysis Methods

As mentioned above in the discussion of the Tacoma experiment, the U.S. Environmental Protection Agency in recent years has attempted to apply risk analysis methods to various environmental problems. The readings presented here explain and evaluate these methods more fully. These readings also indicate that risk assessment and risk management methods may provide more objective bases for setting regulatory priorities and, in any event, are likely to become an increasingly common aspect of regulatory issues addressed by environmental lawyers. As one commentary has noted, "Risk assessment is a new science, but it has clearly occupied the high ground in government and many intellectual circles and will expand in the decades to come." Charles Perrow, Normal Accidents: Living with High-Risk Technologies 305 (1984).

In examining these materials, consider the extent to which the influence of the types of factors discussed earlier in this chapter would be reduced in the making of environmental policy if risk analysis were used more extensively. In what aspects of policy making might such factors be entirely eliminated from consideration? Also, to the extent that these more scientific analytical and decisional approaches could supplant less technical influences on policy making, would you consider that a salutary development? Would it promote or impede the achievement of one or more concepts of justice regarding the distribution of environmental burdens? And how might it change the role of environmental lawyers relative to other types of environmental experts?

The first reading explains basic tools of risk analysis, the second discusses the use of these methods by the federal government, and the third criticizes some of the current uses of risk analysis.

$$*********************$$

Carnegie Commission on Science, Technology, and Government, Risk and the Environment: Improving Regulatory Decision Making 73-74, 76-78 (1993)

The fundamental problem in regulatory decision making at the agency level, as at the presidential and interagency level, is how to set priorities. It is a great challenge for science-based regulatory agencies to compare and rank individual risks and families of risks within the universe they regulate.

This difficulty can be partly ascribed to organizational fragmentation within agencies, which in turn stems at least partly from the patchwork of statutory provisions the agencies administer. More than anything else, though, its cause lies outside the agencies. Agencies are buffeted by a torrent of forces exerted by the public, the media, industry, the Executive Office of the President, legislators, and the courts. The decisions agencies make frequently seem to equal the vector sum of these forces. At one level this is good: our regulatory agencies are responsive to the people and to other government institutions. Yet, by the same token, setting priorities on a "chemical of the month" basis may result in overregulation of some hazards, underregulation of others, and reduction of agency credibility.

Our relative ignorance of the facts further complicates the task of making sound decisions about regulating risks. Data on many environmental, health, and safety risks are scarce. For example, few or no data are available on most chemicals in commerce, and data on the remainder are often insufficient for reliable risk assessment. It is also possible for reasonable people to interpret data in different ways—and this is often the case in regulatory decision making. Moreover, science by its very nature is provisional; new findings drive out old ones after a time.

Finding and organizing those data that exist is frequently difficult. Data bases in different agencies and even in different offices within agencies often cannot be readily cross-accessed. This compartmentalization of information impedes efforts by top agency management to put the universe of risks they regulate into perspective. Also hampering attempts to order risks in an agency's domain sensibly is the historical preoccupation with carcinogens (and to a much lesser extent respiratory irritants and teratogens, agents which cause birth defects). Recently, agencies have begun to focus more on certain noncancer health risks and ecological risks, but further attention is needed.

Risk assessment is a composite of established disciplines, including toxicology, biostatistics, epidemiology, economics, and demography. The goals of risk assessment are to characterize the nature of the adverse effects and to produce quantitative estimates of one or both of the following fundamental quantities: (1) the *probability* that an individual (a hypothetical or identified person) will suffer disease or death as a result of a specified exposure to a pollutant or pollutants; and (2) the *consequences* of such an exposure to an entire population (i.e., the number of cases of disease or death).

Risk assessment can be either generic (e.g., an estimate of the number of excess annual cancers caused by all 189 hazardous air pollutants identified in the 1990 Clean Air Act Amendments) or site- and/or chemical-specific (e.g., the probability that a specified child will suffer neurological impairment as a result of exposure to lead in his household drinking water).

The regulatory process is generally thought to encompass two elements, risk assessment and risk management. The distinction between these two components is important, though controversial. Risk assessment is usually conceived as the "objective" part of the process, and risk management the subjective part. In risk assessment the analyst decides how big the problem is, while in risk management political decision makers decide what to do about the problem. The "conventional wisdom" (which some believe needs rethinking) stresses that risk management must not influence the process and assumptions made in risk assessment, so the two functions must be kept conceptually and administratively separate.

Numerical estimates derived from risk assessment serve as inputs to several different kinds of decisions, including (1) "acceptable risk" determinations (wherein action is taken if the risk exceeds some "bright line," which can be zero); (2) "cost-benefit" determinations, where the risks reduced by a proposed action are translated into benefits (e.g., lives saved, life-years extended), expressed in dollar amounts, and compared to the estimated costs of implementing the action and some rule of thumb regarding how much cost it is wise to incur to achieve a given level of benefit (e.g., $10 million to save one additional life); and (3) "cost-effectiveness" determinations, where the action that maximizes the amount of risk reduction (not necessarily expressed in dollar terms) per unit cost is favored.

Since at least 1983 (with the publication of the National Research Council's "Redbook"), the dominant paradigm for risk assessment has been a sequential, four-step process:

- ■ *Hazard identification* — in which a qualitative determination is made of what kinds of adverse health or ecological effects a substance can cause. Typically, agencies have focused on cancer as the effect that drives further analysis and regulation. So, for example, a typical hazard identification for vinyl chloride released from industrial facilities would involve the collection and critical analysis of short-term test-tube assays (for mutagenicity, etc.), of long-term animal assays (typically two-year rodent carcinogenicity tests), and of human epidemiologic data — either cohort studies (in which populations exposed to vinyl chloride are followed to assess whether their rates of any disease were significantly greater than those of unexposed or less-exposed populations) or case-control studies (which focus on victims of a particular disease to see whether they were significantly more likely to have been exposed to vinyl chloride than similar but disease-free individuals).

- ■ *Exposure assessment* — in which a determination is made of the amounts of a substance to which a hypothetical person (usually the "maximally exposed individual") and/or the total population are exposed. To return to the vinyl chloride example, this part of risk assessment would bring to bear techniques of emissions characterization (how much vinyl chloride leaves the plant in a given time?), fate-and-transport analysis (how is the chemical dispersed in the atmosphere and transformed into other compounds?), uptake analysis (how much air do people breathe, both outdoors and indoors?), and demographic analysis (how many hours per day do people spend in various locations near the plant, and how long do they reside in one locale before moving away?).

- ■ *Dose-response assessment* — in which an estimate is made of the probability or extent of injury at the exposure levels determined above, by quantifying the "potency" of the chemical in question. For vinyl chloride again, scientists would determine its carcinogenic potency by fitting the animal bioassay data (number of tumors produced at different exposure levels) to a mathematical model (usually one that is linear at low doses), and then transforming the resultant potency estimate for rodents into a human potency estimate through the use of a "scaling factor" (usually, a ratio of the body surface areas of the two species). Additionally, human epidemiologic data could be used to validate or supplant the animal-based potency estimate.

- ■ *Risk characterization* — in which the results of the above steps are integrated to describe the nature of the adverse effects and the strength of the evidence and to present one or more "risk numbers." For example, EPA might say, "This vinyl chloride plant is estimated to produce up to 3 excess cases of liver cancer every 70 years among the 100,000 people living within 1 mile of the facility" or "the maximally exposed individual faces an excess lifetime liver cancer risk of 5.4×10^{-4}."

Risk assessment is essentially a tool for extrapolating from scientific data to a risk number. The tool is made up of a host of assumptions, which are an admixture of science and policy. Sometimes either science or policy predominates, but it is often difficult to get a broad consensus that this is so.

A view among some in industry and elsewhere is that risk assessment systematically overestimates risk and frightens the public: as they see it, the typical risk assessment takes a trivial emission source, pretends that people are pressed up against the fence line of the source 24 hours a day for 70 years, gauges the toxicity of the pollutant released by exposing ultrasensitive rodents to huge doses in the laboratory, and then uses the most "conservative" dose-response model to estimate a risk to humans at the low ambient exposures of interest. The view of some in environmental and public interest groups, and elsewhere, is that risk assessment may often inherently underestimate the true magnitude of the problem, by ignoring complicating but salient factors, including synergies among exposures, vast variations in susceptibility among humans, and unusual exposure pathways (e.g., inhalation of steam in showers containing volatilized chemicals from contaminated water).

Because the science underlying most risk assessment assumptions is inconclusive, arguments over whether or not an assumption is scientifically valid often distill down to debates about whether it is better to err on the side of "false positives" (if there is an error, it will more likely be a false indication of danger) or "false negatives" (if there is an error, it will more likely be a false indication of safety). Those who might be harmed by the substance being assessed will generally favor false positives; those who would gain from the substance will generally favor false negatives.

Two practical consequences of risk assessment's reliance on poorly substantiated assumptions are that numerical risk estimates tend to be highly uncertain and highly variable. Uncertainty refers to how likely a given estimate (expressed as a range of values) is to be true. However close a number is to being correct, it is correct only for a particular scenario—for example, average exposure level, or average individual susceptibility to the adverse effect at issue. Yet we know that exposures typically vary across space and time, and individuals probably vary widely in their susceptibility to different toxicants. Thus, any statement that "the risk is $A \times 10^{-B}$" is really a shorthand for the general truth that "we are Y% sure that the risk is no more than $A \times 10^{-B}$ for Z% of the population." If Y and Z were both very close to 100%, EPA and other agencies would not be seriously misleading themselves and the public with these shorthand statements, but that assumption is highly speculative in many cases.

Risk assessment can be most useful when those who rely on it to inform the risk management process understand its nature and its limitations, and use it accordingly. This means that decision makers must at least understand that the process is assumption-and value-laden; that they understand what assumptions were used in the assessment in question, and what values they reflect; that the risk estimate with which they work is expressed as a range, with the level of certainty that the true average is in that range quantified; and, that variability is expressed to the degree that it is known, i.e., how many and what kind of persons (e.g., children) will likely be at significantly higher or lower risk than the hypothetical average individual. Risk managers must take all these factors into account in making a decision, along with political and economic factors extrinsic to the risk assessment.

****

U. S. Environmental Protection Agency Science Advisory Board, Reducing Risk: Setting Priorities and Strategies for Environmental Protection 1-4, 6, 16-17, 22 (1990)

The Concept of Risk

Over the past 20 years this country has put in place extensive and detailed government policies to control a number of environmental problems. Smog in heavily populated areas, the eutrophication of lakes, elevated levels of lead in the blood of millions of children, the threat of cancer from exposure to pesticide residues in food, and abandoned drums of hazardous wastes are a few of the problems that have driven the enactment of more than a dozen major Federal laws and the current public and private expenditure of about $100 billion a year to protect the environment.

Those efforts have led to very real national benefits. The staggering human health and ecological problems apparent throughout eastern Europe suggest the price this country would be paying now had it not invested heavily in pollution controls.

Yet despite the demonstrable success of past national efforts to protect the environment, many national environmental goals still have not been attained. Factors like the growth in automobile use and common agricultural practices have caused national efforts to protect the environment to be less effective than intended.

Furthermore, with hindsight it is clear that in many cases those efforts have been inconsistent, uncoordinated, and thus less effective than they could have been. The fragmentary nature of U.S. environmental policy has been evident in three ways:

In Laws. As different environmental problems were identified, usually because the adverse effects—smog in major cities, lack of aquatic life in stream segments, declining numbers of bald eagles—were readily apparent, new laws were passed to address each new problem. However, the tactics and goals of the different laws were neither consistent nor coordinated, even if the pollutants to be controlled were the same. Many laws not passed primarily for environmental purposes also had major effects on the environment.

In Programs. The Environmental Protection Agency (EPA) was established as the primary Federal agency responsible for implementing the nation's environmental laws. EPA then evolved an administrative structure wherein each program was primarily responsible for implementing specific laws. Consequently, the efforts of the different programs rarely were coordinated, even if they were attempting to control different aspects of the same environmental problem. This problem is compounded by the fact that EPA is not the only agency whose activities affect the environment.

In Tools. The primary tools used to protect the environment have been controls designed to capture pollutants before they escape from smokestacks, tailpipes, or sewer outfalls, and technologies designed to clean up or destroy pollutants after they have been discharged into the environment. These so-called "end-of-pipe" controls and remediation technologies almost always have been applied because of Federal, State, or local legal requirements.

For a number of reasons, this kind of fragmented approach to protecting the environment will not be as successful in the future as it has been in the past. In this country the most obvious controls already have been applied to the most obvious problems. Yet complex and less obvious environmental problems remain, and the aggregate cost of controlling those problems one-by-one is rising.

Moreover, this country—and the rest of the world—are facing emerging environmental problems of unprecedented scope. Population growth and industrial expansion worldwide are straining global ecosystems. Never before in history have human activities threatened to change atmospheric chemistry to such an extent that global climate patterns were altered.

Given the diversity, complexity, and scope of the environmental problems of concern today, it is critically important that U.S. environmental policy evolves in several fundamental ways. Essentially, national policy affecting the environment must become more integrated and more focused on opportunities for environmental improvement than it has been in the past.

The environment is an interrelated whole, and society's environmental protection efforts should be integrated as well. Integration in this case means that government agencies should assess the range of environmental problems of concern and then target protective efforts at the problems that seem to be the most serious. It means that society should use all the tools—regulatory and non-regulatory alike—that are available to protect the environment. It means that controlling the end of the pipe where pollutants enter the environment, or remediating problems caused by pollutants after they have entered the environment, is not sufficient. Rather, waste-generating activities have to be modified to minimize the waste or to prevent the waste from being generated at all. Most of all, integration is critically important because significant sources of environmental degradation are embedded in typical day-to-day personal and professional activities, the cumulative effects of which can become serious problems. Thus protecting the environment effectively in the future will require a more broadly conceived strategic approach, one that involves the cooperative efforts of all segments of society.

One tool that can help foster the evolution of an integrated and targeted national environmental policy is the concept of environmental risk. Each environmental problem poses some possibility of harm to human health, the ecology, the economic system, or the quality of human life. That is, each problem poses some environmental risk. Risk assessment is the process by which the form, dimension, and characteristics of that risk are estimated, and risk management is the process by which the risk is reduced.

The concept of environmental risk, together with its related terminology and analytical methodologies, helps people discuss disparate environmental problems with a common language. It allows many environmental problems to be measured and compared in common terms, and it allows different risk reduction options to be evaluated from a common basis. Thus the concept of environmental risk can help the nation develop environmental policies in a consistent and systematic way.

Scientists have made some progress in developing quantitative measures for use in comparing different risks to human health. Given sufficient data, such comparisons are now possible within limits. Although current ability to assess and quantify ecological risks is not as well developed, an increased capacity for comparing different kinds of risks more systematically would help determine which problems are most serious and deserving of the most urgent attention. That capacity would be even more valuable as the number and seriousness of environmental problems competing for attention and resources increase.

An improved ability to compare risks in common terms would have another value as well: it would help society choose more wisely among the range of policy options available for reducing risks. There are a number of ways to reduce the automobile emissions that contribute to urban smog; there are a number of ways to decrease human exposure to lead. The evaluation of relative risks can help identify the relative efficiency and effectiveness of different risk reduction options.

There are heavy costs involved if society fails to set environmental priorities based on risk. If finite resources are expended on lower-priority problems at the expense of higher-priority risks, then society will face needlessly high risks. If priorities are established based on the greatest opportunities to reduce risk, total risk will be reduced in a more efficient way, lessening threats to both public health and local and global ecosystems.

The Environmental Protection Agency squarely faced the question of relative risk for the first time when it established an Agency task force to assess and compare the risks associated with a range of environmental problems. In 1986 and 1987, about 75 senior career managers and staff compared the relative risks posed by 31 environmental problems within four broad categories of risk: 1) human cancer risk, 2) human non-cancer health risk, 3) ecological risk, and 4) welfare risk. The task force limited its comparison to those risks that remain after currently-required controls have been applied (i.e., residual risks). The results of this effort were presented in *Unfinished Business: A Comparative Assessment of Environmental Problems.*

Unfinished Business was a landmark study. For the first time, the many environmental problems of concern to EPA were compared to each other in a non-programmatic context. Moreover, the report explicitly pointed out the disparity between residual risk and resource allocation at EPA. The problems that the authors judged to pose the most serious risks were not necessarily the problems that Congress and EPA had targeted for the most aggressive action.

However, the report did find a correlation between EPA's programmatic priorities and the apparent public perceptions of risk. That is, Congress and the Agency were paying the most attention to environmental problems that the general public believed posed the greatest risks.

The Ten Recommendations

1. EPA should target its environmental protection efforts on the basis of opportunities for the greatest risk reduction. Since this country already has taken the most obvious actions to address the most obvious environmental problems, EPA needs to set priorities for future actions so the Agency takes advantage of the best opportunities for reducing the most serious remaining risks.

2. EPA should attach as much importance to reducing ecological risk as it does to reducing human health risk. Because productive natural ecosystems are essential to human health and to sustainable, long-term economic growth, and because they are intrinsically valuable in their own right, EPA should be as concerned about protecting ecosystems as it is about protecting human health.

3. EPA should improve the data and analytical methodologies that support the assessment, comparison, and reduction of different environmental risks. Although setting priorities for national environmental protection efforts always will involve subjective judgments and uncertainty, EPA should work continually to improve the scientific data and analytical methodologies that underpin those judgments and help reduce their uncertainty.

4. EPA should reflect risk-based priorities in its strategic planning processes.

5. EPA should reflect risk-based priorities in its budget process.

6. EPA – and the nation as a whole – should make greater use of all the tools available to reduce risk. Although the nation has had substantial success in reducing environmental risks through the use of government-mandated end-of-pipe controls, the extent and complexity of future risks will necessitate the use of a much broader array of tools, including market incentives and information.

7. EPA should emphasize pollution prevention as the preferred option for reducing risk. By encouraging actions that prevent pollution from being generated in the first place, EPA will help reduce the costs, intermedia transfers of pollution, and residual risks so often associated with end-of-pipe controls.

8. EPA should increase its efforts to integrate environmental considerations into broader aspects of public policy in as fundamental a manner as are economic concerns.

9. EPA should work to improve public understanding of environmental risks and train a professional workforce to help reduce them.

10. EPA should develop improved analytical methods to value natural resources and to account for long-term environmental effects in its economic analyses. Because traditional methods of economic analysis tend to undervalue ecological resources and fail to treat adequately questions of intergenerational equity, EPA should develop and implement innovative approaches to economic analysis that will address these shortcomings.

EPA Should Emphasize Pollution Prevention as the Preferred Option for Reducing Risk

The costs of cleaning up and disposing of pollutants after they have been generated can be enormous. The costs of the Superfund program, the planned cleanup of the Department of Energy's nuclear weapons plants, and the cancellation and disposal of chemicals already in use are painful examples of that lesson.

Thus end-of-pipe controls and waste disposal should be the last line of environmental defense, not the front line. Preventing pollution at the source—through the redesign of production processes, the substitution of less toxic production materials, the screening of new chemicals and technologies *before* they are introduced into commerce, energy and water conservation, the development of less-polluting transportation systems and farming practices, etc.—is usually a far cheaper, more effective way to reduce environmental risk, especially over the long term.

More widespread use of pollution prevention techniques holds enormous environmental and economic promise for a number of reasons. For one thing, some environmental problems—like global warming—simply cannot be remediated in any practical way using only end-of-pipe controls.

Pollution prevention also minimizes environmental problems that are caused through a variety of exposures. For example, substituting a non-toxic for a toxic agent reduces exposures to workers producing and using the agent at the same time as it reduces exposures through surface water, groundwater, and the air.

Pollution prevention also is preferable to end-of-pipe controls that often cause environmental problems of their own. Air pollutants captured in industrial smokestacks and deposited in landfills can contribute to groundwater pollution; stripping toxic chemicals out of groundwater, and combusting solid and hazardous wastes, can contribute to air pollution. Pollution prevention techniques are especially promising because they do not move pollutants from one environmental medium to another, as is often the case with end-of-pipe controls. Rather, the pollutants are not generated in the first place.

The advantages of pollution prevention also are becoming apparent as the nation tries to address some of the environmental risks that remain after end-of-pipe controls are applied. Ongoing growth in the amount of wastes generated in this country is quickly overcoming the ability of landfills and incinerators to absorb it, especially since landfills are no longer an option for hazardous waste disposal. Society must find more ways to reduce the amount of waste requiring disposal. Similarly, as the nation attempts to reduce the environmental risks still posed by urban smog more than a decade after automobile emissions were reduced sharply by end-of-pipe technology, it is clear that preventing pollution—e.g., through mass transit, car pools, and the combustion of alternative fuels—is a promising long-term option.

In addition, pollution prevention techniques often bring substantial economic benefits to the sources that use them. Business can avoid the cost of end-of-pipe controls, waste cleanup and disposal, and liability by preventing pollution instead of controlling it. Moreover, some pollution prevention techniques, like using energy more efficiently and recycling process materials, can pay for themselves quite apart from environmental considerations. One reason that Japan and Western Europe are formidable economic competitors is that they use energy and raw materials so efficiently. To compete in the global marketplace, American businesses also must use them more efficiently.

****

Peter Huber, "Exorcists vs. Gatekeepers in Risk Regulation," Regulation, November 1983, p. 23[7]

Two Goals, Two Procedures

Risk regulation has two overarching goals—goals that are distinct and often contradictory. It aims, on the one hand, to reduce the "old" risks of our environment. I am referring here to risks that accompany such familiar activities as driving a car, or digging for coal, or stepping out for a breath of air. On the other hand, risk regulation seeks to impede technological changes that threaten to introduce "new" hazards into our lives. I have in mind here risks associated with the likes of nuclear power, artificial food additives, and new toxic chemicals.

These two goals—the control of old risks and the exclusion of new ones—lead to profoundly different legislative commitments. The first is made when Congress wakes up one day to discover that things somewhere out there are intolerably hazardous. The resulting "something ought'a be done" laws are transformational. They demand a change in the established order—clean-up programs, if you will. The second kind of commitment is the child of a Panglossian dream, in which Congress sees the ominous unknown encroaching on this safest-of-all-possible worlds. So the "don't let it happen" laws are exclusionary. They demand protection of the presumptively safe status quo—like antilittering programs.

The two different legislative objectives spawn two quite different regulatory procedures: "standard setting" and "screening." Under a standard-setting regime of regulation, reserved for old risks, you go about your business until Washington, in its own good time, comes to you and tells you how to do it better. OSHA is an example of a standard-setting agency. "Screening," which applies to new hazards, is regulation by advance licensing. *Before* undertaking a new venture, you go to Washington to ask for permission. The Food and Drug Administration (FDA) is a screening agency. OSHA and the FDA regulate chemically similar toxins, but use fundamentally different regulatory tools.

Standard setting is initiated by the regulatory agency. If a standard-setting agency promulgates a standard based on inadequate scientific evidence of the underlying risk, the standard will be thrown out by the courts. Screening places the burden of initiating the regulatory process on the regulatee. A screening agency can survive a judicial challenge by proving its complete ignorance about the hazard involved. It is up to the would-be licensee, the person trying to pass through the screening system, to prove that the screened product is acceptable.

Standard setting is an incremental transformational approach. Standard-setting agencies aspire for a safer world: they exorcize the devils we know. Screening agencies,

---

[7] *See also* Peter Huber, "The Old-New Division in Risk Regulation," 69 Virginia Law Review 1025 (1983).

on the other hand, serve to protect the universe of risk from deterioration; they act as guardians at the gate, making yes-no kinds of decisions, protecting us from the ominous unknown.

Congress generally decrees that standards shall be set for old products, old sources of risk, and that screening will be used to regulate new products, new risks. Standard setting is reserved for our "familiar killers" – risks that society has come to tolerate before the decision to regulate is reached. Screening regulates new risks that loom on the horizon – risks that threaten to undermine the perceived safety of the status quo.

Thus, we set standards for cars, but screen aircraft. We set standards to control the old hazards of burning coal, but screen new nuclear power plants. Under the Toxic Substances Control Act (TOSCA), EPA is supposed to screen all major new productions of "new" chemicals, but is directed merely to set standards for the production and handling of old ones. EPA screens new pesticides but for the most part leaves the old ones alone. Numerous other examples could be cited. Of course, some statutes, like the Clean Air Act, combine elements of standard setting (in establishing ambient standards) and screening (to set individual new source emission limits). But overall, the old/new line falls remarkably close to the standard-setting/screening division.

Indeed, Congress exerts itself mightily to preserve the division. TOSCA . . . divides the regulatory universe of toxic chemicals between old chemicals – in this case chemicals in significant use before 1973 – and new ones. The Clean Air Act calls for the screening of new major sources of pollution, but only sets standards for old ones. The Federal Water Pollution Control Act contemplates more stringent regulation of new emitters than of old ones. New pesticides are regulated more severely than the old ones. Again, numerous other examples can be found.

Process and Reality

So what? Who cares if the procedures for regulating old and new risks are different? The answer, I think, is found in the words of Alfred North Whitehead: "The process is itself the actuality." There is a difference between Mohammed going to the mountain and the mountain coming to Mohammed. Procedures *do* make a difference.

The Supreme Court's decision in *Industrial Union Department v. American Petroleum Institute* [448 U.S. 605] (1980) – the benzene case – was about procedures. OSHA had come to realize that regulating occupational exposures to carcinogens through standard setting is difficult and time-consuming. So it set about promulgating its own, in-house Delaney Amendment. Under its proposed carcinogen policy, no employer could introduce into a work place chemicals that had been found to be carcinogenic in test animals. OSHA would make no assessment of actual risk to humans; it would be up to employers to prove, if they could, that non-zero occupational exposures to animal carcinogens were safe. Through the magic of the Federal Register OSHA would turn itself into a screening agency, shifting burdens of proof from the agency to the regulatee. OSHA's benzene standard, though promulgated just before the agency's official carcinogen policy, reflected the evolving philosophy.

But the Supreme Court would not go along. It ruled, in effect, that OSHA was constituted as a standard-setting agency and would have to behave like one. It is up to OSHA to demonstrate that its standards will mitigate a "significant risk," not up to employers to show that their work places are "safe."

For a standard-setting agency this result made perfect sense. For a screening agency it would have been extraordinary. When the FDA declines to license a new food additive and thereby effectively bans the additive, the agency is not required to show that the additive poses a significant risk. The FDA may simply insist that it is ignorant, that safety has not been proven by the regulatee to the agency's satisfaction. The same is true for the NRC when it declines to grant an operating license to a new plant, or for the FAA when it holds up on licensing a new aircraft, or for the EPA when it declines to license a new pesticide, or for any other screening agency, when the information available does not support an affirmative finding of acceptability.

The different procedures for regulating old and new risks — standard setting and screening — can thus have profoundly different substantive consequences. Screening, first of all, regulates at the "strict" margin of scientific uncertainty, standard setting regulates at the "lenient" margin. A screening system admits only the "acceptably safe," while a standard-setting system excludes only the "unacceptably hazardous." There is often a wide gap in between those two criteria.

Screening systems also place the cost of acquiring the information needed for regulation on the regulatee; standard-setting systems place that cost on the agency. This makes all the difference when the product or process targeted for regulation is only marginally profitable. A pesticide manufacturer may have to spend $20 million on tests needed for licensing. Even if a pesticide is completely safe, it will never even be submitted for review if the manufacturer stands to make only $19 million from its sale.

The cost problem also impels screening systems to favor big-ticket products and operations — a broad spectrum drug, a new pesticide that will kill everything from aphids to dung beetles, the largest nuclear power plants. As in most other ventures, there are economies of scale in paying the price of being screened. Securing regulatory approval of a single 1000 MW power plant will certainly cost less than securing approval of two 500 MW plants. So our nuclear plants tend to get bigger and bigger, our pesticides less and less specific. Standard-setting systems, in contrast, tend to place the greatest burdens on the largest regulatory targets because it is there that the standard-setting agency can have the biggest impact. A small generator of an unusual type of risk is often beneath the standard-setting agency's attention.

Another component of cost is delay. Under a screening system it is the regulatee who bears the risk and cost of regulatory delay. Delay postpones the return on R&D costs and allows the clock to tick on crucial patents. In standard setting, delay postpones the cost of compliance until an agency acts — which may mean forever, especially if you have a good lawyer litigating avidly on your side.

The final and most important difference between standard setting and screening — that is, between the regulation of old and new risks — is found in the statutory criteria for regulation. Standard-setting statutes almost always limit in some manner the *costs* that a regulatory scheme may impose on regulatees. Screening statutes rarely contain analogous cost-conscious provisions.

Origin of the Double Standard

Old risks subject to standards are systematically treated more leniently than new risks that are screened. What accounts for the double standard?

Some suggest that informational problems are at the root of the division. We set standards for old risks because they are familiar and therefore well understood. We screen new hazards because we know less about them. Yet those in the business know that informational problems are pervasive even for hazards as old as asbestos and wood fires. Others have suggested that the psychological dimension of risk accounts for the old-new division. "Rare catastrophes" provoke different legislative responses than "common killers." Again I am skeptical. Rare catastrophes are caused by old sources of risk every bit as much as by new ones. Somewhat more convincing is Robert Crandall's suggestion that the old-new division results from the raw politics of competition between the industrially old, politically powerful Frost Belt and the industrially new, less powerful Sun Belt.

Though all of these factors undoubtedly play some role, I am convinced that the old-new division is primarily attributable to something much more pedestrian. Congress thinks that it is much more expensive to regulate old risks than new ones. That belief is understandable enough. Cleaning up the risk environment requires direct cash outlays. Regulated industries rebel at these transition costs; consumers are dismayed to lose products to which they have become habituated. People are usually of the view that it is better that things be settled than that they be settled right.

In contrast, excluding new risky products or activities seems relatively painless. Manufacturers do not have to readjust production processes, consumers do not have to change established patterns of consumption. The only cost that *is* incurred by the regulation of new types of risk is the price society pays whenever it decides not to do something — a lost opportunity cost. Congress, it seems plain, systematically judges this type of cost to be relatively small or at least obscure.

Congress's belief that it is cheaper to exclude one unit of new risk than to neutralize one unit of old risk is both plainly wrong and readily understandable. It is plainly wrong because lost opportunity costs are not uniformly negligible. To cite just one example, uniquely therapeutic drugs are often licensed in this country years after they are approved elsewhere. The people who lose the opportunity to be treated in the interim definitely pay a very real price. More generally, this misapprehension about costs reflects the alarming view that there is little to be lost in obstructing technological and scientific change.

But Congress's view about costs is also readily understandable because legislators care more about *political* costs than economic ones. Old risks derive from established technology and their regulation presents unwelcome production and consumption choices. Old risks have identifiable and self-aware constituencies. In contrast, the regulation of new risks attracts much less political heat. Under a rigid, predictable screening system industry loses little – it just steers clear of the field. Consumers lose, of course, but – here's the political kicker – they don't know it.

Formula for Regression

To sum up, we have established a systemic preference for old sources of hazard and a systemic bias against new sources of risk. Imbue this system with the widely held belief that life is too dangerous, encourage it with vocal demands that life be made safer, and you have a formula for inexorable technological regression.

Two things, I believe, have brought us to where we are now. First, there has been a change in the national mood. Somewhere along the way we lost our taste for technological exploration and adventure. Ours seems to be what Arthur Kantrowitz, an engineer and scientist, dubbed the era of "neo-Malthusianism." We share, he believes, a profound belief that "mankind cannot manage the great power that it is able to unleash." Second, we have progressively changed the way in which we regulate risk, and that has greatly affected the conclusions we reach about the acceptability of risk.

There was a day when risks were regulated only *after* the accident, after the bodies had fallen, through liability rules administered by the courts. The incentive not to create a risk was that if the risk was an unreasonable one, you might end up paying compensation, and perhaps punitive damages, to the person you injured.

This retrospective regulatory system was cumbersome, it diverted too much to the lawyers, it placed on injured persons an often insurmountable burden of proving causation, it was erratic and unpredictable. But it had one large advantage. To recover in the courts you had to prove *harm*. A cardinal rule of tort litigation is that the courts do not compensate exposure to risk – "the neighbors your dog doesn't bite"; they compensate those who are bitten. This means, first, that risks have to be real before they are regulated by the courts, and second, that the "acceptability" of a risk is evaluated at a time when the social utility of the risk-creating activity is known.

But risk regulation is becoming an increasingly prospective business. Agency standard setting is the first step in this direction. Once a pattern of unacceptable harm becomes clear, an agency intervenes to mandate across-the-board correction. Like a court, the standard-setting agency must have evidence of harm before it regulates. But unlike a court, the standard-setting agency regulates wholesale, not retail, once that evidence is found. Both the suspected risk-creators and the proven harm-causers are regulated uniformly.

Screening moves regulation yet another step forward in time. Screening regulation occurs before any pattern of harm is apparent or predictable. It is grounded on some generalized anxiety about risk in a particular area. A screening agency regulates not on the basis of proven harm, but on the basis of unproven safety. This is the ultimate step in prospective intervention – you cannot move regulation any earlier.

There are two central problems with pushing regulation earlier and earlier, as we seem determined to do. First, the earlier we regulate, the harder it is to assess the *benefits* of the product or activity regulated. A century ago people agitated to ban vaccination. It seems unlikely that the eventual eradication of smallpox figured prominently in the debate. More recently, we have witnessed attempts to curtail significantly experiments in genetic engineering. Who can begin to assess what benefits we would forgo if such research were in fact halted?

Second, the earlier we regulate, the harder it is to evaluate *risk* accurately. Of course, we regulate early precisely because we do not want to count bodies later. But without bodies it is very easy to overestimate risk, especially when the national mood is receptive to claims of new and lurid risk. Indeed, early regulation can become something of a self-fulfilling prophecy. We start with unfocused anxiety about a product and set up a strict regulatory regime. The public infers from that action that the product is especially dangerous. Enthusiasm for strict regulation grows, impelling the politically responsive agency to regulate even more strictly. And of course the public infers from the stricter regulatory regime that there is even more danger out there than originally thought.

Which brings me full circle. The paradox of risk regulation is that too much of it makes life more dangerous. Not just more expensive, not just less convenient, but *more dangerous*. The introduction of new, safer products is slowed; safer (but not perfectly safe) products recently introduced to the market are driven out, and consumption shifts back to the old and common killers, which are entrenched and therefore too costly to regulate seriously.

Proposals for Change

What is to be done? The most popular reform proposal these days seems to be risk-benefit balancing—monetize both the injuries and the benefits of the hazardous activity and then bring in chartered accountants to balance the books. I fear the proposal is up against insuperable political obstacles. Moreover, if you propose cost-benefit balancing, I ask, by whom? The last thing a regulatee whose product is to be screened should want is an additional requirement that *it* prove the acceptability of the product in risk-benefit terms.

Other promising proposals would standardize the screening process in various fields. For example, if nuclear plants are ever built again in this country, the NRC will undoubtedly push for an extremely standard plant that can be approved once and then built by all. Again, the purpose would be to cut down on the staggering transaction costs associated with screening regulation. Finally, it is also occasionally proposed to force some cost-consciousness on to screening agencies. The proposal usually takes the form of a threshold risk criterion. Screening agencies would be required to establish the likelihood of a given degree of harm before deciding to ban an established product from the marketplace.

I believe there is one politically feasible possibility for more far-reaching reform. One of the most common, and most profoundly fallacious assumptions made in the risk-regulation trade is that new products and processes generally add to the risk burden of our environment. In fact, most new products do not "add to," they "substitute for." Yet under most existing regulatory statutes, the agency is clearly and flatly prohibited from comparing the risks of a new product with the risks of the old products for which it will substitute.

Examples abound. The artificial sweetener saccharin, although thought to present some risk, has been kept legal by special act of Congress. After ten years of delay, the FDA recently approved a new dietetic sweetener called aspartame. But the agency had to establish that aspartame met an objective level of safety; it could not lawfully have approved aspartame simply by establishing that aspartame was safer than saccharin.

The NRC, and its myriad consultants and contractors, have become extremely expert at estimating nuclear risks. Understandably, nearly all their efforts are directed at estimating risks of nuclear power. EPA devotes vastly fewer resources to assessing the risks of the non-nuclear alternatives that it regulates – coal power, for example. Neither agency is encouraged, nor perhaps even permitted, to base its regulatory decisions on a comparison of the risks presented by the alternative generating technologies.

Our regulatory system must find a way to recognize that most things in life are substitutes, not additions. The uncomfortable truth, widely ignored, is that banning one risky product may decrease societal risk, or it may increase it. It depends entirely on what is left behind.

In recognition of this painful reality, risk agencies should be restructured around natural "risk markets." The hazards of all sources of electric power should be placed under one regulatory umbrella. In the area of occupational safety and health, the regulator must recognize that strict regulation of safer jobs tends to drive workers toward more hazardous ones. We should abandon the artificial divisions between old and new drugs, old and new emitters of air pollutants, old and new pesticides, old and new chemicals, at least when the new target for regulation promises to substitute for an old product or process. Functional substitutes should be regulated within a single agency according to more or less uniform decisional criteria.

Reorganizing our risk agencies around natural risk markets would have some obvious advantages.

First, a comparative approach to risk regulation can operate in perfect harmony with our reluctance to regulate old risks precipitately. If we are determined to proceed with circumspection in our regulation of old risks, those risks provide the perfect benchmark for a comparative system.

Comparative regulation would also make risk regulation more credible. It is always much easier to compare risks than to make determinations of absolute safety. Critics might complain less about the overfeeding of rats if the data simply showed one group of live and healthy aspartame-fed rats and another group of dead or ailing saccharin-fed rats.

Finally, comparative regulation would help to avert the most intolerable of all possible risk regulations – regulations that aggravate the hazard they are supposed to mitigate. Again, historical examples of the problem are easy to come by . . . .

Some time ago the FDA banned bottles made of acrylonitrile because small amounts of the carcinogenic plastic leach into the drink. But an "all-natural" *glass* bottle containing soda under pressure has much in common with a hand grenade, with an unexpected defect in the glass playing the role of the firing pin. Before the advent of plastic bottles, exploding glass bottles caused tens of thousands of injuries in this country every year. Plastic bottles have been a great setback for the trial lawyers of America. Yet at no time was the FDA legally empowered to ask how the risks of acrylonitrile bottles compare with those of glass bottles.

The Reaction

The idea of comparing interchangeable sources of risk before deciding which to regulate, or how strictly, seems so simple, so obviously reasonable. It was with some surprise that I discovered that this proposal encounters vehement and vocal opposition. The criticism comes in subtle forms but it has two basic refrains: risks are unmeasurable and risks are incommensurable.

Unmeasurability. This has become quite a crusade. The arguments sound like this. Don't trust the experts. Don't believe any estimates of risk probabilities. Regulate according to maximum conceivable harm, ignore the likelihood of harm. Expand the definition of risk – I quote from one prominent commentator's recently published suggestion – to include all "sociopolitical, biological and geophysical conditions."

This is, of course, intellectual rubbish that can be answered in short order. If risks are unmeasurable, then risk regulation is an utterly futile endeavor. You cannot rationally control what you cannot measure.

Incommensurability. This is a more popular, more credible, and more pernicious attack on comparative risk regulation. It runs something like this. Risks in the nature of carcinogens are special – the public demands particularly strict cancer control. Occupational hazards associated with the production of a hazardous product have attendant benefits (they provide jobs) and so should be treated differently; in effect, labor-intensive risks are more tolerable than capital-intensive risks. Risk regulation tends to reallocate wealth from one group to another; we must attend to the distributional and allocative effects of regulation. Rare catastrophes are different from common but localized hazards; we must regulate the two classes of risk according to different criteria. Some risk decisions have international consequences; we must regulate so as to avoid exporting hazardous technologies. Some hazardous technologies are more susceptible to terrorism and sabotage; regardless of the actual magnitude of risk, these technologies require especially strict treatment.

This incommensurability lament is so varied, and so amorphous, that a short response is difficult to articulate. Suffice it to say that for a governmental agency, well-meaning but with finite resources, this kind of fragmentation of the risk universe is a recipe for utter paralysis. And keep in mind that regulatory paralysis under our regulatory system as presently structured means that new risks will be excluded and old ones accepted.

Despite their weaknesses, the unmeasurability/incommensurability attacks on comparative risk regulation receive a great deal of press. The ascendant belief seems to be that comparing risks is an impossible, fraudulent, or fanciful practice, designed to obscure the issues, avoid the difficult questions, narrow the range of choices – in short, designed to implement what has been denounced as the tyranny of the experts. For my part, I do not for a moment believe that comparative risk regulation would usher in a "tyranny" of any description. And a comparative approach, with a single focus on aggregate risk, is the only one that comes close to being capable of rational implementation by our less than omniscient regulators.

The opposition to comparing risks is, I believe, a perverse reaction to one unshakable and (to many) unacceptable reality: in spite of popular misconceptions on the subject, life is in fact growing safer, not more dangerous. New technologies, new products, new processes are almost uniformly safer than the old ones they replace. Many fear, perhaps with good reason, that a comparative approach to risk regulation will lead to regulatory choices that favor new technologies over old ones, capital-intensive technologies over labor-intensive technologies, and large-scale, centralized projects over small-scale decentralized ones. There may be strong and good political and sociological reasons for resisting any or all of these trends. Those reasons, if they exist, should be aired in the appropriate political arenas. They should not, however, concern regulatory agencies whose task — already difficult enough — must be to monitor and improve our risk environment. If we insist on asking our risk agencies to do too much, they will do too little. Measuring and comparing risks is no small task. Risk-regulating agencies should not be concerned with promoting jobs, allocating wealth or tending to the psychological health of the nation.

****

Notes

1. Is Huber's argument for greater use of risk comparisons entirely divorced from concerns such as "allocating wealth"? Is there a distributive fairness concern implicit in the argument, at least as between existing economic enterprises and proposed new ventures, or as between large businesses and small businesses? Would the approach to risk regulation he advocates be likely to produce a safer environment, fairer regulatory outcomes, both, or neither?

2. Ten years after the Huber article, news reports suggested that a greater receptiveness to comparative risk analysis might be developing, at least in the realm of federal pollution control. For example, the New York Times reported:

> A three-year study of pollution and how best to clean it up at a small Amoco Corporation refinery [in Yorktown, Virginia] is prompting the Clinton Administration to consider a sharply different approach to the way the nation's environmental laws are written. The study, conducted jointly by Amoco and the Environmental Protection Agency, found that Federal regulations forced the refinery to solve relatively minor pollution threats at major expense while far more important problems were overlooked.
>
> Specifically, Amoco was required under a change in the Clean Air Act to spend $31 million to rebuild the refinery's waste water treatment plant to prevent

benzene, a toxic chemical, from evaporating into the air. But investigators found that the major source of benzene pollution was coming from a part of the plant not yet addressed by the Clean Air Act: the marine terminal in the York River, where ships unload oil and load gasoline. Controlling benzene pollution there would have cost only about $6 million, the company said.

Using the Yorktown study as a model, the Clinton Administration plans to ask Congress for money for analyses of pollution at up to a dozen other plants serving the automobile, paper, chemical, steel and food processing industries, among others. In addition, the E.P.A. has begun examining the nation's laws that regulate air and water pollution and control hazardous wastes to try to eliminate overlapping rules that are often in conflict.

In some respects, the Administration wants to return to the approach to environmental regulation developed in the 1970's. Then Congress set broad policy goals that depended on regulations for specifics. But in the 1980's because members believed that the Reagan and Bush Administrations were hostile to environmental protection, Congress itself provided the specifics and took away the discretion earlier given to agencies to write regulations.

Keith Schneider, "Unbending Regulations Incite Move to Alter Pollution Laws," New York Times, November 29, 1993, p. A1. Recalling the observations of Professors Dwyer and Ely in Chapter 3(B), *supra*, are you comforted by this report that a return to broad legislative formulations is contemplated?

3. What types of changes in federal environmental statutes would be needed in order to effect more sophisticated comparison of environmental risks and their related control costs? Do you prefer a system in which Congress makes these comparisons and the corresponding choices of control strategies, or one that imposes that responsibility on environmental agencies such as the EPA? To what extent should the comparisons and choices be made by the regulated entities themselves, rather than by the government? What are the environmental lawyer's functions in serving different types of clients under each of these different models?

As of February, 1995 the United States House of Representatives was actively considering comparative risk assessment and cost-benefit analysis requirements in Title III of H.R. 9, the proposed Job Creation and Wage Enhancement Act of 1995.

4. In what respects is Huber's analysis of the screening approach to new risks an accurate explanation of the type of opposition to the siting of polluting and risk-creating facilities examined in Chapter 7, *infra*? Does his analysis offer any basis for distinguishing such opposition by affluent or middle-class, white communities from opposition by poor, racial minority communities?

E. Risk Analysis and Equity

During the same period in the 1980's when the Environmental Protection Agency was increasing its attention to risk analysis, the environmental justice movement was developing in strength and visibility.[8] This coincidence meant, rather ironically, that a trend toward more technical and objective bases for setting environmental priorities was to be confronted by claims for greater reliance on less technical, more equitable grounds. As one commentator has observed,

> Environmental equity takes current environmental protection strategies as a given at a time when the science and ethics of environmental protection are undergoing a profound re-evaluation. For example, mainstream environmental protection is moving toward more rational risk assessment and management, pollution source reduction, and ecosystem protection strategies, each of which potentially undercuts the environmental equity movement's focus on the status quo.

A. Dan Tarlock, "City Versus Countryside: Environmental Equity in Context," 21 Fordham Urban Law Journal 461, 465 (1994).[9]

In recognition of these parallel developments, the EPA began to focus on the relationship between them, as the following excerpt from a 1992 EPA report indicates.

****

U.S. Environmental Protection Agency, "Environmental Equity: Reducing Risk for All Communities" 1-4 (1992)

The U.S. Environmental Protection Agency (EPA) is continually attempting to improve its approach to environmental protection. Traditionally, environmental programs at all levels of government have set broadly applicable standards for individual pollutants released by specific types of sources with the goal of protecting the environment and all people. Recognizing that not everyone is affected in the same ways by pollution, these standards have often been set to protect the most susceptible, such as asthmatics, children or pregnant women.[10]

Environmental protection has progressed from this initial strategy to include risk-based priority setting. The EPA Science Advisory Board, in its report *Reducing Risk: Setting*

---

[8] Historical background on the environmental justice movement is presented in Chapter 7(B), *infra*.

[9] As discussed in Chapter 7(B), *infra*, some opponents of the siting of new hazardous waste facilities on environmental justice grounds also have expressed an objective of promoting pollution prevention. *See generally* Nicholas Freudenberg *et al.*, "Not in Our Backyards: The Grassroots Environmental Movement," in America Environmentalism: The U.S. Environmental Movement, 1970-1990 (Riley E. Dunlap *et al.*, eds. 1992), at 27, 35 ("Critics of NIMBY groups also fail to acknowledge that many local groups move beyond simple nay-saying to support socially constructive alternatives that express a NIABY [not in anyone's back yard] philosophy. Thus, many groups opposing the construction of garbage incinerators become advocates for recycling and waste reduction measures such as packaging controls.").

[10] [Ed.] EPA's risk assessment methods are criticized, particularly for giving inadequate attention to variations in different groups' vulnerability to environmental insult, in Samara F. Swanston, "Race, Gender, Age, and Disproportionate Impact: What Can We Do about the Failure to Protect the Most Vulnerable?" 21 Fordham Urban Law Journal 577 (1994).

Priorities and Strategies for Environmental Protection, urged EPA to target its environmental protection efforts based on the opportunities for reducing the most serious remaining risks. In response, EPA began to examine and target its efforts on those environmental problems which pose the greatest risks nationwide to human health and the environment, using comparative risk analyses to rank environmental problems according to severity. One approach EPA now employs to prioritize environmental efforts based on risk is geographic targeting, where attention is focused on the problems faced by individual cities or regions, such as the Chesapeake Bay, the Great Lakes and the Gulf of Mexico.

In the context of a risk-based approach to environmental management, the relative burden borne by low-income and racial minority communities is a special concern. A low-income community which is surrounded by multiple sources of air pollution, waste treatment facilities and landfills and which has lead-based paint in the residences is clearly a community that faces higher than average potential environmental risks. A racial or cultural group whose children commonly have harmful levels of lead in their blood is also living with a greater environmental risk. In addition, as a result of factors affecting health status, such communities may be more likely than the general population to experience disease or death due to a given level of exposure. Poor nutrition, smoking, inadequate health care and stress can all contribute to an increased rate of health effects at a given pollutant level. Hence, to the extent these communities are subject to these factors, they are also more likely to actually experience harm due to these exposures.

Issues such as these, and how government agencies respond, have come to be known today as issues of *environmental equity*. Environmental equity refers to the distribution of environmental risks across population groups and to our policy responses to these distributions. While there are many types of equity, all of which are important to EPA, this report focuses on racial minority and low-income populations.

EPA has begun to assess how patterns of environmental problems converge on different places, how people who live in those places are affected and how environmental programs should be further refined to address identified differences. The causes of these differences are often complex and deeply rooted in historical patterns of commerce, geography, state and local land use decisions and other factors that affect where people live and work. With respect to some types of pollutants, race and income, however, appear to be correlated with these distributions.

Clearly, environmental equity is important to those who might bear high risks. But everyone has a stake in environmental equity because it results in better environmental protection generally. Environmental equity is an important goal in a democratic society. It involves ensuring that the benefits of environmental protection are available to all communities and an environmental policy-making process that allows the concerns of all communities to be heard, understood, and addressed.

In response to a variety of concerns raised by EPA staff and the public, in July 1990, EPA Administrator William K. Reilly formed the EPA Environmental Equity Workgroup with staff from all EPA offices and regions across the Agency. The Workgroup was directed to assess the evidence that racial minority and low-income communities bear a higher environmental risk burden than the general population, and consider what EPA might do about any identified disparities.

This report to the Administrator reviews existing data on the distribution of environmental exposures and risks across population groups. It also summarizes the Workgroup's review of EPA programs with respect to racial minority and low-income populations. Based on the findings from these analyses, the Workgroup makes initial recommendations.

Summary of Findings

1. There are clear differences between racial groups in terms of disease and death rates. There are also limited data to explain the environmental contribution to these differences. In fact, there is a general lack of data on environmental health effects by race and income. For diseases that are known to have environmental causes, data are not typically disaggregated by race and socioeconomic group. The notable exception is lead poisoning: A significantly higher percentage of Black children compared to White children have unacceptably high blood lead levels.

2. Racial minority and low-income populations experience higher than average exposures to selected air pollutants, hazardous waste facilities, contaminated fish and agricultural pesticides in the workplace. Exposure does not always result in an immediate or acute health effect. High exposures, and the possibility of chronic effects, are nevertheless a clear cause for health concerns.

3. Environmental and health data are not routinely collected and analyzed by income and race. Nor are data routinely collected on health risks posed by multiple industrial facilities, cumulative and synergistic effects, or multiple and different pathways of exposure. Risk assessment and risk management procedures are not in themselves biased against certain income or racial groups. However, risk assessment and risk management procedures can be improved to better take into account equity considerations.

4. Great opportunities exist for EPA and other government agencies to improve communication about environmental problems with members of low-income and racial minority groups. The language, format and distribution of written materials, media relations, and efforts in two-way communication all can be improved. In addition, EPA can broaden the spectrum of groups with which it interacts.

5. Since they have broad contact with affected communities, EPA's program and regional offices are well suited to address equity concerns. The potential exists for effective action by such offices to address disproportionate risks. These offices currently vary considerably in terms of how they address environmental equity issues. Case studies of EPA program and regional offices reveal that opportunities exist for addressing environmental equity issues and that there is a need for environmental equity awareness training. A number of EPA regional offices have initiated projects to address high risks in racial minority and low-income communities.

6. Native Americans are a unique racial group that has a special relationship with the federal government and distinct environmental problems. Tribes often lack the physical infrastructure, institutions, trained personnel and resources necessary to protect their members.

Summary of Recommendations

Although large gaps in data exist, the Workgroup believes that enough is known with sufficient certainty to make several recommendations to the Agency. These recommendations are also applicable to other public and private groups engaged in environmental protection activities. The job of achieving environmental equity is shared by everyone.

1. EPA should increase the priority that it gives to issues of environmental equity.
2. EPA should establish and maintain information which provides an objective basis for assessment of risks by income and race, beginning with the development of a research and data collection plan.
3. EPA should incorporate considerations of environmental equity into the risk assessment process. It should revise its risk assessment procedures to ensure, where practical and relevant, better characterization of risk across populations, communities or geographic areas. These revisions could be useful in determining whether there are any population groups at disproportionately high risk.
4. EPA should identify and target opportunities to reduce high concentrations of risk to specific population groups, employing approaches developed for geographic targeting.
5. EPA should, where appropriate, assess and consider the distribution of projected risk reduction in major rulemakings and Agency initiatives.
6. EPA should selectively review and revise its permit, grant, monitoring and enforcement procedures to address high concentrations of risk in racial minority and low-income communities. Since state and local governments have primary authority for many environmental programs, EPA should emphasize its concerns about environmental equity to them.
7. EPA should expand and improve the level and forms with which it communicates with racial minority and low-income communities and should increase efforts to involve them in environmental policy-making.
8. EPA should establish mechanisms, including a center of staff support, to ensure that environmental equity concerns are incorporated in its long-term planning and operations.

****

Robert D. Bullard, "Conclusion: Environmentalism with Justice," in Confronting Environmental Racism: Voices from the Grassroots 195-99, 201 (Robert D. Bullard, ed., 1993)

Environmental Equity: Reducing Risk for All Communities, published in February 1992 by the federal Environmental Protection Agency [and] which took the EPA over eighteen months to complete, was written as a response to several scholars of color active in the environmental justice movement who wrote to the EPA's top administrator, William Reilly, asking that the agency finally address the disproportionately high environmental risks borne by people of color and low-income communities. Yet, despite more than eighteen months of study, the EPA failed to grasp the interplay of race and class biasing environmental decision making. The weaknesses of the report are worth analyzing.

The EPA's report is best seen as part of the EPA's "outreach strategy" to mount a public relations campaign to drive a wedge between grassroots environmental justice activists and mainstream civil rights and environmental groups rather than offer a substantive effort to address environmental problems that disproportionately harm people of color and low-income citizens.

Contrary to the EPA's self-serving claim of "substantial investment in environmental equity and cultural diversity," their environmental equity report reveals itself as a public relations ploy to diffuse the issue of environmental racism. The EPA staff that produced the Equity Report did not produce one piece of original research or develop a single piece of new information. More importantly, the report appears to reflect a half-hearted and less-than-serious treatment of its own subject matter. The report contains, for instance, a very selective, biased, and superficial review of the literature on the nature and severity of environmental problems faced by low-income populations and communities of color in the United States. The systematic omission of important works that document the impact of discriminatory land-use planning, differential enforcement of regulations and laws, and inequitable facility siting is quite glaring, in fact.

The report only makes passing reference to a handful of studies that document the relationship between the sociodemographic characteristics of communities and the quality of their physical environment.

Tellingly though, the EPA report implies that lead poisoning is the only environmental hazard for which clear and unambiguous evidence exists of differential exposure due to race and class differences. At the same time, it does not explain why the EPA has done so little to protect those who are "most vulnerable" to lead poisoning. The agency has consistently delayed and dragged its feet on the problems posed by lead-contaminated paint, soil, and drinking water. Even being armed with sufficient facts and documented "proof" is not a strong enough incentive for the EPA to tackle the environmental and health problems involving mostly people of color. For millions of lead-exposed, inner-city children, the agency's delaying tactics are tantamount to a life sentence in lead-contaminated environments.

This pattern of obscuring environmental racism is consistent throughout the report. For example, the report glosses over the pesticide problem faced by farm workers and those who live in migrant labor camps.

It is usually a community's business and political elites (not the ordinary residents of the community) who seek waste facilities as an economic development program. This is particularly true in Native-American reservations. They have become prime targets for waste-disposal firms. The leaders of more than a hundred reservations have been approached in recent years by such firms. Nearly all of the proposals were defeated through grassroots opposition. The threat to Native lands hovers from Maine to Alaska. Both the U.S. Department of Interior and the Bureau of Indian Affairs are promoting the construction of waste facilities on Native lands as a form of economic development. Native Americans, however, are not beating down the doors to recruit polluting industries for the reservations. The EPA's report, however, attempts to blame the victims.

Note

An examination of the Presidential and Congressional materials presented in Chapter 7(D), *infra*, will reveal that, not surprisingly, the relationship between risk analysis methods and the distributional concerns of environmental justice advocates is still in a formative stage, particularly as embodied in federal law. *See also* "Supporters Contend Risk Assessment Vital to Environmental Equity," Inside EPA, August 27, 1993, at 12 ("Supporters of risk analyses are urging the House to add a risk assessment provision to its EPA Cabinet elevation bill, arguing that the provision is vital to identifying the risks to poor and minority neighborhoods . . . . Environmentalists and some congressional sources say the linkage between the two areas is starting to be addressed, but they charge that traditional risk assessments may not provide an accurate measurement of the environmental risks facing low-income and minority populations.")

Chapter 4
Selecting Enforcement and Cleanup Targets

A. Overview

The preceding chapter explored factors that help determine the goals and intended beneficiaries of environmental protection, and the setting of priorities among them. As these determinations evolve, and the resulting regulatory agenda is incorporated into binding legal requirements, it becomes necessary for environmental agencies to promote compliance and to respond to violations. Regulators then must select specific targets for enforcement action, whether they be individuals, businesses, other government agencies, or other types of institutions.

The criteria by which enforcement targets are identified raise fairness questions of great concern to environmental lawyers, especially those representing potential targets. As in the setting of regulatory agendas at the outset, here too a range of possible factors can apply. Some of these factors are closely linked to concepts of justice such as those presented in Chapter 2. Thus the importance of a potential defendant's fault or lack thereof, and the weight to be given to diligent, good faith compliance efforts, ultimately depend upon corrective justice norms. These norms are most critically at issue when violators are selected for possible imposition of criminal penalties.

Similarly, corrective justice issues show up frequently in one of the most active realms of environmental practice, the imposition of contaminated site cleanup costs among responsible parties. Thus the continuing debates in this context over application of strict liability, and joint and several liability, are an ongoing exercise in the delineation of just treatment of parties who arguably should bear some responsibility to redress this type of environmental harm.

Competitive advantages and disadvantages as among different polluters also may be a relevant factor, bearing on distributional fairness in the exercise of enforcement discretion. Attention to the specific type of community benefitted by government selection of one environmental violator rather than another also bears on distributive justice concerns. Community impact is a factor not only in the usual enforcement context, but also in the realm of site cleanup. When government agencies select areas of soil and groundwater contamination, and potentially responsible parties, as targets for governmental enforcement or cleanup measures, the differential community impacts of these choices may be significant. Because it recently has been charged that racial discrimination has been a factor in environmental enforcement and cleanup, this chapter includes some readings on that accusation, as well as numerous cross-references to Chapter 7's more extensive examination of "environmental racism."

This chapter also will touch upon the question of whether risk assessment methods of the sort discussed in Chapter 3 can provide a fair and rational basis for setting priorities among different, possible targets of enforcement action. Other factors examined here, however, are much less substantive, relating instead largely to practical and political concerns. For example, the need for choices to be made among possible enforcement or cleanup targets partially arises out of the perennial limits on public resources — in both dollars and personnel — for environmental protection efforts.

B.   Exercises

1. You have been designated as the chairperson of a state interagency committee which is drafting a unified policy to guide enforcement of the state's environmental laws by all major enforcement agencies, e.g., the state attorney general, the state environmental protection agency, other state natural resource agencies, cities and counties, district attorneys, special districts, etc. Some of these laws, of course, facilitate the state's implementation of federal environmental statutes.

With the aid of the readings that follow, prepare an outline of the major factors that you believe ought to be included in the unified policy to guide the identification of environmental violators against whom enforcement proceedings will be brought. Try to identify which of these factors are more closely linked to environmental objectives and which are more closely linked to one or more concepts of justice.

Try also to rank these factors in terms of which should have greater or lesser bearing on the determination of whether proceedings should be brought against a particular violator. You might also expand your outline to correlate the weight of specific factors with different levels of enforcement proceedings — e.g., administrative, civil, or criminal.

Finally, are there factors that you believe should influence enforcement decisions — or inevitably will influence enforcement decisions — but that you would feel uncomfortable spelling out in a written, public policy? If so, what is the basis for your reticence, and should it be overcome?

2. Assume that you are the attorney for the clients listed below, each of which is under consideration as a possible target for enforcement action. In each instance, you are preparing for a meeting with the government attorneys who will be making the final decision on whether proceedings will be brought against your client.

What arguments would you make, and especially what factors would you urge be given greatest weight, in order to try to persuade the government lawyers that your client should be spared, i.e., that proceedings should not be initiated? Which of these arguments are more closely linked to environmental objectives and which are more closely linked to one or more concepts of justice?

With the aid of the readings that follow, develop your responses to these questions with respect to each of the following, separate clients. You may wish to identify additional facts that it would be helpful to obtain in order to develop the most cogent arguments.

A paint manufacturing company some of whose employees recently spilled a small quantity of product on the ground at one of the company facilities. The employees quickly cleaned up the spill, but not before a portion of it had flowed into a nearby creek. The company failed to report this spill, in violation of applicable environmental regulations.[1]

A large, city-owned electrical generating plant that has modified some equipment without seeking the necessary air pollution permits and without installing the expensive, advanced air pollution abatement controls required by law.

A retail dry cleaning store, owned by a racial minority family, that has modified some equipment without seeking the necessary air pollution permits and without installing the expensive, advanced air pollution abatement controls required by law.

A company that manufactures large metal storage shelves for use in various types of warehouses, and that has violated regulations on the proper methods of both temporary storage and final disposal of a few hazardous wastes such as spent cleaning solvents and used lubricating oils. These regulations are part of a large volume of hazardous waste management regulations that frequently are amended pursuant to federal or state authority. This company has been in business for many years but has been only marginally profitable for the past few years. It relies upon its plant manager to keep up with environmental compliance requirements, since the company cannot afford to hire a specialized environmental affairs manager.

C. Enforcement Strategies

Kenneth A. Manaster, "Early Thoughts on Prosecuting Polluters," 2 Ecology Law Quarterly 471, 474-80 (1971)

The first question the environmental prosecutor faces is the practical determination of which polluters and which pollution will be the focus of his efforts. The limitations of his staff and resources make such choices inevitable, and a number of factors usually will influence these decisions.[2] It is not realistic to expect agencies of government to

---

[1] This example also appears in Chapter 1(B), *supra*.

[2] [Ed.] *See* Sheldon M. Novick (ed.), Law of Environmental Protection sec. 8.01[4] (1987, 1992), stating as follows:

"All of the traditional variable factors that must be considered by an enforcement official in deciding whether to pursue a case are present under the environmental statutes: the severity of the violation, the deterrence value of an enforcement action, the strength of the case, the resources available, the choice of remedies and forums, and so on. But there are many factors not present in other contexts. There is a delicate federalist balance at work under most of the environmental statutes . . . . There is a broader array of remedies under the statutes than is addressed by the courts."

be reliable, frequent litigators in opposition to proposed public construction projects or other governmental acts which may have adverse environmental effects. The reason for this is that the government lawyer not only often works with the officials directly responsible for public projects, but would most likely be called upon to defend those officials if they were sued by other parties even on environmental grounds. This is true of the Justice Department at the national level, of the attorney general's office of any state, or of the attorney for a given county or municipality. Therefore, prospective suits seeking to halt such projects or to force disclosure of environmental impact information must, as a general rule, be initiated by citizens and citizen groups.

This is not to say, however, that the attorney for one level of government will never sue for injunctive relief against a project proposed under the auspices of a different level of government.

When the prosecutor turns his attention to non-governmental polluters, his usual targets are individual offenders. It is also very useful, or even essential, to focus at times on categories of polluters in coordinated prosecution efforts. Categories may be selected on the basis of various criteria. For example, the prosecutor may find reason to concentrate upon air pollution cases, in preference to water or land pollution problems. He may wish to take a geographic perspective and concentrate upon elimination of pollution in a particularly troublesome area, perhaps zeroing in on all the air pollution problems in a specific locale or even on air, water, land, noise and other pollution problems there. As a third category, efforts may be coordinated into sets of prosecutions against a particular industry identified as causing a specific type of pollution in a number of areas from basically the same equipment or process. Such a group approach is helpful for inducing a particular industry to develop or put into operation a new form of control technology. This is true especially if the technology is so costly as to call for considerable investment and risk if only one member of the industry were forced to consider it alone.

Prospective or anticipatory lawsuits against private polluters are not as likely to occur as are suits with respect to existing pollution or past incidents. This is so presently because there are so many existing problems to contend with that it is difficult to deal with these and simultaneously to venture into areas of potential pollution. This is not to say that such foresight would not be tremendously valuable.

The deterrent effect of pollution prosecutions does seem to be considerable. That is, it is highly likely that vigorous prosecution of a certain type of polluter will be noticed by other polluters of the same type. The polluter on the sidelines quickly begins to envision and assess his posture in similar litigation. Often the result is either a quiet but prompt cleanup or an inquiry to the prosecuting authorities as to just what he must do in order to avoid being next. This logical tendency on the part of polluters, whether they be business concerns or public entities, such as municipalities and sanitary districts, brings us to the question of whether prosecution efforts are best directed at a smaller number of larger cases or at a large, random number of small or medium-sized cases. There is no easy answer to this question, and it would seem that a blend is probably inevitable. The responsible environmental prosecutor cannot avoid attending at least to some of the major sources of pollution in his area. At the same time, especially if he holds an elective office or has been appointed by an elected official, he cannot afford to ignore the large number of citizen complaints concerning relatively small sources of pollution.

The prosecutor generally should not be dissuaded from action by virtue of the fact that he knows that claims of hardship will be heard by way of defense or mitigation for the polluter. In some instances it undoubtedly will be apparent to the prosecutor that certain types of relief will not be granted by the court in view of obvious hardship or detriment to significant numbers of employees, to the provision of basic public services, or to the survival of a marginally profitable but socially useful enterprise. In such situations the prosecutor either must decide that action in court is realistically out of the question, or he must seek to develop a conception of other, suitable relief which might be obtained in court or elsewhere. In any event, the responsible prosecutor must be sensitive to these questions. In part this sensitivity will include a sharp ability to assess the credibility of polluters' claims of hardship and impending economic disaster if compliance with the law is required.

****

LeRoy C. Paddock, "Environmental Enforcement at the Turn of the Century" 21 Environmental Law 1516 (1991)

Since the mid-1980s, the context within which environmental enforcement is conducted has changed. A vast array of new programs has been enacted affecting tens of thousands of facilities, many of which are small businesses such as service stations and print shops. These new programs are beginning to supplant the older environmental programs that concentrated on far fewer, larger pollution sources as the principal focus for many environmental enforcement officials. This increased emphasis on the issues associated with the large numbers of smaller facilities is likely to continue.

This new context for environmental enforcement will demand major alterations in the way enforcement is carried out. Some of these changes are quite advanced while others have barely emerged.

One of the principal changes in environmental enforcement has been a rapid shift to the use of administratively imposed penalties. Administrative penalties differ from judicially imposed civil penalties in two important respects. First, administrative penalties can be imposed by an administrator of an environmental agency without having to resort to a court. Second, administrative penalties frequently have lower ceilings than judicially imposed penalties. The principal advantages of administrative penalties are that they usually can be imposed more quickly and that they require less staff time than filing a judicial action or negotiating a settlement of a potential court action.

All of the major federal environmental laws now authorize the Administrator of the EPA to impose penalties for violations of environmental laws.

A second significant change in enforcement programs has been the introduction of criminal law as a tool for environmental enforcement. Although some environmental criminal cases were filed in the early 1980s, criminal enforcement was not used widely by environmental agencies until late in the decade. Today thirty-three states have felony laws that apply to illegal disposal of hazardous waste and about one-half of the states have active environmental criminal enforcement programs at the state or local level. Still, criminal enforcement is not used extensively outside of the hazardous waste field.

There are two principal reasons for the increased use of criminal enforcement. First, it is now clear that some environmental violations are not prevented by the threat of civil penalties. This is especially true when substantial money can be made through illegal conduct. Hence, the agencies see the more severe penalties, such as prison sentences available under the criminal law, as the only effective tool to address these violations.

The second and more important reason for increased criminal enforcement is related to the large number of regulated facilities. Since facilities may only rarely be inspected under some environmental programs, it is important to deter serious violations. Criminal enforcement is believed to be an effective method of deterring environmental violations. As one commentator noted: "The deterrent effect of the environmental statutes is enhanced . . . if responsible individuals within the corporation know they may not sanction or participate in illegal activity without subjecting themselves personally to the possibility of substantial fines and/or imprisonment." Criminal enforcement is rapidly becoming a routine enforcement tool in environmental cases. This trend is likely to continue throughout the remainder of this decade.

Another emerging approach to enforcement is the wider use of strategic planning techniques, including multimedia enforcement, targeting, and risk-based enforcement. Multimedia enforcement is designed to use inspection and enforcement personnel more effectively by reviewing all aspects of a facility's environmental compliance at one time rather than in a series of uncoordinated, single media inspections and enforcement actions. Targeting involves selecting categories of facilities for enforcement either on an industry or geographic basis. The technique is designed to achieve a high level of compliance through individual cases and the related deterrent effect of those cases in the selected industry or geographic area. The final strategic planning tool is risk-based enforcement. This technique is designed to focus enforcement resources on the violations that present the most serious risks to health and the environment.

The increasing use of strategic planning techniques indicates a growing understanding that limited enforcement resources must be leveraged to obtain the maximum degree of compliance in the most important areas of concern. It is clear that federal and state enforcement officials will not be able to inspect and initiate enforcement proceedings against the hundreds of thousands of regulated entities. Rather, much like a tax auditing system, it will be necessary to conduct a number of well-planned enforcement initiatives designed to achieve a significant "enforcement presence" in the area of concern.

D. Social and Political Factors

Marianne Lavelle *et al.*, "Unequal Protection: The Racial Divide in Environmental Law," The National Law Journal (September 21, 1992), at S2

In a comprehensive analysis of every U.S. environmental lawsuit concluded in the past seven years, the NLJ found penalties against pollution law violators in minority areas are lower than those imposed for violations in largely white areas. In an analysis of every residential toxic waste site in the 12-year-old Superfund program, the NLJ also discovered the government takes longer to address hazards in minority communities, and it accepts solutions less stringent than those recommended by the scientific community.

This racial imbalance, the investigation found, often occurs whether the community is wealthy or poor.

The following are key National Law Journal findings, gathered over an eight-month period, and based on a computer-assisted analysis of census data, the civil court case docket of the Environmental Protection Agency, and the agency's own record of performance at 1,177 Superfund toxic waste sites:

- Penalties under hazardous waste laws at sites having the greatest white population were about 500 percent higher than penalties at sites with the greatest minority population. Hazardous waste, meanwhile, is the type of pollution experts say is most concentrated in minority communities.

- For all the federal environmental laws aimed at protecting citizens from air, water and waste pollution, penalties in white communities were 46 percent higher than in minority communities.

- Under the giant Superfund clean-up program, abandoned hazardous waste sites in minority areas take 20 percent longer to be placed on the national priority action list than those in white areas.

- In more than half of the 10 autonomous regions that administer EPA programs around the country, action on cleanup at Superfund sites begins from 12 percent to 42 percent later at minority sites than at white sites.

- At the minority sites, the EPA chooses "containment," the capping or walling off of a hazardous dump site, 7 percent more frequently than the cleanup method preferred under the law, permanent "treatment," to eliminate the waste or rid it of its toxins. At white sites, the EPA orders treatment 22 percent more often than containment.

[A]ctivists who have been working in communities inundated by waste say that the hundreds of seemingly race-neutral decisions in the science and politics of environmental enforcement have created a racist imbalance. Through neglect, not intent, they say minorities are stranded on isolated islands of pollution in the midst of the nation that produced the first, most sophisticated environmental protection laws on earth.

"People say decisions are made based on risk assessment and science," says Prof. Robert D. Bullard, a sociologist at the University of California, Riverside, who has been studying environmental racism for 14 years. "The science may be present, but when it comes to implementation and policy, a lot of decisions appear to be based on the politics of what's appropriate for that community. And low income and minority communities are not given the same priority, nor do they see the same speed at which something is perceived as a danger and a threat."

The most striking imbalance between whites and minorities in The National Law Journal's analysis of the EPA's enforcement effort was a 506 percent disparity in fines under the Resource Conservation and Recovery Act—the 13-year-old [sic] law intended to assure the safe handling and disposal of hazardous waste. The average fine in the areas with the greatest white population was $335,566, compared to $55,318 in the areas with the greatest minority population.

The other type of case in which minority areas also saw far lower fines than white areas was in the 28 cases brought using multiple law charges that the EPA has concluded during the past seven years. In those, fines were 306 percent higher in white than in minority areas, $239,000 compared to $59,429.

Only in Superfund enforcement cases, lodged mainly against polluters who have been recalcitrant about cleaning up abandoned toxic waste sites, did fines in minority areas come out higher than in white areas, by 9 percent. Minority communities saw lower average penalties in federal enforcement of the Clean Water Act, by 28 percent, the Clean Air Act, by 8 percent and the Safe Drinking Water Act, by 15 percent.

The EPA says that many factors go into its determination of penalties, such as the seriousness of an offense, the ability of a polluter to pay, the polluter's history and level of cooperation, as well as the vagaries of judges and the legal system.

The Law Journal's investigation of the EPA's Superfund program shows that for the sites with the most minorities, it took an average of 5.6 years from the date a toxic dump was discovered to place it on a Superfund list. That's 20 percent longer than the 4.7 years it took for the sites with the highest white population.

In six of the EPA's 10 regional field offices across the country, where most Superfund decisions are made, the pace from the discovery of a site to the beginning of cleanup is from 8 percent to 42 percent faster at white sites than at minority sites. The greatest disparity was in Midwestern Region 5, with the most sites at 257, where the pace from discovery to cleanup was 13.8 years for minority sites compared to 9.7 years for white sites. In one area, Mid-Atlantic Region 3, the pace for minority and white sites is dead even.

In three regions, cleanup begins more quickly at minority sites than white sites: in the Deep South, Region 4, by 8 percent; in New York/New Jersey, Region 2 by 11 percent; and in the Pacific Northwest, Region 10, by 36 percent.

One indication of how successfully residents have lobbied for permanent and complete cleanup of superfund waste is in the "remedial decisions" arrived at by the EPA, polluters, state authorities and other interested parties through negotiation. The EPA categorizes these decisions each year as "treatment" or "containment" in response to Congress' order in 1986 to make treatment the preferred choice.

The more intensive treatment choice was chosen 22 percent more frequently than containment at the white sites. At minority sites, containment was chosen 7 percent more frequently.

In the Superfund decision-making realm, the EPA argues that its decisions are based on the science of particular sites, not on race. But in a program as massive and costly as Superfund, political clout certainly does help a community to get solutions. Unfortunately, environmental justice activists argue, white communities usually have been better able to wield this access than minority communities.

[A]ctivists . . . are asking the EPA to begin to take into account disparate racial impact in addition to the scientific analysis the agency makes in its decisions. This would be analogous to the Reagan-era directives that now require federal agencies to consider the cost to industry with every decision.

The Rev. Ben Chavis, executive director of the United Church of Christ's Commission on Racial Justice and a founder of the environmental justice movement, agrees that the EPA needs to rethink how it does business. "So much of the methodology of the last 12 years in environmental protection has been risk-assessment and therefore risk-management, and too little attention has been paid to equal enforcement of the law," he says.

EPA officials, without concluding that racist results flow from their current methods, have begun to study how to do their job more "equitably."

****

Note

Further information on the EPA's initial response to the "environmental equity" issue is presented in Chapter 3(E), *supra*. More extensive background on the development of the environmental justice movement is presented in the context of siting disputes in Chapter 7, *infra*. The final portion of that chapter presents the 1994 Presidential Executive Order on environmental justice. To what extent do that Order and the accompanying Presidential Memorandum respond to the charge that federal enforcement of environmental laws has been discriminatory?

****

Richard J. Lazarus, "Pursuing 'Environmental Justice': The Distributional Effects of Environmental Protection," 87 Northwestern University Law Review 787, 816-819 (1993)

The absence of any systematic consideration of minority interests in environmental protection has . . . likely affected the implementation of environmental protection laws. The siting of hazardous waste treatment, storage, and disposal facilities is a prime example. EPA is currently placing significant pressure on states to establish licensed hazardous waste facilities with the capacity to handle hazardous wastes generated within their borders. Under the federal Superfund law, EPA is required to deny Superfund monies for remedial cleanups to states that do not meet these "capacity assurance requirements." In choosing a location, the relevant state agency, as well as any private company involved, inevitably must consider the political implications of the siting, including the potential for effective, local political opposition. Few proposals survive the volatile public review that often accompanies announcement of the recommended siting of a hazardous waste facility.

Similar considerations are also likely to affect the development and implementation of environmental enforcement priorities, including the allocation of resources necessary for inspections of polluting facilities and other factfinding investigations. *Potential* and *realized* programmatic benefits and burdens are not the same. Congress may enact a statute, or an agency may promulgate a generic rule, but neither detecting the violation of an environmental statute in the first instance, nor the subsequent bringing of an enforcement action to compel compliance, automatically follows from passage of the law.

Whether, where, and when such detections occur, and whether, where, and when they lead to enforcement actions, are the complex product of a host of "extra-legal" variables. Significant among these variables are the complex relationships between those charged with monitoring and enforcement responsibilities, the regulated community, those adversely affected by the violation, and any watchdog organizations overseeing the law's enforcement. Just as these relational factors apply when the substance of an environmental statute or regulation is fashioned in the first instance, they continue to influence enforcement priorities and policies at both the regional and local level where the impact of an environmental law on environmental quality is ultimately determined.

In the environmental law context, substantial resources are generally required to discover a violation of a prescribed environmental quality standard, to bring an enforcement action against the violator, and to monitor for future violations. However, given the sheer breadth of federal environmental protection laws, any comprehensive enforcement scheme capable of ensuring compliance with the laws' requirements is wholly impractical. The federal government never has, and likely never will, allocate the resources necessary to guarantee such compliance. At best, there has been a "half-hearted" commitment of federal resources to the monitoring and enforcement of federal environmental restrictions.

Similarly, state governments have proven unwilling or unable to commit the resources or efforts to ensure such compliance. And, public interest organizations have never been capable of enlisting those resources necessary to bring the huge number of citizen suit enforcement actions that would be required to fill the enforcement gap. Nor is it clear, given the needs of other competing social welfare programs, that the government's (or public interest organizations') failure to do so is incorrect from either an economic efficiency or social justice perspective. Be that as it may, what remains clear is that the allocation of those resources necessary to ensure actual compliance – whether the enforcer be the federal, state, or local governments, or a public interest organization – is a significant determinant in the distribution of benefits and burdens ultimately realized. Compliance will necessarily be greater in both those substantive and geographic areas where the government decides to allocate its limited investigative and enforcement resources. And, in the absence of such governmental initiative, compliance is more likely where the community members possess the resources necessary to launch an independent, citizen-based, enforcement effort.

Some evidence supports the claim that, because of inequities in the distribution of enforcement resources, environmental quality is actually less in minority than in nonminority areas.[3] This may be reflected in less generous cleanup remedies, lower fines, slower cleanups, or more frequent violations of pollution control laws, in areas where minorities reside in greater percentages than nonminorities. For example, "nonattainment" areas under the Clean Air Act are primarily urban areas where minority populations are disproportionately high. Additionally, among those reasons cited for the continuing problem of lead poisoning in minority communities are that "federal efforts to create the necessary infrastructure to abate high-priority lead hazards from paint are still essentially at ground zero, and funding for abatement activities in low-income communities is grossly inadequate." Finally, reportedly ninety percent of farm workers in the United States are persons of color, and those workers are routinely exposed to pesticides in their work because EPA has generally been unable to implement — as mandated by the Federal Insecticide Fungicide and Rodenticide Act — the necessary protective regulations for a majority of pesticides covered by the law.

****

Note

Among the "extra-legal variables" affecting government actions in the environmental realm at any time are various, broad political objectives. Among the leading instances of the impact of such variables was the early implementation of the Superfund program under the Reagan Administration. Studies of that period have shown that expenditure of Superfund money then was severely constrained by the Administration's desire to curb inflationary spending and obviate the need for reauthorization of the fund in later years. *See, e.g.*, Frederick R. Anderson, "Negotiation and Informal Agency Action: The Case of Superfund," 1985 Duke Law Journal 261, 279. Even more vivid political influences on Superfund implementation at that time related to efforts to direct Superfund resources to sites whose cleanup would aid Republican candidates and to withhold funding that would help Democrats. *Id.* at n. 55.

****

---

[3] *See generally* Marianne Lavelle & Marcia Coyle, *Unequal Protection — The Racial Divide in Environmental Law*, Nat'l L.J., Sept. 21, 1992, at S1-S12.

[Ed.] Professor Lazarus notes that the National Law Journal writers' "use of the term 'minority community' to describe the community with the lowest white population is somewhat misleading; most of the communities falling under that label are in fact predominantly white. However, the authors point out that, in light of segregated residential patterns, even communities with an 80% white population may have a different character, or at least be perceived different than communities that are nearly 100% white."

Mary Bryant, "Unequal Justice? Lies, Damn Lies, and Statistics Revisited" SONREEL [American Bar Association Section of Natural Resources, Energy, and Environmental Law] News (September-October 1993) at 3

It has been more than a year since the National Law Journal (NLJ) printed its groundbreaking, award-winning article on environmental racism . . . . Since that time, Congress has held hearings on the issue, EPA has established an Office of Environmental Equity, and dozens of publications have jumped on the "environmental justice" band-wagon. But no one has seriously questioned NLJ's premise.

The NLJ conducted a statistical analysis of EPA enforcement data from 1985 to 1991 to reach its conclusion. [T]he statistics appear compelling. When stripped of the supporting narrative, however, they do not hold up. A few of the more glaring problems are itemized below.

Key terms are undefined or badly defined. For example, at no point in its twelve-page supplement does the NLJ say exactly what it means by "minority" and "white" communities. The greatest differences cited by NLJ, between those communities with the largest white populations and the largest minority populations, involve, for the white communities, populations that are at least 98% white, and for minority communities, populations that are at least 79% white. Because the population of the country is more than 85% white, NLJ suggests that a community that is only 79% white is a "minority" community.

The NLJ's statistics are further suspect because at no time do they give an idea of the size of the studied communities, in terms of either population or area. (The "communities" are defined by zip code). There is no breakdown of the studied communities by region of the country, rural vs. urban, or any other factors that might promote greater understanding of the numbers.

Sample sizes are not given. It is axiomatic that the results of a random sample of 1,000 are more reliable than the results of a random sample of 10. NLJ did not disclose the size of its sample, leaving the reader unable to evaluate independently the results.

NLJ does not report the statistical significance of any element of its study. Statistical significance reflects the margin of error in the results, and is stated in terms of the percentage of the time the study's results would have occurred by chance alone.

The data are not adjusted for time. Anyone who has defended environmental enforcement actions over a period of years can testify that the penalties for similar violations have steadily increased. If enforcement occurred first in minority communities, it would be reasonable to conclude that penalties could have been lower for those facilities without reflecting racial bias. By not asking the question, NLJ leaves it open.

Failure to control for time in Superfund cases raises a similar question. NLJ reports that EPA chooses "containment" seven percent more frequently than "permanent treatment," "the cleanup method preferred under the law," at minority sites, while the reverse is true for 22 percent of white sites. "Permanent treatment" has been the preferred method only since enactment of the Superfund Amendments and Reauthorization Act in late 1986, so sites that were cleaned up or for which Records of Decision

(ROD) had been issued prior to implementation of SARA are more likely to have had containment as the chosen remediation method. If so-called minority sites were listed first (again, failing to ask the question leaves it open), that could account for the difference, if any, in remedy selection.

This article is not meant to belittle the pollution problems of minority communities. . . . But a badly presented, quasi-statistical study is not the way to promote environmental justice.

****

Note

For further debate about the methods and results of data gathering in the environmental justice realm, see Chapter 7(B)(2), *infra*.

****

Richard J. Lazarus, "Pursuing 'Environmental Justice': The Distributional Effects of Environmental Protection," 87 Northwestern University Law Review 787, 842-44, 846 (1993)

A better accounting of the distributional implications of environmental protection will likely also require substantive reform of the federal environmental laws. This is in part because EPA has historically resisted embracing a distributional mandate in its enforcement of these laws. The agency has consistently viewed "sociological" concerns, such as distributional impacts, as outside the purview of its purely "technical" mandate of establishing technically effective, and economically efficient, pollution control standards.

Notwithstanding EPA's apparent assumption, the agency's failure to take distributional equity into account has not resulted in a neutral distribution of the benefits and burdens of environmental protection. Indeed, the agency's position may instead have facilitated a distributional skewing unfavorable to those persons, such as racial minorities, less able to influence the legislative, regulatory, and enforcement agendas that ultimately determine who will receive the benefits and burdens of a particular legislative initiative.

Two kinds of statutory reforms could address this problem. One possibility would be to require formal agency consideration of the distributional impacts associated with a particular decision. Such consideration could be required where the agency establishes rulemaking agendas, promulgates implementing regulations, and determines enforcement priorities. It could also be required when the agency allocates grant monies and technical assistance. The second, more ambitious, reform would be to establish equitable benchmarks that would provide standards for judging discretionary agency determinations with significant distributional impacts.

Neither substantive reform is as radical a proposal as it might seem. Indeed, there is plenty of applicable precedent for infusing distributional factors into the fashioning of legal standards and agency priorities. For example, environmental impact statements, prepared pursuant to the National Environmental Policy Act, have long included discussions of the socioeconomic effects of certain proposed federal actions.[4] Even more broadly, federal and state natural resource laws have routinely included substantive distributional standards. The purpose of these standards was generally to ensure a fair distribution of the nation's natural resource wealth. It should be equally acceptable to ensure that the risks associated with environmental protection are also fairly distributed. For example, homestead, mining, mineral leasing, and reclamation laws historically included acreage limitations. These limitations were intended to promote a fair and equitable distribution of public resources.[5]

In one notable respect, moreover, the nation's natural resources laws take explicit account of their distributional impact on an identifiable minority group: Native American tribes. The Bureau of Indian Affairs within the Department of the Interior is charged, inter alia, with honoring the United States' treaty obligations and general fiduciary duties to Native American tribes. The existence of that formal voice within the executive branch may, in part, explain why some federal environmental protection laws articulate specific exemptions aimed at ameliorating some of the distributional impacts that those laws may have on Native Americans, particularly when those laws adversely affect some of their subsistence ways of life.

****

Note

Given the traditional wisdom that a certain quantum of discretion is essential in environmental enforcement and cleanup decisions, can you envision a statutory formulation that could effectively address racial and economic inequities in the implementation of environmental laws?[6] How likely is it that a statute on this subject would partake of some of the characteristics of "symbolic legislation" described by Professor Dwyer in Chapter 3(B), *supra*?

---

[4] [Ed.] Does the discussion of NEPA in Chapter 7(C)(4), *infra*, support this assertion?

[5] [Ed.] *See, e.g.,* Kenneth A. Manaster, "Squatters and the Law: The Relevance of the United States Experience to Current Problems in the Developing Countries," 43 Tulane Law Review 94, 120 (1968) ("[T]he public domain was to be settled in small farms, so that the largest number of persons could benefit by gaining legal holdings.").

[6] For the argument that "an explicit statutory mandate is needed to ensure that regulatory agencies administer and enforce environmental programs equally across all population groups," *see* Deeohn Ferris, "A Broad Environmental Justice Agenda: Mandating Change Begins at the Federal Level," 5 Maryland Journal of Contemporary Legal Issues 115, 123 (1993).

Consider whether the Executive Order and legislative proposals discussed in Chapter 7(D), *infra*, offer any such formulations. Consider also whether inequities could be adequately addressed through the type of agency enforcement policy you were invited to draft in Exercise 1, *supra*.

E. The Choice of Criminal Charges

Sheldon M. Novick (ed.), Law of Environmental Protection, section 8.01[9] (1987, 1992)

The basic enforcement sections of the environmental statutes provide that persons who knowingly violate specified requirements or prohibitions of the Act in question shall be fined, imprisoned, or both. They may double the potential punishment for second offenders and may contain a separate sanction for false statements. Over time Congress has increased many of the sanctions and recently it has added severe sanctions for knowing violations that recklessly endanger human life. In general they are short and straightforward provisions and raise few questions on their face. It should be recognized, of course, that many violations of environmental statutes may also violate provisions of the criminal code: for example, conspiracy, mail fraud, or obstruction of justice. Where this occurs, U.S. attorneys should be expected to use these, to them, more familiar tools in place of or in addition to the environmental violations.

There have been few reported decisions in criminal cases under the statutes, reflecting the relative scarcity of criminal prosecutions by EPA. Indeed, it was not until the early 1980s that EPA recognized the desirability of establishing a criminal investigative unit with a modest staff of experienced criminal investigators. This infusion of resources has had a dramatic impact on criminal charges and prosecutions.[7] Those convicted before 1984 were not sentenced to imprisonment, whereas today imprisonment is common. During each of the last three years convicted defendants have been sentenced to an average aggregate of 328 months in prison. This reflects both a greater familiarity by courts with environmental crimes and the effect of the sentencing guidelines. As EPA's criminal investigative program develops, more states undertake analogous efforts, and courts become more used to dealing with environmental crimes, penalties will undoubtedly become more severe and the number of reported decisions will increase.

---

[7] [Ed.] "Since the Department of Justice formed its Environmental Crimes Section in 1982, it has imposed fines of more than $26 million in 430 pleas and convictions." Celia Campbell-Mohn, ed., Environmental Law: From Resources to Recovery 142 (1993).

"[T]he Department of Justice and the EPA, working with the FBI, have shown some willingness to enforce what criminal provisions there are in our environmental laws. From 1983 to 1991, they brought a total of 813 indictments for environmental crimes. Pleas or convictions were obtained in 613 cases." Hearing on H.R. 5305, "Environmental Crimes Act of 1992," before the Subcommittee on Crime and Criminal Justice, Committee on the Judiciary, House of Representatives, 102nd Congress, 2nd Session at 14 (Statement of Representative Charles E. Schumer). H.R. 5305 was not enacted.

The criminal sanctions apply to a ''person'' who violates the statutes. ''Person'' is defined in the general definitional sections of most of the environmental statutes, but the definitions vary, requiring a separate inquiry under each statute. In addition, some of the criminal sanctions have their own definition of ''person'' or modify the statute's. The primary objective of special treatment of the definition is to particularize the criminal liability of officers and employees. Clean Air Act section 113(c)(6) and Clean Water Act section 309(c)(6), for instance, specify that the term includes ''any responsible corporate officer.'' EPA's emphasis on prosecuting individuals within corporations lends particular interest to these provisions. As far as this author can determine, EPA's prosecutions to date have been directed at corporate officials or employees with real knowledge of and participation in the alleged violations. This is not strictly necessary for imposing criminal liability on corporate officials with ultimate responsibility for compliance with statutory mandates, particularly when the statute in question is for the protection of public health. It is clear that courts are willing to utilize this rationale in convictions of corporate officers on a respondeat superior theory under the environmental statutes. Lower level employees who participate in violations are also subject to prosecution and conviction. Thus, in *United States v. Johnson & Towers, Inc.*,[8] the court was not hesitant to convict a foreman and truck service manager of several counts arising from pumping hazardous waste into a creek.

The enforcement sections typically provide criminal sanctions for specified violations. These may or may not be the same violation for which civil penalties are authorized. Each statute must be examined separately in this regard to determine if a particular violation is subject to criminal sanctions, although it can be assumed with some degree of assurance that all mainline violations will be.

Of great interest to potential defendants is whether the government will proceed against a particular violation civilly, criminally, or both. Statistically, of course, almost all enforcement actions are civil and administrative. Moreover, for a violation to be pursued criminally, it will usually have an element that makes it worthy of criminal prosecution, a touchstone of egregiousness in the violation or in its consequences that sets it apart from ordinary violations. This may be of small comfort to the potential defendant, however, because whether a violation appears worthy of prosecution depends upon the eye of the beholder and the prosecutor's eye may be very different than the potential defendant's eye. Indeed, there may even be an element of chance involved: the decision whether to prosecute criminally or civilly may turn on who investigates the case first. If a FBI agent or one of EPA's special agents initiates the investigation, it is much more apt to be pursued criminally than if the initial inspection is conducted by EPA's regular inspectors. Moreover, even an ordinary violation may be prosecuted criminally if the criminal investigation process has become deeply involved but has not uncovered a violation more worthy of prosecution. This is particularly likely if there has been a grand jury investigation. It is unlikely, however, that both civil and criminal

---

[8] 741 F.2d 662 (3d Cir. 1984).

processes will proceed simultaneously, because such parallel proceedings require separation of functions and personnel that is taxing on the bureaucracy. Separation is necessary to assure that the confidentiality of grand jury proceedings won't be breached and that limited government criminal discovery won't be unduly augmented. It is, of course, possible for the government to maintain parallel proceedings and it will do so when there is reason to, e.g., to stop a release of hazardous substances causing an imminent and substantial endangerment while conducting a grand jury investigation. Normally, however, it will not do so and may even seek a stay of civil proceedings to allow a grand jury investigation to go forward unencumbered.

While most of the sections specify that criminal sanctions are applicable only where a violation is "knowing," Clean Water Act section 309(c) makes them applicable to either negligent or knowing violations, but provides greater penalties for knowing violations. As a practical matter there may not be a great deal of difference between the two because of the clear proof of culpability that most prosecutors require before initiating a criminal case, and the relaxed showing of scienter necessary to prove convictions of statutes designed to protect health and safety. The knowledge to satisfy the scienter requirement under such statutes is merely of the action taken, i.e., the disposal of hazardous wastes without a permit, rather than the fact that such disposal is illegal. CWA, CAA, and RCRA provide especially severe penalties for violations that are knowing and that the actor also knows will put another at risk of serious bodily harm or death. And some of these elements for which knowledge is required may be established by inference. Indeed, "willful blindness" is no defense where the defendant deliberately avoided learning of such facts to construct a defense. This relaxed scienter has been especially well developed in cases arising under the Endangered Species Act.

****

Note

Can you construct a hierarchy of levels of fault that would tend to indicate when a criminal prosecution should be pursued and when noncriminal enforcement avenues are more apt?[9] In doing so, consider the readings in Chapter 2 with regard to approaches to corrective justice.[10] Recalling some of the concepts suggested there, should the major emphasis in environmental enforcement be upon the "the goodness or badness of the person," "the damage" done, the "deep pockets" of "activities, however carefully controlled" that can cause environmental harm, the value of "a warning" conveyed to other potential offenders, or some other bases?

---

[9] One commentator has observed that public strategies for dealing with environmental noncompliance "theoretically range from draconian criminal sentences to subsidies for compliance." Joseph F. DiMento, Environmental Law and American Business: Dilemmas of Compliance 39 (1986).

[10] *See also* Symposium, "Environmental Crime," 59 George Washington Law Review 775 (1991); Symposium, "Criminal Enforcement of Environmental Laws," 22 Environmental Law 1315 (1992).

F. The Significance of Diligence

In an area of law such as environmental law, in which violations can be based upon a broad spectrum of culpable conduct, the incentive is great for alleged violators to assert their past diligence, good faith, honorable motives, etc. as grounds for being excused from legal responsibility for their apparent misdeeds and the resulting harms. The fundamental validity of these assertions in some circumstances is acknowledged by the presence in virtually all states' environmental legislation, and under some federal statutes as well, of provisions allowing variances for activities that involve violations, but justifiable ones.[11]

Another, increasingly popular justification for avoiding punishment for violations stems from the trend toward more environmental auditing by regulated entities, i.e., voluntary and thorough examination of one's own compliance status. The essence of the argument is that the violator who has been attentive and responsible enough to find and fix a problem should not be penalized for it. Auditing is one type of responsible activity that can be a double-edged sword, however, for although it may enable the pollution source to identify and correct violations, it also can generate evidence of the violations that unsympathetic enforcement agencies may seek to use against the source. Some of the complexities of this tension are explored in the following federal policy statement, which implicitly addresses both corrective justice standards and procedural fairness in the selection of enforcement targets.

****

U. S. Department of Justice, "Factors in Decisions on Criminal Prosecutions for Environmental Violations in the Context of Significant Voluntary Compliance or Disclosure Efforts by the Violator" (July 1, 1991)

Introduction

It is the policy of the Department of Justice to encourage self-auditing, self-policing and voluntary disclosure of environmental violations by the regulated community by indicating that these activities are viewed as mitigating factors in the Department's exercise of criminal environmental enforcement discretion. This document is intended to describe the factors that the Department of Justice considers in deciding whether to bring a criminal prosecution for a violation of an environmental statute, so that such prosecutions do not create a disincentive to or undermine the goal of encouraging critical self-auditing, self-policing, and voluntary disclosure.

---

[11] *See generally* Daniel P. Selmi *et al.*, State Environmental Law 8-39 (1989, 1991) ("The primary safety valve available to regulated entities is the variance process. Typically an adjudicatory board or hearing officer is vested with the power to grant variances, or temporary exemptions, from regulatory requirements for sources demonstrating good cause for such relief.").

This guidance and the examples contained herein provide a framework for the determination of whether a particular case presents the type of circumstances in which lenience would be appropriate.

Factors to be Considered

Where the law and evidence would otherwise be sufficient for prosecution, the attorney for the Department should consider the factors contained herein, to the extent they are applicable, along with any other relevant factors, in determining whether and how to prosecute. It must be emphasized that these are examples of the types of factors which could be relevant. They do not constitute a definitive recipe or checklist of requirements.

Voluntary Disclosure: The attorney for the Department should consider whether the person made a voluntary, timely and complete disclosure of the matter under investigation. Consideration should be given to whether the person came forward promptly after discovering the noncompliance, and to the quantity and quality of information provided. Particular consideration should be given to whether the disclosure substantially aided the government's investigatory process, and whether it occurred before a law enforcement or regulatory authority (federal, state or local authority) had already obtained knowledge regarding noncompliance. A disclosure is not considered to be "voluntary" if that disclosure is already specifically required by law, regulation, or permit.

Cooperation: The attorney for the Department should consider the degree and timeliness of cooperation by the person. Full and prompt cooperation is essential, whether in the context of a voluntary disclosure or after the government has independently learned of a violation. Consideration should be given to the violator's willingness to make all relevant information (including the complete results of any internal or external investigation and the names of all potential witnesses) available to government investigators and prosecutors. Consideration should also be given to the extent and quality of the violator's assistance to the government's investigation.

Preventive Measures and Compliance Programs: The attorney for the Department should consider the existence and scope of any regularized, intensive, and comprehensive environmental compliance program; such a program may include an environmental compliance or management audit. Particular consideration should be given to whether the compliance or audit program includes sufficient measures to identify and prevent future noncompliance, and whether the program was adopted in good faith in a timely manner.

Compliance programs may vary but the following questions should be asked in evaluating any program: Was there a strong institutional policy to comply with all environmental requirements? Had safeguards beyond those required by existing law been developed and implemented to prevent noncompliance from occurring? Were there regular procedures, including internal or external compliance and management audits, to evaluate, detect, prevent and remedy circumstances like those that led to the noncompliance?

Were there procedures and safeguards to ensure the integrity of any audit conducted? Did the audit evaluate all sources of pollution (*i.e.*, all media), including the possibility of cross-media transfers of pollutants? Were the auditor's recommendations implemented in a timely fashion? Were adequate resources committed to the auditing program and to implementing its recommendations? Was environmental compliance a standard by which employee and corporate departmental performance was judged?

Additional Factors Which May Be Relevant

Pervasiveness of Noncompliance: Pervasive noncompliance may indicate systemic or repeated participation in or condonation of criminal behavior. It may also indicate the lack of a meaningful compliance program. In evaluating this factor, the attorney for the Department should consider, among other things, the number and level of employees participating in the unlawful activities and the obviousness, seriousness, duration, history, and frequency of noncompliance.

Internal Disciplinary Action

Effective internal disciplinary action is crucial to any compliance program. The attorney for the Department should consider whether there was an effective system of discipline for employees who violated company environmental compliance policies. Did the disciplinary system establish an awareness in other employees that unlawful conduct would not be condoned?

Subsequent Compliance Efforts

The attorney for the Department should consider the extent of any efforts to remedy any ongoing noncompliance. The promptness and completeness of any action taken to remove the source of the noncompliance and to lessen the environmental harm resulting from the noncompliance should be considered. Considerable weight should be given to prompt, good-faith efforts to reach environmental compliance agreements with federal or state authorities, or both. Full compliance with such agreements should be a factor in any decision whether to prosecute.

****

Notes

1. Reexamine the violations by each of the four clients described in Exercise 2, *supra*. In each instance, if the violation first was identified by the polluter itself, how likely is it that application of these Department of Justice factors would prevent a criminal prosecution? Should factors of this type also protect the violator from other types of enforcement remedies and penalties?

2. In 1986 the EPA issued an "Environmental Auditing Policy Statement." 51 Federal Register 25004 (July 9, 1986). More recently, as part of ongoing review of that Policy Statement, the Agency issued a "Restatement of Policies Related to Environmental Auditing." 59 Federal Register 38455 (July 28, 1994).[12] The Restatement reiterates "regulated entities' need to self-evaluate environmental performance with some measure of privacy," and it indicates that "EPA will take into account a facility's efforts to audit in setting inspection priorities and in fashioning enforcement responses to violations." *Id.* at 38457. Nonetheless, the Restatement affirms "EPA's authority to request and receive any relevant information – including that contained in audit reports – under various environmental statutes or in other administrative or judicial proceedings." EPA emphasizes that "[e]nvironmental audits are in no way a substitute for regulatory oversight."

Among other important points, the Agency also notes:

> Four states (Colorado, Indiana, Kentucky, and Oregon) have recently enacted legislation which, with some variations, creates a 'self-evaluative' privilege for audit reports.[13] EPA has consistently opposed this approach, principally because of the risk of weakening State enforcement programs, the imposition of unnecessary transaction costs and delays in enforcement actions, and the potential increase in the number of situations requiring the expenditure of scarce Agency resources, including the [federal] 'overfiling' of State enforcement actions." *Id.* at 38459.

In view of the various conflicting considerations touched upon by the Restatement, how would you resolve the question of whether environmental audit information should be subject to a privilege of confidentiality relative to enforcement agencies or other litigants?[14]

One recent commentary has argued against a broad privilege, but in favor of a policy that would preclude imposition of penalties for past violations "discovered by a voluntary self audit and voluntarily reported to EPA, unless the past violation was intentional or resulted from reckless conduct." Stanley W. Legro, "Self Audits and EPA Enforcement," The Environmental Forum, Volume 11, Number 6, November-December 1994,

---

[12] Also, on January 12, 1994 EPA issued a memorandum on "The Exercise of Investigative Discretion" to guide "all EPA employees working in or in support of the criminal enforcement program." The memorandum "sets out the specific factors that distinguish cases meriting criminal investigation from those more appropriately pursued under administrative or civil judicial authorities." EPA stated that the selection of cases for criminal treatment will be guided by "two general measures – significant environmental harm and culpable conduct." Culpable conduct is not limited to an assessment of criminal intent, but also includes such factors as a history of repeated violations, falsification of records, tampering with monitoring or control equipment, operation without permits, etc.

[13] [Ed.] *See also* "Illinois Legislature Approves Measure to Grant Confidentiality for Environmental Audits," 25 Environment Reporter (BNA) 1621 (December 16, 1994); "Effects of Oregon's Audit Privilege Law Still Unclear after First Year," *id.*

[14] Varying judicial responses to a claimed "self-evaluative" or "self-critical analysis" privilege to protect environmental information from discovery during litigation can be found at *U.S.v. The Dexter Corporation*, 132 F.R.D. 8 (D. Conn. 1990) (privilege rejected) and *Reichhold Chemicals, Inc. v. Textron, Inc.*, 1994 U.S. Dist. LEXIS 13806 (N.D. Fla. September 20, 1994) (privilege allowed). *See also Olen Properties Corp. v. Sheldahl, Inc.*, 1994 WL 212135 (C.D. Cal. April 12, 1994) (environmental audit covered by attorney-client privilege).

at 8. Legro's argument is premised on his belief that, in contrast to earlier periods in the development of enforcement policy, "now there is a high degree of awareness" of environmental requirements among regulated entities and the general public, and there is "relatively little incidence" of knowing or intentional violations. Accordingly, he urges that the enforcement emphasis should shift to the creation of incentives for developing more information about environmental problems and for voluntary compliance, through methods such as environmental audits.[15]

Do you agree with these premises? Can you reconcile them with the increasing emphasis on criminal enforcement methods discussed in the preceding section of this chapter?

---

[15] For a discussion of the November, 1993 Draft Corporate Sentencing Guidelines for Environmental Violations, and of their proposed treatment of voluntary compliance efforts in the calculation of punishment, *see* Joe B. Whitley *et al.*, "Increased Prosecution is Predicted: New Sentencing Guidelines for Organizations May Lead to More Frequent Charges against Corporations for Environmental Crimes," The National Law Journal (December 5, 1994) at C1.

Chapter 5
Administering and Enforcing Environmental Standards

A. Overview

Environmental lawyers frequently are called upon to address the fairness of the processes by which environmental standards are applied to a particular regulated entity. This concern for fair procedure is an especially important focus of the work of lawyers representing regulated businesses, for they are most directly affected by the normal administrative functions required by environmental statutes, such as rulemaking, inspections, and permitting. In those contexts, the lawyer's efforts to promote fair treatment usually consist of a variety of communications with the regulatory agency aimed at persuading officials to implement certain basic components of fair process.

When regulatory efforts culminate in enforcement proceedings regarding alleged violations, the lawyer for the regulated entity must seek to promote fair treatment in a more structured manner. The lawyer then can express procedural fairness concerns in two formats: defenses based on alleged procedural irregularities in the earlier administrative phases, and demands for procedural fairness in the conduct of the enforcement proceedings themselves.

This chapter will examine both of these types of concerns. They embody various concepts of procedural justice, such as those discussed in Chapter 2. For example, Hart's emphasis on impartial consideration of competing claims to different benefits as a prerequisite to legislative action is reflected here. Similarly, Rawls's discussion of perfect and imperfect procedural justice is echoed, with regard to the search both for clear criteria for correct outcomes and for effective adjudicatory arrangements that ''may reasonably be expected in different circumstances to yield the right results,'' i.e., results that correspond with the factual truth.

Although the present chapter presents a potpourri of administrative and enforcement process issues, it does not purport to address all of the hard questions of procedural fairness that environmental lawyers encounter. Also, as should become evident, these questions sometimes are addressed in terms of constitutional requirements, and at other times only statutorily mandated procedures are at issue. More generally, the environmental practitioner often argues for procedural fairness simply in broad, equitable terms, without resorting to any specific procedural requirements set forth in the law. On all of these levels, the pervasiveness of procedural justice as an element of environmental law practice cannot be overstated.

The first section explores a variety of overlapping fairness concerns regarding the regulatory standards being applied. As will be seen, the constitutional adequacy of environmental standards has been challenged with respect to their clarity, as well as their rationality in terms of equal protection requirements. Constitutional questions also occasionally have been raised as to whether legislative power has been improperly delegated to executive branch agencies. The material presented regarding the right to be heard addresses familiar and fundamental demands for procedural due process.

It is, of course, relatively infrequent that attorneys find it necessary to mount constitutional challenges to environmental requirements. Nonetheless, it is ultimately critical for the fairness of environmental law that the values these challenges seek to protect are constantly respected, and that lawyers remain ready and able to protest on behalf of their clients when these values are in jeopardy.

Finally, although not usually rising to the level of constitutional objections, some problems of unpredictability, delay, and overlapping enforcement will be noted, for they also raise practical concerns for procedural fairness.

B. The Applicable Standards

1. Clarity

State v. Normandale Properties, Inc., 420 N.W.2d 259 (Minn. App. 1988)

Normandale is charged with attempted violations of two statutes, based on the criminal attempt statute, Minn. Stat. §609.17 (1986). Count 1, attempted willful or negligent unlawful disposal of hazardous waste, is based on the following statute:

willfully or negligently violating any provision relating to hazardous waste of this chapter or chapter 116, or any standard [or] rule * * * adopted by the [Minnesota pollution control] agency under such a provision * * *.

Minn. Stat. § 115.071, subd. 2a(a) (1986).

Count 2, attempted unlawful disposal of hazardous waste, is based on this statute:

Any person who knowingly, or with reason to know, disposes of hazardous waste in a manner contrary to any provision of this chapter or chapter 116, or any standard or rule adopted in accordance with those chapters relating to disposal, is guilty of a felony.

Minn. Stat. § 115.071, subd. 2b (1986).

Hazardous waste is defined as follows:

''Hazardous waste'' means any refuse, sludge, or other waste material or combinations of refuse, sludge or other waste materials in solid, semisolid, liquid, or contained gaseous form which because of its quantity, concentration, or chemical, physical or infectious characteristics may (a) cause or significantly contribute to an increase in mortality or an increase in serious irreversible, or incapacitating reversible illness; or (b) pose a substantial present or potential hazard to human health or the environment when improperly treated, stored, transported, or disposed of, or otherwise managed. Categories of hazardous waste materials include, but are not limited to: explosives, flammables, oxidizers, poisons, irritants, and corrosives. Minn. Stat. § 116.06, subd. 13 (1986)

Agency rules contain lists of chemicals considered hazardous wastes. Only the statutory definition of hazardous waste applies here, however.

The United States and Minnesota Constitutions require that statutes meet due process standards of definiteness.

[T]he void-for-vagueness doctrine requires that a penal statute define the criminal offense with sufficient definiteness that ordinary people can understand what conduct is prohibited and in a manner that does not encourage arbitrary and discriminatory enforcement.

Vagueness challenges to statutes that do not involve first amendment freedoms must be examined in light of the facts of the particular case. A person whose conduct is clearly proscribed "cannot complain of the vagueness of the law as applied to others." The person charged must show the statute "lacks specificity as to his own behavior and not as to some hypothetical situation."

Normandale argues the statutory definition of hazardous waste is void on its face. A statute that does not implicate first amendment freedoms is facially void for vagueness only if it is vague in all its applications. Unless the statute proscribes no comprehensible course of conduct at all, it will be upheld against a facial challenge.

This court has upheld prosecutions based on the statutes at issue here. Those cases in effect hold the statutes are not facially void.

The state argues that the statutory definition of hazardous waste is not unconstitutionally vague as applied to the facts of this case. We agree.

The statute defines hazardous waste to include

any * * * combinations of * * * waste materials in * * * liquid * * * form which because of its quantity [or] concentration * * * may * * * pose a substantial * * * hazard to human health or the environment when improperly * * * disposed of * * * [H]azardous waste materials include * * * flammables [and] poisons * * *.

The statute provides adequate notice that it covers the approximately forty gallons of highly flammable lacquer thinner at issue here. Indeed, under these circumstances Normandale had more than adequate notice. The wastes emitted a strong solvent odor and were in containers labeled "hazardous waste" or "flammable" or both. Normandale attempted to dispose of them after a waste hauler had refused to take them at another location. Although the statutory definition might conceivably raise due process concerns in some situations, it does not here.

Normandale's main argument is that the statute is void for vagueness because it fails to specify what substances in what amounts and concentrations are covered. The fact that the legislature could have defined hazardous waste more precisely does not make the statute unconstitutional.

We are not persuaded, moreover, that a list of chemical compounds would have provided Normandale better notice than the statute's more general criteria. It is more likely Normandale knew that the lacquer thinner was flammable and "posed a substantial * * * hazard to human health or the environment" than it is they knew its chemical composition.

The hazardous waste statute is not unconstitutionally vague on its face or as applied to the facts of this case.

****

Exxon Company, U.S.A. v. State of Texas, 646 S.W.2d 536 (Tex. App. 1982)

This is an appeal from a conviction for the offense of air pollution under the provisions of Article 4477-5b of Vernon's Ann. Civ. Stat. The evidence was presented to the trial court by way of an agreed stipulation.

The phrase "interference with the normal use and enjoyment of property" has a long legal history in the civil law of nuisances. Nuisances have been defined as, and damages have been awarded for, conditions which interfere with the use and enjoyment of property.

Due process only requires that a statute define terms in understandable language so that men of common intelligence do not have to guess at its meaning or differ as to its application. *Connally v. General Construction Co.*, 269 U.S. 385, 46 S. Ct. 126 (1926). Thus, we hold that the phrase "interfere with the normal use and enjoyment of property" is not unconstitutionally vague.

****

Notes

1. The *Normandale* court states that the statutory definition of hazardous waste "might conceivably raise due process concerns in some situations." What might those be? Does the result hinge upon the presence, as in this case, of labels that used the same terms as the statute? Does this procedural fairness concern for adequate notice of proscribed behavior always answer the basic corrective justice question, *viz.*, whether a statute imposes fault-based or strict liability? In this regard, consider the linkage between notice and scienter presented in *People v. Martin*, *infra*.

2. What are the implications of the *Normandale* court's suggestion that it is less likely the defendant knew of the wastes' chemical composition than that it knew of their potential hazards? Could a defendant specifically charged with improper disposal of a

listed compound have a stronger defense than Normandale did? Consider in this regard the final client described in Exercise 2 in Chapter 4(B), *supra*.

3. In view of the proliferation of detailed regulations in many fields of environmental law, including hazardous waste management and air pollution control, is it anomalous, as well as unfair to potential violators, to prosecute on the basis of general prohibitions? Alternatively, are such statutory prohibitions both a necessary foundation for the detailed regulations and a valuable supplement to them?

More broadly, have we reached a point in environmental law at which enforcement sometimes is unfair because a proscription is too general, and at other times is unfair because a proscription is too specific?

****

Ross Neely Express, Inc. v. Alabama Department of Environmental Management, 437 So. 2d 82 (Ala. 1983)

This is an appeal from a judgment of the Circuit Court of Montgomery County, enjoining Ross Neely Express, Inc. (RNE) from violating certain rules and regulations of the Alabama Department of Environmental Management (ADEM). In issuing the injunction, the trial court found that RNE was in violation, and that the rules violated were not unconstitutional. The pertinent portions of the rules allegedly violated are as follows:

4.2.1 No person shall cause, suffer, allow, or permit . . . a road to be used . . . without taking reasonable precautions to prevent particulate matter from becoming airborne. Such reasonable precautions shall include, but not be limited to, the following: . . . .
(b) Application of asphalt, oil, water, or suitable chemicals on dirt roads, materials stock piles, and other surfaces which create airborne dust problems; . . . .
4.2.2 Visible Emissions Restrictions Beyond Lot Line. No person shall cause or permit the discharge of visible fugitive dust emissions beyond the lot line of the property on which the emissions originate.
Statutes and regulations are void for overbreadth if their object is achieved by means which sweep unnecessarily broadly and thereby invade the area of protected freedoms.

In applying the above cited principles to the regulations challenged in the case before us, we find that both 4.2.1 and 4.2.2 are constitutionally defective. Regulation 4.2.1 requires that RNE not allow its road to be used without taking "reasonable" precautions to prevent particulate matter from becoming airborne, and lists certain precautions which shall be included. While "reasonableness" has been upheld as a legal standard in some cases, the fact remains that the regulation before us is so vague that men of common intelligence must necessarily guess at its meaning and differ as to its application. See Connally v. General Construction Co., 269 U.S. 385, 46 S. Ct. 126 (1926). How often should RNE have taken "reasonable" precautions? Must it take all of the suggested precautions, as well as others? If the precautions taken fail to eliminate airborne particulate matter completely, has RNE failed to take reasonable precautions per se?

The stipulated facts show that RNE used 50 to 60 truckloads of slag in the construction of the road in 1974. Since that time, on at least four occasions, slag and chert had been added to the road surface. On three occasions oil was applied to the surface. (We note that this was one of the suggested "reasonable precautions" contained in the regulation itself.) But in 1981, ADEM alleged that RNE was in violation of § 4.2.1 because dust had been observed rising from the road, and the trial court agreed. This appears to be a classic example of a case where men of common intelligence must necessarily guess as to the requirements of the regulation.

Regulation 4.2.2 is unconstitutionally restrictive. Visible fugitive dust emissions may not be permitted to float beyond the lot line of the property on which the emissions originate. Thus, the Department of Public Health memorandum of May 12,1981, noted in the agreed statement of facts, showed a violation when it stated, "This writer observed fugitive dust which was created when a pickup truck drove to the plant. The fugitive dust went onto a vacant lot in front of A Liquid Air Inc. The wind was out of the southwest." Such a regulation is clearly overbroad, encompassing every situation in which visible fugitive dust emissions move across a lot line, without regard to damage, injury, or inconvenience caused, reasonable attempts at control, etc. This invades the area of protected freedom, severely restricting the use of property, and creates a situation where discriminatory enforcement is almost inevitable.

We find both of the regulations under consideration to be unreasonable. ADEM argues that they are a proper exercise of the police power of the State of Alabama, going to the protection of health, public convenience, public welfare, protection of property, and the maintenance of good order. While the above matters are clearly subject to the police power, and while the control of air pollution is greatly to be desired, we find that the restraint imposed by the two regulations before us, as written, imposes a restraint upon the use of private property that is disproportionate to the amount of evil that will be corrected. Thus, they fail the test of constitutionality . . . .

****

Note

Is the Alabama court's conclusion consistent with the Texas court's view in *Exxon*? What "area of protected freedoms" does the Alabama court believe to be at issue? Is vagueness of the regulations the only basis for the result that court reaches? Is the court declaring the regulations "unreasonable" just because they rely upon "reasonableness"? Reconsider these questions after examining the next section on rationality.

2. Rationality

Daniel P. Selmi and Kenneth A. Manaster, State Environmental Law, Section 5.05[1] (1989, 1994)

State and local environmental regulations occasionally have been challenged as violating substantive due process and equal protection of the laws, concepts embedded in the Fourteenth Amendment. The specific tests applied under these doctrines are very similar. The basic inquiry in each instance is whether the regulatory enactment under challenge represents a rational exercise of legislative authority. In pursuing this inquiry, the courts have taken a very deferential approach to legislative power. Accordingly, they are extremely reluctant to overturn economic regulatory legislation on these grounds. Only when a fundamental right is threatened or a suspect classification can be shown is a court very likely to uphold a substantive due process or equal protection attack. Because interests of this sort are seldom involved in environmental disputes, such a result is extremely unlikely with regard to most environmental legislation.

The overlapping nature of the tests applied under these two constitutional doctrines is evident in *Minnesota v. Clover Leaf Creamery Company*[1]. The Supreme court there considered a challenge to a Minnesota statute banning the retail sale of milk in plastic, nonreturnable containers. The essence of the challengers' equal protection argument was that the classification scheme for containers chosen for regulation by the state legislature was irrational. . . . The court applied the "familiar 'rational basis' test," which will uphold legislative classifications so long as they are rationally related to the achievement of legitimate state interests. It rejected the various arguments that the classification between plastic and nonplastic nonreturnable containers was not rationally related to the legislature's stated purposes. Thus the equal protection argument failed.

The Court noted that the state statute also was being attacked on substantive due process grounds. This argument also essentially challenged the rationality of the legislation. The Court said, "From our conclusion under equal protection, however, it follows *a fortiori* that the Act does not violate the Fourteenth Amendment's Due Process Clause." Clearly the acceptability of the legislature's classification scheme suffices to overcome the irrationality claim under both equal protection and substantive due process analyses."

****

Rockford Drop Forge Company v. Pollution Control Board, 402 N.E.2d 602 (Ill. 1980)

The appellants, 22 Illinois forging companies and the Forging Industry Association (the forging companies), filed a petition . . . to review rules adopted by the Pollution

---

[1] 449 U.S. 456, 101 S. Ct. 715 (1981).

Control Board of the State of Illinois (the Board) for noise emissions from stationary, or "property line," sources. The rules were upheld by the appellate court, and we granted the forging companies' petition for leave to appeal. The Board has taken a cross-appeal.

The forging companies contended in the appellate court that the noise pollution provisions of the Environmental Protection Act were unconstitutional because of vagueness and improper delegation. The companies also asserted that the regulations exceeded the power granted the Board under the Act, which, according to the forging companies, confined the Board to the prevention of public nuisances. The companies asserted further that the regulations violated the equal protection clauses of the United States Constitution and the Constitution of Illinois because comparable rules had not been adopted for other sources of noise emissions. These claims are renewed on this appeal.

Although we hold that the appellate court should have considered the objections to the validity of the Act, we do not reverse its judgment on that account, for we conclude that those objections are without merit. The first of them is that section 24 of the Act is so vague and indefinite as to violate due process. Section 24, the violation of which is made a criminal offense by section 44, is as follows:

> "No person shall emit beyond the boundaries of his property any noise that unreasonably interferes with the enjoyment of life or with any lawful business or activity, so as to violate any regulation or standard adopted by the Board under this Act."

We do not inquire whether the phrase "unreasonably interferes with the enjoyment of life," standing alone, would be too vague to pass muster, for what is proscribed is conduct which violates any regulation or standard adopted by the Board. The forging companies' argument under this heading thus relates more properly to its next charge, which is that the Act makes an unconstitutional delegation of legislative power.

In the discussion of that question the forging companies do not identify the points at which they consider the Act vulnerable, and in the treatment of the point in their brief they fail to mention [certain] recent decisions . . . . In those decisions this court reappraised the constitutional limitations upon rule-making under a comprehensive regulatory statute, and adopted as the criteria of validity that the statute sufficiently identify the persons and activities subject to regulation, the harm sought to be prevented, and the general means intended to be made available to prevent the harm. It is plain without further discussion that the provisions of [the statute], including the legislative declaration, the definition of the acts prohibited, and the specification of permissible regulations, . . . amply satisfy constitutional requirements.

The forging companies also contend, somewhat inconsistently, that in adopting these rules the Board exceeded its powers. The thrust of the argument is that the Act permits the Board to limit noise emissions only to the extent that they would be actionable at common law under the doctrine of public nuisance, but that the regulations adopted are more stringent.

The companies' argument is bottomed on section 23, which defines the Board's powers. It directs that the Board shall "categorize the types and sources of noise emissions that unreasonably interfere with the enjoyment of life, or with any lawful business, or activity, and shall prescribe for each such category the maximum permissible limits on such noise emissions.'' The objectives stated in section 25 may reflect in general terms the same concerns as those which underlie the common law. The legislative purpose, however, was to vindicate those concerns through a comprehensive regulatory system. Such an approach might well be thought to require that noise be limited on the basis of an objective, quantitative standard, rather than by its qualitative impact upon a particular affected individual as would be done under the common law method. We cannot say that the legislature contemplated that each regulation must be tailored to some common law decision on tort liability.

The forging companies' final contention is that the rules violate the equal protection clauses in that the board has established four categories of noise emission – stationary sources, ground transportation sources, construction site sources, and airport sources – but had adopted rules only for the first of these by 1973, and since that time has adopted additional rules only for vehicles on public highways.

This contention is largely disposed of by *Illinois Coal Operators Association v. Pollution Control Board* (1974), 59 Ill.2d 305, 312-13, 319 N.E. 2d 782, 786, where the court stated: ''The legislature may address itself to one stage of a problem and not take action at the same time as to other phases.'' The forging companies invite us to reconsider that decision in the light of the fact that as of the date when their petition for leave to appeal was filed the board had still not promulgated regulations for all the other noise source categories.

The forging companies also assert that the standards governing noise emissions for vehicles on the highway are substantially less stringent than those for stationary sources. We have considered this objection, and we judge that the companies have not shown that the classification complained of is unreasonable or arbitrary. For the reasons given in this opinion the judgment of the appellate court is affirmed.

****

Notes

1. In addition to the equal protection argument, the Illinois court also is faced with a claim that the statutory noise prohibition is void for vagueness. Is the court's conclusion on this point consistent with the Alabama court's decision in *Ross Neely*? Note an apparent anomaly that the more specific Alabama statutory provision is held to be void for vagueness, while the more general Illinois provision is saved by its reference to subsequent administrative standards. In linking the vagueness objection with an objection based on improper delegation of legislative power, is the Illinois court adequately addressing each of these constitutional grounds?

2. With respect to the equal protection claim raised by the forging companies, might the analysis and result have been different if the Board had finished its promulgation of noise regulations for all four categories of emission sources? What evidence could the companies then offer to bolster an equal protection claim? Consider the following formulation: ''It is elementary that the Legislature may in its judgment create classifications so

long as they are not arbitrary and are based upon actual differences in classes which differences bear a substantial rational relation to the public purpose sought to be accomplished by the statute." *In Re Spring Valley Development*, 300 A.2d 736 (Maine 1973).

3. Delegation of Powers

People v. Martin, 211 Cal. App. 3d 699, 259 Cal. Rptr. 770 (1989)

California regulates the transportation and disposal of hazardous waste through the Hazardous Waste Control Act. The act affixes criminal liability for violation of a standard of ordinary care. We hold that the act is constitutional, that it is not vague or ambiguous, that it does not unlawfully delegate legislative authority, and that it is not superseded by federal law which exempts "empty" hazardous waste containers from regulation.

Ray E. Martin is the president and principal operating officer of the Chem-O-Lene Company, a chemical blending plant located next to the Ventura River in Ventura County. Martin also owns and operates Unico Chemicals, located in Bakersfield. Chemicals blended at Chem-O-Lene are sold and transported to Unico, which sells them for use in oil drilling operations.

On March 15, 1985, Martin was arrested and charged with knowingly disposing of hazardous waste, or knowingly causing others to dispose of hazardous waste, at the Chem-O-Lene plant in violation of section 25189.5, subdivision (b). In the week following his arrest, Martin directed employees at Chem-O-Lene to truck 182 metal barrels from Chem-O-Lene to the Unico facility. At Unico, a number of those barrels were smashed, their contents spilling into ground.

Martin was convicted of two counts alleging the transporting and disposal of hazardous waste at the Unico facility in violation of section 25189.5, subdivision (c).

The trial court suspended imposition of sentence and placed Martin on five years felony probation. The court also imposed a $75,000 fine and a mandatory penalty assessment of $52,500.

Martin argues that section 25189.5 is unconstitutionally vague, ambiguous, and constitutes an unlawful delegation of legislative authority; that the act does not regulate the transportation of empty containers, and that the trial court improperly instructed the jury in this regard; and that the statute may not be constitutionally construed as providing a criminal penalty for merely negligent conduct, and that the trial court erred in instructing the jury that it may convict him for negligent conduct.

Martin contends that section 25189.5 is "vague, ambiguous and not susceptible to any definition that would have meaning to the average person" and so is unconstitutional. He specifically argues that the term "hazardous waste" as defined by the code "lack[s] any common sense basis upon which the average person can determine if they are in violation of the law, and provide[s] absolutely no objective standards or measurements" for the purpose of law enforcement. We disagree.

"'[A] statute which either forbids or requires the doing of an act in terms so vague that men of common intelligence must necessarily guess at its meaning and differ as to its application, violates the first essential of due process of law.'" Due process "requires a statute to be definite enough to provide (1) a standard of conduct for those whose activities are proscribed and (2) a standard for police enforcement and for ascertainment of guilt."

"If an accused can reasonably understand by the terms of the statute that his conduct is prohibited, the statute is not vague. In determining the sufficiency of the notice, a statute must of necessity be examined in the light of the conduct with which the defendant is charged. Furthermore, in the field of 'regulatory statutes governing business activities, where the acts limited are in a narrow category, greater leeway is allowed' than in statutes applicable to the general public."

Section 25117 defines "hazardous waste" as: "[A] waste, or combination of wastes, which because of its quantity, concentration, or physical, chemical, or infectious characteristics may either:

(a) Cause, or significantly contribute to an increase in mortality or an increase in serious irreversible, or incapacitating reversible, illness.
(b) Pose a substantial present or potential hazard to human health or environment when improperly treated stored transported, or disposed of or otherwise managed . . . ."

At the time of the events in this case, section 25124 defined "waste" in part as either of the following: "(a) Any material for which no use or reuse is intended and which is to be discarded. (b) Any recyclable material."

These statutory definitions for those who produce or handle hazardous waste provide adequate notice and adequate standards for enforcement for those who police such businesses. Regulated businesses "can be expected to consult relevant legislation in advance of action . . . [and] may have the ability to clarify the meaning of the regulation by its own inquiry, or by resort to an administrative process." In order to convict Martin, the jury must have found that he knew or should have known that he was causing the disposal and transportation of hazardous waste. (§ 25189.5, subds. (b), (c).) The scienter requirement itself guarantees adequate notice. "Where as here dangerous substances are involved, and the probability of regulation is great, the trier of fact may infer knowledge on the part of those engaged in the business of using such substances.

Further, the regulations promulgated by the Department of Health Services (the department) pursuant to the code contain a list of hundreds of materials designated potentially hazardous, and include mathematical formulas and scientific standards by which hazardous materials are identified. Even though statutes need not be of mathematical certainty, these are.

A waste may be designated hazardous if it meets any of four criteria. One of these is toxicity, which may be measured by the effect of the waste material on fish. Another criteria is ignitability: a material is a hazardous waste if it is liquid and has a flash point of less than 140° Fahrenheit. These and other tests were performed on chemical samples taken from Chem-O-Lene and Unico, and the results were entered into evidence.

Martin contends that the Legislature, by directing the department to "prepare, adopt and . . . revise . . . a listing of the wastes which are determined to be hazardous . . .", delegated to the department the authority to broaden and alter the definition of hazardous waste. He argues that such a delegation is improper when those definitions are applied to criminal sanctions such as those under section 25189.5.

"An unconstitutional delegation of legislative power occurs when the Legislature confers upon an administrative agency unrestricted authority to make fundamental policy decisions . . . . The Legislature must make the fundamental policy determinations, but after declaring the legislative goals and establishing a yardstick guiding the administrator, it may authorize the administrator to adopt rules and regulations to promote the purposes of the legislation and to carry it into effect."

Here, the Legislature expressed its intent to protect public health and environmental quality by establishing regulations for the handling, treatment, recycling and disposing of hazardous wastes, and granted to the department the authority to implement such a program. The Legislature defined hazardous waste and directed the department to prepare a list designating wastes which are hazardous and to adopt by regulation "criteria and guidelines for the identification of hazardous wastes." This is a reasonable grant of power to an administrative agency, providing adequate standards for administrative application of the statutory scheme.

That the department's list of hazardous waste and criteria for identifying hazardous waste is used in a criminal prosecution does not make this an unconstitutional delegation of legislative power. The Legislature, not the department, created the criminal sanction and fixed the penalties. "A rule does not assume 'a legislative character because the violation thereof is punished as a public offense.'"

****

Note

Are there any practical alternatives to the type of delegation of power approved in this case and in *Rockford Drop Forge*? Does either of these statutory schemes suffer from the vices discussed in Chapter 3(B), *supra*?

C. The Right to be Heard

Horn v. County of Ventura, 24 Cal. 3d 605, 156 Cal. Rptr. 718 (1979)

In this mandamus action, we consider whether approval by defendant county of a tentative subdivision map is an "adjudicatory" function which, under principles of due process, requires that both appropriate notice and an opportunity to be heard be given to persons whose property interests may be significantly affected. We will hold that such approval is "adjudicatory," and that rights to prior notice and hearing are accordingly invoked. We will further conclude that the county's general procedures for public notice of environmental decisions were constitutionally inadequate to apprise concerned landowners of government actions affecting their property interests.

Plaintiff's principal argument is that because the approval of subdivisions constitutes "quasi-adjudicatory" acts of local government, those persons affected by such land use decisions are therefore constitutionally entitled to notice and an opportunity to be heard prior to the rendition of final decisions. In response, both defendant and real party characterize the actions as "quasi-legislative," prescribing no prior notice and hearing. As will appear, we agree with plaintiff.

Due process principles require reasonable notice and opportunity to be heard before governmental deprivation of a significant property interest.

It is equally well settled, however, that only those governmental decisions which are *adjudicative* in nature are subject to procedural due process principles. *Legislative* action is not burdened by such requirements.

The rationale of the "legislative-adjudicatory" distinction was well expressed many years ago by Justice Holmes in *Bi-Metallic Co. v. Colorado*, (1915) 239 U.S. 441 [60 L. Ed. 372, 36 S. Ct. 141]: "Where a rule of conduct applies to more than a few people it is impracticable that every one should have a direct voice in its adoption. The Constitution does not require all public acts to be done in town meeting or an assembly of the whole. General statutes within the state power are passed that affect the person or property of individuals, sometimes to the point of ruin, without giving them a chance to be heard. Their rights are protected in the only way that they can be in a complex society, by their power, immediate or remote, over those who make the rule."

We adopted similar reasoning recently in *San Diego Bldg. Contractors Assn. v. City Council* (1974) 13 Cal.3d 205 [118 Cal. Rptr. 146, 529 P.2d 570], in which we concluded that the enactment of a general zoning ordinance by a city's voters under the initiative process, being "legislative" in character, required no prior notice and hearing, even though it might well be anticipated that the ordinance would deprive persons of significant property interests. In so holding, we distinguished "adjudicatory" matters in which "the government's action affecting an individual [is] determined by facts peculiar to the individual case" from "legislative" decisions which involve the adoption of a "broad, generally applicable rule of conduct on the basis of general public policy."

We expressly cautioned in *San Diego* that land use planning decisions less extensive than general rezoning could not be insulated from notice and hearing requirements by application of the "legislative act" doctrine. We noted: "We are thus not faced in the instant case with any of the great number of more limited 'administrative' zoning decisions, such as the grant of a variance or the award of a conditional use permit, which are adjudicatory in nature and which thus involve entirely different constitutional considerations."

Subdivision approvals, like variances and conditional use permits, involve the application of general standards to specific parcels of real property. Such governmental conduct, affecting the relatively few, is "determined by facts peculiar to the individual case" and is "adjudicatory" in nature.

The test for "legislative" and "adjudicatory" acts described by us in *San Diego* does not exclude from the latter category decisions of local governing bodies. Subdivisions are subject to environmental evaluation under [the California Environmental Quality Act]. Moreover, the Subdivision Map Act, as in effect both during October-December 1975 and at present, mandates rejection of a subdivision plan if it is deemed unsuitable in terms of topography, density, public health and access rights, or community land use plans. It is significant that several of these statutory concerns are precisely those which the plaintiff seeks to raise. Additionally, at the time of approval of the instant map, the Ventura County subdivision ordinance (of which we may take judicial notice) extended similar approval standards even to tract divisions which were not covered by the state act.

Resolution of these issues involves the exercise of judgment, and the careful balancing of conflicting interests, the hallmark of the adjudicative process. The expressed opinions of the affected landowners might very well be persuasive to those public officials who make the decisions, and affect the outcome of the subdivision process.

In therefore rejecting the concept that subdivision approvals are purely "ministerial" acts requiring no precedent notice or opportunity for hearing, we thereupon proceed to consider defendant and real party's secondary arguments.

Real party urges that plaintiff suffered no significant deprivation of property which would invoke constitutional rights to notice and hearing. However, . . . land use decisions which "substantially affect" the property rights of owners of adjacent parcels may constitute "deprivations" of property within the context of procedural due process. Plaintiff herein alleges that the subdivision plan as currently constituted will substantially interfere with his use of the only access from his parcel to the public streets, and will increase both traffic congestion and air pollution. From a pleading standpoint, plaintiff has thus adequately described a deprivation sufficiently "substantial" to require procedural due process protection.

The general application of due process principles is flexible, depending on the nature of the competing interests involved. The extent of administrative burden is one of the factors to be considered in determining the nature of an appropriate notice. However, where, as here, prior notice of a potentially adverse decision is constitutionally required, that notice must, at a minimum, be reasonably calculated to afford affected persons the realistic opportunity to protect their interests.

The notice provided by the county's CEQA regulations fails to meet the foregoing standard. By limiting itself to the posting of environmental documents at central public buildings, and mailings of notice to those persons who specifically request it, the county has manifestly placed the burden of obtaining notice solely on the concerned individuals themselves. While such posting and mailing may well suffice to encourage the generalized public participation in the environmental decision making contemplated by CEQA, they are inadequate to meet due process standards where fundamental interests are substantially affected. Those persons significantly affected by a proposed subdivision cannot reasonably be expected to place themselves on a mailing list or "haunt" county offices on the off-hand chance that a pending challenge to those interests will thereby be revealed. Other forms of notice appear better calculated to apprise directly affected persons of a pending decision.

We deliberately refrain from describing a specific formula which details the nature, content, and timing of the requisite notice. Rather, we leave to the affected local governments these determinations. We do observe, however, that depending on (1) the magnitude of the project, and (2) the degree to which a particular landowner's interests may be affected, acceptable techniques might include notice by mail to the owners of record of property situate within a designated radius of the subject property, or by the posting of a notice at or near the project site, or both. Notice must, of course, occur sufficiently prior to a final decision to permit a "meaningful" predeprivation hearing to affected landowners.

****

Daniel P. Selmi and Kenneth A. Manaster, State Environmental Law, Section 5.05[3] (1989, 1994)

Probably the best known of the Constitution's constraints on state government is the Fourteenth Amendment's prohibition of any state depriving any person of "life, liberty, or property, without due process of law." In many cases this provision has been held to mean that before government may impair an individual's interests, certain procedural steps must be observed. At times these required procedures are in the nature of a trial-type hearing, while in other instances the procedures are more flexible and informal. In each case, however, the fundamental problem the courts face is ascertaining what constitutes basic, procedural fairness when the government acts with the effect of impairing individual rights.

The Supreme Court has long struggled with the two major, problematic prongs of procedural due process analysis: First, what constitutes a personal "liberty" or "property" interest which is entitled to this constitutional protection? Second, what are the elements of "due process" when a protectible interest is threatened by state action? None of the Court's major, recent cases on these points has involved environmental regulation, centering instead mostly on the rights of persons whose ongoing status is closely linked to government programs. Thus the Court has addressed extensively the procedural rights of government welfare recipients, government employees, public school students, and prisoners.

In some environmental cases in the state courts, however, procedural due process problems have arisen. They demonstrate that environmental controversies often involve disputes over constitutionally protected property rights. In particular, these cases usually raise either the property rights of the proponents of regulated business or development projects, or the rights of persons adversely affected by such activities. In order to understand the state judges' resolution of these disputes, the practitioner first must be familiar with the basic analytic framework established by the Supreme Court decisions.

The question of what constitutes constitutionally protected liberty or property was addressed by the Supreme Court in *Board of Regents of State Colleges v. Roth*[2]. Although the Court's general language there does help in finding the answer to this question in a given case, a succession of later Court opinions has demonstrated the difficulty of finding a precise and satisfactory formulation for all cases. The Court in *Roth* recognized "that the property interests protected by procedural due process extend well beyond actual ownership of real estate, chattels, or money." It also said,

> It is a purpose of the ancient institution of property to protect those claims upon which people rely in their daily lives, reliance that must not be arbitrarily undermined. . . . Property interests, of course, are not created by the Constitution. Rather, they are created and their dimensions are defined by existing rules or understandings that stem from an independent source such as state law—rules or understandings that secure certain benefits and that support claims of entitlement to those benefits.

In *Mathews v. Eldridge*[3] the Court clarified the analysis to be used in determining the specific procedural requirements called for by due process when government is acting to deprive a person of a protected interest. The Court said that

> [I]dentification of the specific dictates of due process generally requires consideration of three distinct factors: first, the private interest that will be affected by the official action; second, the risk of an erroneous deprivation of such interest through the procedures used, and the probable value, if any, of additional or substitute procedural safeguards; and finally, the government's interest, including the function involved and the fiscal and administrative burdens that the additional or substitute procedural requirement would entail.

This flexible approach has been widely followed in the federal and state court cases addressing claims that state agencies are attempting to deprive an individual of a protected right without due process.

In California, due process objections have been raised in cases challenging actions taken under the extensive scheme for regulation of coastal development. For example, in *Stanton v. San Diego Coast Regional Commission*[4], the owner of a commercial building within the regulated coastal zone contested the procedures used by the Coastal Commission in denying a permit for his remodeling project. The court found the procedures constitutionally acceptable, stating that

> [Plaintiff] is correct in that a fundamental requirement of due process is the opportunity to be heard and the principles of due process are fully applicable to administrative proceedings which are quasi-judicial in nature. Yet no particular form of

---

[2] 408 U.S. 564, 92 S. Ct. 2701 (1972).

[3] 424 U.S. 319, 96 S. Ct. 893 (1976).

[4] 101 Cal. App.3d 38, 161 Cal. Rptr. 392 (1980).

proceeding is required so long as the statute provides for a "reasonable" opportunity to be heard. What is a "reasonable" opportunity to be heard will "not turn solely on the fact that a constitutionally protected interest is affected by government action . . . the nature of the claimed procedural rights, the extent of interference with the private interest, and the government interest" all coalesce to define the scope of due process.

This type of flexible analysis of what constitutes due process most often leads to judicial approval of agency procedures. In an earlier California environmental case [*Horn v. County of Ventura*], however, the California Supreme Court followed this approach and found a denial of due process. As is often the case, there was no dispute about whether plaintiff as a landowner had the requisite property interest entitled to due process protection. At issue was the adequacy of a county's procedures for advising landowners of proposed government actions affecting their property.

A similar claim by owners of property in the vicinity of a recently constructed asphalt plant [in Texas] was considered and rejected by the court in *Kettlewell v. Hot-Mix, Inc.*[5] The property owners attacked the procedures through which the Texas Air Control Board issued a construction permit to Hot-Mix without providing them with notice or an opportunity to be heard. Applying the *Mathews v. Eldridge* criteria, the court gave considerable weight to the availability of notice and hearing *after* the construction was completed but before an operating permit was issued. The court concluded,

> If the hearing had been held prior to the granting of the construction permit, permission to build the facility might have been denied without giving Hot-Mix the opportunity to demonstrate—at its risk—that the emissions would not be worse than the parties have here stipulated. Under the facts of this case it appears that giving of notice and setting a hearing after construction but before the granting of the operating permit was a reasonable procedure. It adequately protected the [plaintiffs'] rights to due process while placing on Hot-Mix the risk of building the plant without knowing an operating permit would be issued.

****

Note

As Chapter 6 will explore more fully, much of the work of environmental lawyers consists of efforts to maximize clients' access to decisional processes and to data generated by the regulatory process. The procedural due process principles presented in this chapter provide the basic constitutional framework underlying those efforts.

---

[5] 566 S.W.2d 663 (Tex. Civ. App. 1978).

D. Unpredictability, Delay, and Overlapping Enforcement

Monsanto Company v. Environmental Protection Agency, 19 F.3d 1201 (7th Cir. 1994)

The Monsanto Company brings this petition for review of an Environmental Protection Agency decision that denied Monsanto's request for additional time to comply with certain hazardous emissions standards under the Clean Air Act. For the reasons given below, we grant the petition and reverse the agency's decision.

At issue in these proceedings is Monsanto's compliance with the EPA's emissions limit for benzene. The standard was promulgated by the EPA on September 14, 1989, and became effective for new or modified sources on that date. However, it did not apply to existing sources, such as Monsanto's monochlorobenzene manufacturing facility in Sauget, Illinois, until 90 days after its effective date. The Clean Air Act also gave the EPA Administrator authority to grant a waiver to existing sources for a period of up to two years "if he finds that such period is necessary for the installation of controls and that steps will be taken during the period of the waiver to assure that the health of persons will be protected from imminent endangerment."

Monsanto was not prepared to comply with the new benzene standard in December 1989 and, therefore, requested a waiver until August 15, 1990, to allow the company to install water scrubbing equipment designed to satisfy the standard. The EPA granted this request. However, after the equipment was installed, Monsanto discovered that the equipment did not perform as anticipated. Instead of achieving the 95 percent emissions reduction that the benzene standard requires, the water scrubber system appeared to be operating at about an 80 percent reduction level. The company, therefore, asked the EPA for an extension of the waiver so that it could install a carbon adsorption system as a secondary means of filtering out the harmful emissions that were not captured by the primary system. The EPA denied this second request, leading to the pending petition for review under § 307(b) of the Clean Air Act.

The EPA granted Monsanto's initial request for a waiver. Thus, there appears to be no dispute that as of December 1989, the company needed additional time in which to install the equipment needed to control its benzene emissions. The question is whether it was "necessary" for Monsanto to have an extension of the original waiver when the company discovered in August 1990 that its control technology did not perform as predicted and, therefore, the company could not demonstrate that it was meeting the benzene emissions standard.

In stating its intent to deny the request for an extension, the EPA found that Monsanto's request did not provide sufficient information to show that an additional waiver of compliance was necessary. Many of the concerns identified by the EPA were valid. However, Monsanto subsequently submitted a thorough response to each of these concerns. The company explained that in designing its original system, it had decided to install a water scrubber system because that system would allow the company to recover and reuse the benzene and other organic chemicals. The company decided against using the alternative control measure of carbon adsorption, which uses carbon filters to reduce benzene emissions, because this ''end-of-the-pipe'' technology would produce benzene-contaminated carbon. In short, instead of recapturing and reusing the benzene, carbon adsorption would create a hazardous waste that would require special treatment or disposal.

The company similarly decided against incineration because that ''end-of-the-pipe'' alternative would produce waste gases. Carbon adsorption and incineration also had several other disadvantages that were not present in the water scrubber system. In upholding its preliminary decision to deny the extension, the EPA maintained its position that additional time was not ''necessary'' because Monsanto could have installed carbon adsorption in the first place.

The EPA expressly rejected Monsanto's claim that it ''proceeded reasonably in terms of developing and implementing controls,'' and that carbon adsorption was ''a choice of last resort because it offered the least opportunity for waste immunization [sic] and the greatest concern for safety.''

> The CAA does not authorize the Administrator to grant a waiver of compliance in order to allow a source more time to ''proceed reasonably'' in experimenting with the various available technologies, saving those technologies the source believes cause ''considerable expense'' and increase ''safety concerns'' for last. . .
> If a source can install technology that will control the emissions, it must; only if additional time beyond the required compliance date ''is necessary for the installation of controls,'' may the Administrator grant it additional time.

The EPA's explanation grossly mischaracterizes Monsanto's approach. The company was not ''experimenting'' with the various technologies; rather, it had made a scientifically and environmentally sound decision to proceed with the water scrubber system. The system was designed to achieve better than the 95 percent emissions removal required by the statute and had performed up to those standards during a limited test. Thus, Monsanto, as well as the EPA, had every reason to believe that the company was installing technology that would control the emissions.

The EPA's decision also ignores the fact that Monsanto chose the water scrubber system to comply with the EPA's own pollution prevention policy.

The EPA's decision appears to suggest that if Monsanto could have installed a carbon adsorption system in less time than it took to install the water scrubber system, then the EPA would find that it was not ''necessary'' to give Monsanto whatever additional time the water scrubber system would require. In other words, EPA seems to be saying that if a ''quick fix'' is available, sources are required to employ that ''quick fix'' without regard to its adverse environmental ramifications. This viewpoint is short-sighted and bad environmental policy. Instead of eliminating an environmental problem, the EPA's ''quick fix'' would merely change the form of the problem – i.e., it would remove the environmental hazard from the air but create a hazardous waste disposal problem.

The Clean Air Act's waiver provision does not require the source to install the controls that will achieve compliance at the earliest possible date. Instead, it gives the EPA authority to grant a waiver of up to two years as long as there is no imminent endangerment to the public in the interim. Therefore, if a company like Monsanto has a choice between two control strategies, the EPA has the authority to grant a waiver for a pollution prevention strategy even if that strategy would take slightly longer to implement than the less desirable strategy. This assumes, of course, that the pollution prevention strategy will work and can be installed within the two year waiver period.

Those requirements were satisfied in this case. Monsanto's water scrubber system was designed to achieve full compliance with the statute—and has achieved full compliance once the secondary carbon adsorption controls were added. Although full compliance was not achieved within the eleven-month time frame that Monsanto first envisioned, it was accomplished within two years after the statutory deadline. Neither Monsanto nor the EPA had any reason to believe that Monsanto's initial system of choice would not perform up to expectations. Thus, it was arbitrary and capricious to deny Monsanto the additional time it needed to perfect its system.

In sum, Monsanto's original choice of the water scrubber system was environmentally and scientifically sound. The system was designed to achieve full compliance within the initial waiver period granted by the EPA. Although the system did not live up to its full expectations, Monsanto promptly asked the EPA for additional time to add a carbon adsorption process that would bring the system into full compliance with the emissions standard within the two years allowed by the statute. The reasons given by the EPA for denying the request have no foundation in the record. Therefore, we find that the EPA was arbitrary and capricious in denying Monsanto's request for an extension of its waiver. Accordingly, we hereby grant Monsanto's petition for review and reverse the EPA's decision.

EASTERBROOK, Circuit Judge, dissenting.

The majority says that the question on the merits is "whether it was 'necessary' for Monsanto to have an extension of the original waiver when the company discovered in August 1990 that its control technology did not perform as predicted." Putting things in this way shows principally that the wrong question begets the wrong answer.

There might be a problem if the EPA had said something like: We will give you 24 months if you want to install carbon adsorption technology (dirty) but only 11 months if you want to use water scrubbing (clean). What it said, however, is that Monsanto could have 11 months to install water scrubbing and no additional time to add carbon adsorption. Any thumb on the scale favored the cleaner technology. Actually, however, there was no thumb at all. The EPA did not favor either technology; it allowed Monsanto to choose and then insisted that Monsanto keep its word that it would comply by August 1990. If it is apt to apply the word "penalty" to this sequence, then the event penalized is failure. The EPA gave Monsanto enough time to install a control technology of Monsanto's choosing. When this strategy flopped, the EPA concluded that Monsanto rather than the public should pay the price. Although Monsanto contends that it acted in the best of faith—that computer modeling showed that water scrubbing would work, and that it was dismayed when the predictions did not come true—the EPA may insist, as pollution control statutes generally do, on results. An A for effort may affect the selection of a penalty in an enforcement proceeding (or may influence the exercise of prosecutorial discretion), but it does not compel the EPA to give a polluter the maximum waiver permitted by law.

Undergirding the majority's opinion is an independent evaluation of the merits of different pollution-control strategies. Two judges believe that Monsanto "made a scientifically and environmentally sound decision to proceed with the water scrubber system" and that the EPA's view is "short-sighted and bad environmental policy". Yet the record in this case does not demonstrate that Monsanto's system is "sound" or that EPA's view is "bad environmental policy." It contains essentially no evidence on these subjects (although Monsanto's brief is full of self-congratulation, which my colleagues have swallowed). We are not engineers and are in no position to evaluate the evidence it does contain, and at all events we are not the persons to whom Congress delegated the estimation of costs and benefits.

****

Notes

1. The *Monsanto* decision raises a number of questions. First, should a regulatory agency pursue a narrowly focused approach to executing medium-specific statutory duties, or should it enlarge its perspective to encompass broader environmental impacts? Clearly the majority's answer to this question was bolstered by EPA's own efforts to promote pollution prevention and waste minimization, as noted in Chapter 3(D), *supra*. Note that the majority found the Agency's action to be arbitrary and capricious under the statutory review standards, rather than as a matter of consitutional violation.

It would seem unfair for a government agency to urge a regulated entity to take a broad, cross-media approach to environmental compliance, and then to penalize it when a specific violation is prolonged as a result of a broader compliance program. If you agree with this observation, can you explain with more specificity just what the unfairness is or, conversely, what changes in regulatory standards or procedures could prevent this unfair result?

If you were an EPA attorney, what would have been your advice to Agency staff with respect to Monsanto's request to extend the waiver? What advice would Judge Easterbrook's opinion call for?

2. Another issue implicit in this case is the legal significance of delay. As the following commentary suggests, an important aspect of environmental law practice is the timing of actions to be taken.

> As in other fields of the law, environmental practitioners in a multiplicity of ways must be sensitive to the benefits and detriments of delay. Whether the delay be on the part of the regulatory agency, the private protagonist, an intervening environmental group, or some other participant in a particular controversy, it is often the case that the economic and strategic significance of delay is substantial, even determinative.

Sometimes delay is unavoidable, and sometimes it can be orchestrated. Sometimes it would seem to serve broader public interests and sometimes it would seem to undermine them. Whether the question is the issuance of a permit, the initiation of an enforcement proceeding, the duration of a variance, or the conduct of an inspection or test, timing and delay are often key components of strategy within the realm of environmental regulation.

Daniel P. Selmi and Kenneth A. Manaster, State Environmental Law §7.03[6] (1989, 1994). Ethical implications of delay strategies also were touched upon in Chapter 1(B), *supra*.

In *Monsanto* the company appears to have had a strong argument that its delay in complying with the standards was justified at the time they initially went into effect. If you were an attorney for Monsanto then, and assuming you believed the company was taking diligent action toward compliance,[6] what would you have answered if asked by company personnel whether EPA would grant a waiver for the statutory maximum of two years? Obviously the attorney's role when faced with a question like this is to try to reduce the unpredictability of the client's legal status. What sources of information would you explore in order to give your client the most reliable answer to its question?

From the perspective of the regulatory agency in *Monsanto*, what are the risks and benefits of allowing the company a further delay in compliance?

3. Probably the most common delay and unpredictability problems faced by environmental lawyers and their clients arise from the frequent inability of regulatory agencies to give prompt responses to requests for action or information. In some instances, agency delays are an inescapable byproduct of the need to examine complex environmental issues thoroughly. As was noted in a leading, early decision under the National Environmental Policy Act, "[S]ome delay is inherent whenever the NEPA consideration is conducted . . . ." *Calvert Cliffs' Coordinating Committee, Inc. v. Atomic Energy Commission*, 449 F.2d 1109, 1128 (D.C. Cir. 1971).

At many other times, delays result simply because agencies lack the necessary personnel and other resources to manage their heavy workloads efficiently. In those instances, what strategies are available to the attorney who wishes to hasten governmental response to the client? Are there short-term or long-term risks for the client whose attorney initiates litigation or informal means of pressure to induce agency action?

4. One particularly vexing area of delay and unpredictability in environmental practice relates to the overlapping jurisdiction and enforcement powers of federal and state agencies under some of the federal environmental statutes. The most notable example is the Clean Air Act. Under that law, a regulated air pollution source that has obtained temporary protection from state enforcement proceedings through a variance may still

---

[6] The significance of diligence in efforts to obtain variances or avoid enforcement actions is addressed in Chapter 4(F), *supra*.

be subject to federal enforcement action until such time as the state variance is approved by the federal EPA as a revision to the existing state implementation plan (SIP).

The Supreme Court validated this overlap in *General Motors Corporation v. U.S.*, 496 U.S. 530, 110 S. Ct. 2528 (1990). Even though subsequent amendments to the Act specified a time period of 12 months for EPA action on SIP revisions,[7] the risk remains of federal "overfiling" enforcement action that is inconsistent with the state's treatment of the source.[8] What strategies, if any, can the attorney for the regulated source pursue in order to reduce the uncertainty and delay that seem to inhere in this statutory scheme? Consider the following comments:

> Stationary sources obtaining variances from air pollution regulations may be confronted with a brutal choice: (1) operate the facility in violation of applicable rules and hope enforcement officials don't find out; (2) shut down the facility until corrections are made to prevent "offending" air emissions; or (3) seek a variance allowing continued operation under [state] law and risk an EPA enforcement action.

Lawrence J. Straw, Jr., "California Air Pollution Variances: A Federal Enforcement Weapon," 1991 California Environmental Law Reporter 203, 208.

> A practitioner representing a source that faces extraordinary hardship in complying with [an air pollution regulation] should still consider applying for a variance . . . . The "option" of operating in knowing violation poses far too great a risk . . . . At the same time, a prudent practitioner should try to find out as much as possible about the enforcement policies of EPA . . . . Whenever a source is considering a variance, one of the essential steps should be an informed evaluation of the kinds of cases for which an EPA enforcement action may be likely. The *possibility* of federal enforcement action in some cases should not be ignored.

W. Thomas Jennings, "California Air Pollution Variances and Federal Enforcement: A Different Perspective," 1992 California Environmental Law Reporter 111, 115-116.

As attorney for a potential variance applicant, how would you find out "as much as possible about the enforcement policies of EPA"? Could you find out all you wished to know without jeopardizing your client's interests?

---

[7] 42 U.S.C. § 7410(k)(2).

[8] *See* Marc Melnick *et al.*, "Watching the Candy Store: EPA Overfiling of Local Air Pollution Variances," 20 Ecology Law Quarterly 207 (1993).

.

Chapter 6
Access to Decisions and Data

A. Overview

For all types of participants in environmental law and regulation, and thus for their lawyers, access to decisional processes is of vital importance. It is widely agreed among environmental lawyers that procedural justice usually, if not always, means that decisionmaking should be open to full view, as well as open to relevant information and argument. Indeed a great deal of the work of environmental lawyers involves raising, or responding to, claims for greater access to environmental decisions and data.

Chapter 5(C) presented the basic procedural due process principles that guarantee to persons whose interests are at stake an opportunity to have input into adjudicatory decisional processes. In addition to reexamining some problematic features of this right to be heard, the present chapter also examines the pervasive interest in access to the output of regulatory processes. This interest is often referred to nowadays as the "right to know." Virtually all parties interested in environmental policy at one time or another are concerned simply about being able to receive and understand information produced by the regulatory process. There may be many reasons for this concern, starting with a desire simply to be aware of the environmental conditions to which one is subjected. A further reason, of course, may be to enable the individual or community to reassess its position regarding present environmental policies and to gauge the possible need to attempt, in turn, to have input into future decisions to alter those policies.

Concern over access—either to provide input or to receive output—arises in a virtually infinite range of settings. This chapter will note a few examples. The first is one of the earliest access issues in modern environmental law—a citizen's standing to sue to challenge government action. The succeeding examples in this chapter all relate more directly to the regulatory process.

In contrast with the common desire to open regulatory functions for greater access by interested parties, difficult problems arise out of efforts to limit access. As will be seen here, regulated entities sometimes wish to limit public access to trade secret or other proprietary information submitted to a regulatory agency. Also, a dispute over the secrecy of an environmental board's adjudicatory deliberations raises questions about whether open decisional processes are always justified.

Finally, the ability of members of the public to participate effectively in decisionmaking, or simply to understand environmental data, is highlighted by disputes involving the presentation of environmental materials in English, despite the predominance of other languages in the affected communities. This access problem is another facet of the environmental justice movement examined more fully in Chapters 3(E), 4(D), and 7.

****

Daniel P. Selmi and Kenneth A. Manaster, State Environmental Law Section 7.03[7] (1989, 1994)

It is well known that environmental protection activities increased tremendously in the late 1960's in large part because of political pressure exerted by citizens groups concerned about environmental deterioration. In part as a result of these origins, there is an unusually strong and persistent concern among most participants in environmental decision-making for ensuring that the decisional processes are open to public view and participation. The continued involvement of such groups, as well as other special interests, has continued to exert pressure in this regard.

[M]any states have procedural requirements for governmental functions in this field which explicitly provide for public hearings on a broad range of decisions. Numerous opportunities for interested members of the public to comment orally and in writing on proposed government action also are made available. Additionally, opportunities are provided for interested citizens to initiate proceedings of various sorts, such as petitions for proposed rulemaking, appeals of permits, and even some enforcement proceedings. Additionally, of course, standing requirements in some jurisdictions often allow individuals to initiate judicial review of agency action. Although it may have been contemplated originally that the intended beneficiaries of these liberal participation rights would be individuals and groups with an environmental agenda, in practice these access options also have been used by industrial and commercial groups, labor unions, business-oriented public interest law organizations, state and local government units, and other somewhat unexpected parties.

Open, public decision-making has tactical benefits for environmental groups and others who are inclined to challenge decisions they find unsatisfactory. If it can be responsibly asserted that there were procedural errors in the conduct of a proceeding because it should have been more open or public in nature, such assertions may be a relatively easy basis on which an environmental group can challenge the proceeding and its result. For such a group to be restricted to only technical, substantive objections may be much more difficult, in the face of limited expertise and financial resources. In short, for environmental organizations and other segments of the public, requirements of open process not only accomplish the immediate objective of promoting greater access to decisional proceedings, but also provide a ready handle for challenges to the outcome.

The commitment to public decision-making in the environmental field is not always simple to honor. The attorney must be aware of the tension between this commitment and other principles involved in environmental decision-making. One obvious problem arises, for example, when trade secret or other confidential information is submitted in connection with permit applications, variance requests, or other types of proceedings subject to public hearing requirements. Means then must be devised to honor the public's right to know what information goes into government decision-making, while at the same time protecting valid proprietary rights. Similarly, laws requiring government records to be open to the public have to deal with the tension between public access rights and private confidentiality concerns.

****

Richard J. Lazarus, "Pursuing 'Environmental Justice': The Distributional Effects of Environmental Protection," 87 Northwestern University Law Review 787, 850-52 (1993)

Apart from the substance of environmental law, serious consideration should be given to reforming the structure of environmental policymaking so as to enhance minority access to relevant decisionmaking fora.[1] Governmental and nongovernmental organizations that currently dominate the process need to promote minority participation in the dialogue and, even more fundamentally, they need to educate themselves about minority concerns. It is not enough to provide minorities with an opportunity to adequately represent their own interests because correction of distributional equities is not, and should not be, the sole responsibility of racial minorities. Those in positions of authority, whether or not they happen to belong to a racial minority, have an independent responsibility to work toward the fair distribution of environmental benefits and burdens.

Mainstream environmental groups need, therefore, to work towards better representation of minorities within their organizations, both as members and as professional employees. They should likewise lend expertise to local communities in need of financial, legal, and technical assistance, and should also target those communities in their educational programs. There are currently a host of new environmental organizations, more directly involved with environmental issues of special concern to racial minorities, which could greatly benefit from the mainstream groups' sharing of available resources.

Those minority environmental organizations, however, have served notice that any relationship with the mainstream organizations must be as "equals." To that end, those in the mainstream environmental movement need to appreciate what they can learn from the newer minority environmental organizations. They need to increase their awareness and understanding of the potential for inequity in the allocation of benefits and burdens from those environmental protection programs that they have historically supported. They also need to guard against their natural tendency, based on their highly successful fundraising programs, to exploit the "environmental justice" issue in a manner that enhances their own

---

[1] [Ed.] *See also* Sheila Foster, "Race(ial) Matters: The Quest for Environmental Justice," 20 Ecology Law Quarterly 721, 751 (1993) ("Environmental law's process-oriented, public access approach to environmental decisionmaking can provide a vehicle to achieve environmental justice."); Francisco Leal, "Environmental Injustice," 14 Chicano-Latino Law Review 37, 39 (1994) ("the most damaging and perhaps the most obvious causal factor is that our communities do not have access to the decision-making process for the siting of risk-laden projects."); Douglas J. Amy, The Politics of Environmental Mediation 134 (1987) (commenting on politically weak or unorganized groups' unequal access to environmental mediation and negotiation).

fundraising efforts at the expense of minority organizations possessing far fewer resources.

The challenge of opening up existing fora to minority involvement is substantial. Many in the minority community continue to harbor a deep-seated distrust of both mainstream environmentalists, whom they view as too closely tied to industry, and of a federal government that some view as a mere "spokesperson for industry." Environmental organizations are not infrequently characterized as ignoring the legitimate needs of minority communities, valuing those needs less than they do wildlife protection and the preservation of scenic beauty.

In addition, some minority commentators have suggested that both mainstream environmental organizations and governmental officials bear some direct responsibility for the ultimate siting of environmentally risky facilities in minority communities. After all, it is because these same organizations have been so successful in resisting the siting of such facilities in their own neighborhoods (and in those of their membership), that many of the facilities have instead been located in minority neighborhoods. Some minorities have also expressed suspicion of population control proposals, commonly advocated by mainstream environmental groups, based on their perception that those proposals are principally intended to limit the growing populations of persons of color.

Finally, the advantages of a less centralized policymaking regime need to be re-examined in light of environmental justice concerns. As described above, the highly centralized nature of environmental policymaking may be one of the most significant structural causes of existing distributional inequities. There is certainly reason to suspect that racial minorities today possess more real political power in many localities, and in certain state governments, than they do within the federal government. If true, that would add yet another way in which the disadvantages of centralized authority, and the advantages of decentralized decision making, may historically have been underestimated.

****

Note

As the preceding readings suggest, both the historical development of environmental law, and the current dynamics of the environmental justice movement, depend heavily upon the concerns and initiatives of various types of citizens groups. What would you consider to be the ideal structure, skills, and objectives of a citizens group to influence environmental policy in the 1990s?

B. Access to Court

Lujan v. Defenders of Wildlife, __ U.S. __, 112 S. Ct. 2130 (1992)

This case involves a challenge to a rule promulgated by the Secretary of the Interior interpreting § 7 of the Endangered Species Act of 1973 (ESA), 16 U.S.C. § 1536, in such fashion as to render it applicable only to actions within the United States or on the high seas. The preliminary issue, and the only one we reach, is whether the respondents here, plaintiffs below, have standing to seek judicial review of the rule.

The ESA seeks to protect species of animals against threats to their continuing existence caused by man. The ESA instructs the Secretary of the Interior to promulgate by regulation a list of those species which are either endangered or threatened under enumerated criteria, and to define the critical habitat of these species. Section 7(a)(2) of the Act then provides, in pertinent part:

> "Each Federal agency shall, in consultation with and with the assistance of the Secretary [of the Interior], insure that any action authorized, funded, or carried out by such agency . . . is not likely to jeopardize the continued existence of any endangered species or threatened species or result in the destruction or adverse modification of habitat of such species which is determined by the Secretary, after consultation as appropriate with affected States, to be critical."

A . . . regulation, reinterpreting § 7(a)(2) to require consultation only for actions taken in the United States or on the high seas, was proposed in 1983, and promulgated in 1986.

Shortly thereafter, respondents, organizations dedicated to wildlife conservation and other environmental causes, filed this action against the Secretary of the Interior, seeking a declaratory judgment that the new regulation is in error as to the geographic scope of § 7(a)(2), and an injunction requiring the Secretary to promulgate a new regulation . . . .

Though some of its elements express merely prudential considerations that are part of judicial self-government, the core component of standing is an essential and unchanging part of the case-or-controversy requirement of Article III.

Over the years, our cases have established that the irreducible constitutional minimum of standing contains three elements: First, the plaintiff must have suffered an "injury in fact" – an invasion of a legally-protected interest which is (a) concrete and particularized, and (b) "actual or imminent, not 'conjectural' or 'hypothetical.'" Second, there must be a causal connection between the injury and the conduct complained of – the injury has to be "fairly . . . trace[able] to the challenged action of the defendant, and not . . . the result [of] the independent action of some third party not before the court." Third, it must be "likely," as opposed to merely "speculative," that the injury will be "redressed by a favorable decision."

The party invoking federal jurisdiction bears the burden of establishing these elements.

When the suit is one challenging the legality of government action or inaction, the nature and extent of facts that must be averred (at the summary judgment stage) or proved (at the trial stage) in order to establish standing depends considerably upon whether the plaintiff is himself an object of the action (or forgone action) at issue. If he is, there is ordinarily little question that the action or inaction has caused him injury, and that a judgment preventing or requiring the action will redress it. When, however, as in this case, a plaintiff's asserted injury arises from the government's allegedly unlawful regulation (or lack of regulation) of someone else, much more is needed.

Respondents' claim to injury is that the lack of consultation with respect to certain funded activities abroad "increases the rate of extinction of endangered and threatened species." Of course, the desire to use or observe an animal species, even for purely aesthetic purposes, is undeniably a cognizable interest for purpose of standing. See, e.g., *Sierra Club v. Morton*, 405 U.S., at 734, 92 S. Ct., at 1366. "But the 'injury in fact' test requires more than an injury to a cognizable interest. It requires that the party seeking review be himself among the injured." To survive the Secretary's summary judgment motion, respondents had to submit affidavits or other evidence showing, through specific facts, not only that listed species were in fact being threatened by funded activities abroad, but also that one or more of respondents' members would thereby be "directly" affected apart from their "'special interest' in the subject."

With respect to this aspect of the case, the Court of Appeals focused on the affidavits of two Defenders' members--Joyce Kelly and Amy Skilbred. Ms. Kelly stated that she traveled to Egypt in 1986 and "observed the traditional habitat of the endangered Nile crocodile directly," and that she "will suffer harm in fact as a result of [the] American . . . role . . . in overseeing the rehabilitation of the Aswan High Dam on the Nile . . . and [in] developing . . . Egypt's . . . Master Water Plan." Ms. Skilbred averred that she traveled to Sri Lanka in 1981 and "observed th[e] habitat" of "endangered species such as the Asian elephant and the leopard" at what is now the site of the Mahaweli Project funded by the Agency for International Development, although she "was unable to see any of the endangered species;" "this development project," she continued, "will seriously reduce endangered, threatened, and endemic species habitat including areas that I visited . . . [which] may severely shorten the future of these species;" that threat, she concluded, harmed her because she "intend[s] to return to Sri Lanka in the future and hope[s] to be more fortunate in spotting at least the endangered elephant and leopard." When Ms Skilbred was asked at a subsequent deposition if and when she had any plans to return to Sri Lanka, she reiterated that "I intend to go back to Sri Lanka," but confessed that she had no current plans: "I don't know [when]. There is a civil war going on right now. I don't know. Not next year, I will say. In the future."

We shall assume for the sake of argument that these affidavits contain facts showing that certain agency-funded projects threaten listed species—though that is questionable They plainly contain no facts, however, showing how damage to the species will produce "imminent" injury to Mss. Kelly and Skilbred. That the women "had visited" the areas of the projects before the projects commenced proves nothing. As we have said in a related context, "'past exposure to illegal conduct does not in itself show a present case or controversy regarding injunctive relief . . . if unaccompanied by any continuing, present adverse effects.'" And the affiants' profession of an "intent" to return to the places they had visited before—where they will presumably, this time, be deprived of the opportunity to observe animals of the endangered species—is simply not enough. Such "some day" intentions—without any description of concrete plans, or indeed even any specification of *when* the some day will be—do not support a finding of the "actual or imminent" injury that our cases require.

Besides relying upon the Kelly and Skilbred affidavits, respondents propose a series of novel standing theories. The first, inelegantly styled "ecosystem nexus," proposes that any person who uses any part of a "contiguous ecosystem" adversely affected by a funded activity has standing even if the activity is located a great distance away. This approach, as the Court of Appeals correctly observed, is inconsistent with our opinion in [*Lujan v. National Wildlife Federation*, 497 U.S. 871, 110 S.Ct. 3177 (1990)], which held that a plaintiff claiming injury from environmental damage must use the area affected by the challenged activity and not an area roughly "in the vicinity" of it.

Respondents' other theories are called, alas, the "animal nexus" approach, whereby anyone who has an interest in studying or seeing the endangered animals anywhere on the globe has standing; and the "vocational nexus" approach, under which anyone with a professional interest in such animals can sue. Under these theories, anyone who goes to see Asian elephants in the Bronx Zoo, and anyone who is a keeper of Asian elephants in the Bronx Zoo, has standing to sue because the Director of AID did not consult with the Secretary regarding the AID-funded project in Sri Lanka. This is beyond all reason. Standing is not "an ingenious academic exercise in the conceivable," but as we have said requires, at summary judgment stage, a factual showing of perceptible harm. It is clear that the person who observes or works with a particular animal threatened by a federal decision is facing perceptible harm, since the very subject of his interest will no longer exist. It is even plausible – though it goes to the outermost limit of plausibility – to think that a person who observes or works with animals of a particular species in the very area of the world where that species is threatened by a federal decision is facing such harm, since some animals that might have been the subject of his interest will no longer exist. It goes beyond the limit, however, and into pure speculation and fantasy to say that anyone who observes or works with an endangered species, anywhere in the world, is appreciably harmed by a single project affecting some portion of that species with which he has no more specific connection.

Besides failing to show injury, respondents failed to demonstrate redressability.

The short of the matter is that redress of the only injury-in-fact respondents complain of requires action (termination of funding until consultation) by the individual funding agencies; and any relief the District Court could have provided in this suit against the Secretary was not likely to produce that action.

A further impediment to redressability is the fact that the agencies generally supply only a fraction of the funding for a foreign project. AID, for example, has provided less than 10% of the funding for the Mahaweli Project. Respondents have produced nothing to indicate that the projects they have named will either be suspended, or do less harm to listed species, if that fraction is eliminated. [I]t is entirely conjectural whether the nonagency activity that affects respondents will be altered or affected by the agency activity they seek to achieve. There is no standing.

The Court of Appeals found that respondents had standing for an additional reason: because they had suffered a "procedural injury." The so-called "citizen-suit" provision of the ESA provides, in pertinent part, that "any person may commence a civil suit on his own behalf (A) to enjoin any person, including the United States and any other governmental instrumentality or agency . . . who is alleged to be in violation of any provision of this chapter.'' The court held that, because § 7(a)(2) requires inter-agency consultation, the citizen-suit provision creates a ''procedural right'' to consultation in all ''persons''—so that *anyone* can file suit in federal court to challenge the Secretary's (or presumably any other official's) failure to follow the assertedly correct consultative procedure, notwithstanding their inability to allege any discrete injury flowing from that failure. [T]he court held that the injury-in-fact requirement had been satisfied by congressional conferral upon all persons of an abstract, self-contained, non-instrumental ''right'' to have the Executive observe the procedures required by law. We reject this view.

We have consistently held that a plaintiff raising only a generally available grievance about government—claiming only harm to his and every citizen's interest in proper application of the Constitution and laws, and seeking relief that no more directly and tangibly benefits him than it does the public at large—does not state an Article III case or controversy.

We hold that respondents lack standing to bring this action and that the Court of Appeals erred in denying the summary judgment motion filed by the United States.

****

Note

As the Court recognizes, standing to challenge government action is not ordinarily difficult to show when the challenger is ''himself an object of the action (or forgone action) at issue.'' Recognizing, however, that environmental groups often have broader concerns for national or global conditions, standing hurdles such as those enforced by the Court in this case still would seem to limit access to the courts in some cases in which important environmental policies are in dispute.

What are the major justifications presented by the Court for limiting access? Do you find them persuasive? How difficult would it have been for Defenders of Wildlife to satisfy the Court's injury in fact requirements?

C. Access to the Regulatory Process

1. Participation Rights

Phibro Resources Corporation v. State Department of Environmental Regulation, 579 So. 2d 118 (Fla. App. 1991)

Appellants, Phibro Resources Corp. and its corporate parent, Salomon, Inc., appeal a final administrative order entered by the Department of Environmental Regulation (DER or department), dismissing their petitions for formal administrative hearing. In their petitions, appellants had challenged two consent orders entered by the department with Conserv, Inc., the current owner and operator of a phosphate fertilizer manufacturing facility located in Polk County, Florida, and with Mobil Mining and Minerals Company (Mobil), a former owner of the facility. The consent orders represented an attempt to remedy the pollution of groundwater beneath the site of the facility. In its order of dismissal, the department ruled that Phibro, a former owner and operator of the facility, which was not given the opportunity to participate in either of the two consent orders, lacked the requisite standing as a substantially interested party to be allowed a section 120.57 hearing regarding any effect the orders may have had on Phibro's interests. We reverse and remand with directions to accord both Phibro and its corporate parent Salomon a section 120.57 hearing.

The facts alleged in Phibro's petition are as follows: Mobil operated the facility in question until 1968, when it ceased operations. In 1974, Phibro acquired the facility and continued to operate it until 1982, at which time it transferred ownership and operation to its subsidiary Conserv. Subsequently in 1983, Phibro sold Conserv to another owner. In July 1985, DER issued warning notices to Conserv, Phibro, and Mobil, reciting that pollutants exceeding levels permissible in class II groundwaters had been detected at the property boundary of the Conserv facility site. Phibro was specifically warned that former owners like itself could be held responsible for their operations if they had contributed to the present state of contamination.

In 1989, following notice to Phibro and Salomon that DER intended to enter into consent orders with Conserv and Mobil only, Phibro and Salomon petitioned for a formal administrative hearing. Among other measures, the remedial acts in the proposed orders involved construction of a containment system, which would consist of a number of wells surrounding a portion of the facility, designed to act as a hydraulic barrier to prevent the further migration of contaminated groundwater. Phibro and Salomon alleged that this would not restore the groundwater to its former condition, but in fact would allow continued migration of pollutants in such waters and would lead to additional contamination, thereby increasing the liability which DER had asserted against Phibro. The consent orders with Conserv and Mobil specifically recited that the facility had been discharging pollutants into the groundwater on or before 1982, during a period of time which coincided with Phibro's ownership and operation of the facility. The consent orders also reserved all the department's "rights against all past and present owners and operators of the lands" north of the facility. Moreover, the order with Conserv concluded that if it were determined that Conserv had not complied with its obligations under the order, the department reserved the right to enforce the terms of the order "or to take whatever other actions it deems appropriate."

Our conclusion . . . requires that we examine carefully the pertinent provisions of the 1974 Administrative Procedure Act (APA), furnishing adjudicatory proceedings to parties or persons whose substantial interests are affected or may be affected by an agency's actions. Section 120.57 provides that "[t]he provisions of this section apply in *all* proceedings [formal or informal] in which the substantial interests of a party are determined by an agency[.]" (Emphasis added.) As pointed out by a knowledgeable commentator, in order for one to apply the appropriate access standard to administrative proceedings recognized under section 120.57, it is necessary to make "a separate examination of the provision's three essential elements: 'substantial interests,' 'party,' and 'are determined by an agency.'"

In applying the above statutory provisions to the case at bar, we conclude that Phibro was made a party to the proceeding by statute, in that it was served with a written notice of a warning which specified the provision of the statute and rule alleged to have been violated and the facts alleged to constitute a violation . . . . [The statutes] provide that a person served with a notice of violation (NOV) shall be entitled to a section 120.57 administrative hearing within twenty days following service of notice; otherwise the person's right to an administrative hearing shall be deemed waived. Consequently Phibro was made a party pursuant to the above statutory and regulatory provisions once it was served with the notice. Entry of the consent orders with Conserv and Mobil did nothing to change Phibro's party status. Furthermore, Phibro's right of access to a section 120.57 hearing was not dependent upon the department's discretionary act in deciding not to include it as a party to the consent-order proceeding.

Because the agreements entered into between the department and Conserv and Mobil had the potential of affecting the substantial interests of Phibro, a party which was not allowed to participate in the remedial plans set out in the consent orders, the agency erred in denying Phibro such participation. In fact, the department's decision to allow only some of the parties to participate in the consent orders is contrary to the provisions of the agency's own rule, which defines a consent order in part as "a final agency order wherein *all* parties and the Department, by negotiation, have arrived at a mutually acceptable resolution of alleged violations of law . . . ."

Regarding the department's alternative position, that Phibro alleged only economic injury and that this type of interest is not the kind that [the pollution statute] was designed to protect, we respond that Phibro's petition for administrative hearing alleged far more than potential economic injury. Phibro was served with a warning which informed it that the existence of pollutants exceeding permissible levels in groundwaters would constitute a violation . . . , and it was specifically notified that a former owner, which it was, could be held responsible for its previous operations if such operations contributed to the present contamination at the site. Additionally, [the statute] imposes liability against a violator for any damage caused and for civil penalties, and . . . subjects any such violator to the criminal sanction of a misdemeanor of the first degree.

Moreover, Phibro, having a substantial incentive to avoid either the imposition of, or an increase in, civil and penal sanctions, could serve the public interest, as well as its own private interests, by being allowed to participate in the consent orders by presenting evidence or information to aid the agency in making an informed decision regarding whether the remediation efforts submitted were adequate to stem the further migration of contaminated groundwater.

BARFIELD, Judge, dissenting:

I respectfully dissent. It appears the standing issue addressed by the Department of Environmental Regulation is solely directed to its right to settle with less than all of the parties. The effect of the majority opinion is to confer a veto right on any objecting party. I agree with the appellees' argument that all defenses and rights to be heard are preserved to appellant should the State seek to further proceed against it in the future. It may be that further action against it is barred. In the matter of settlement of the State's claims against some of the parties there is no showing of any substantial interest of appellant which will be affected by the consent order. I cannot agree that the parties have a right to be heard on matters that affect only the substantial rights of other parties.

****

Note

In contrast with the constitutional bases for the right to be heard, as presented in Chapter 5(C), the *Phibro* case is decided as an interpretation of the state's Administrative Procedure Act. In what respects are the constitutional and statutory analyses similar, and in what respects are they different? If there were no applicable statute, would Phibro have a procedural due process right to a hearing before the consent orders between the Department and the other parties took effect?

In general, as attorney for a party seeking to compel a hearing before your client's interests are impaired, would you prefer to base your arguments upon constitutional principles, statutory hearing rights, or an agency regulation such as the one apparently disregarded by the Department in this case?

2. Trade Secret Information

Ruckelshaus v. Monsanto Co., 467 U.S. 986, 104 S. Ct. 2862 (1984)

In this case, we are asked to review a . . . determination that several provisions of the Federal Insecticide, Fungicide, and Rodenticide Act (FIFRA) are unconstitutional. The provisions at issue authorize the Environmental Protection Agency to use data submitted by an applicant for registration of a pesticide in evaluating the application of a subsequent applicant, and to disclose publicly some of the submitted data.

Monsanto, like any other applicant for registration of a pesticide, must present research and test data supporting its application. The District Court found that Monsanto had incurred costs in excess of $23.6 million in developing the health, safety, and environmental data submitted by it under FIFRA. The information submitted with an application usually has value to Monsanto beyond its instrumentality in gaining that particular application. Monsanto uses this information to develop additional end-use products and to expand the uses of its registered products. The information would also be valuable to Monsanto's competitors. For that reason, Monsanto has instituted stringent security measures to ensure the secrecy of the data.

It is this health, safety, and environmental data that Monsanto sought to protect by bringing this suit. The District court found that much of these data "contain or relate to trade secrets as defined by the Restatement of Torts and confidential, commercial information.''

Monsanto brought suit in District Court, seeking injunctive and declaratory relief from the operation of the data-consideration . . . and the data-disclosure provisions of FIFRA . . . . Monsanto alleged that all of the challenged provisions effected a ''taking'' of property without just compensation, in violation of the Fifth Amendment. In addition, Monsanto alleged that the data-consideration provisions violated the Amendment because they effected a taking of property for a private, rather than a public, purpose. Finally, Monsanto alleged that the arbitration scheme provided by [the Act] violates the original submitter's due process rights and constitutes an unconstitutional delegation of judicial power.

For purposes of this case, EPA has stipulated that ''Monsanto has certain property rights in its information, research and test data that it has submitted under FIFRA to EPA and its predecessor agencies which may be protected by the Fifth Amendment to the Constitution of the United States.'' Since the exact import of that stipulation is not clear, we address the question whether the data at issue here can be considered property for the purposes of the Taking Clause of the Fifth Amendment.

This Court never has squarely addressed the applicability of the protections of the Taking Clause of the Fifth Amendment to commercial data of the kind involved in this case. In answering the question now, we are mindful of the basic axiom that ''' [p]roperty interests . . . are not created by the Constitution. Rather, they are created and their dimensions are defined by existing rules or understandings that stem from an independent source such as state law.' '' Monsanto asserts that the health, safety, and environmental data it has submitted to EPA are property under Missouri law, which recognizes trade secrets, as defined in § 757, Comment b, of the Restatement of Torts, as property. The Restatement defines a trade secret as ''any formula, pattern, device or compilation of information which is used in one's business, and which gives him an opportunity to obtain an advantage over competitors who do not know or use it.''

Because of the intangible nature of a trade secret, the extent of the property right therein is defined by the extent to which the owner of the secret protects his interest from disclosure to others. Information that is public knowledge or that is generally known in an industry cannot be a trade secret. If an individual discloses his trade secret to others who are under no obligation to protect the confidentiality of the information, or otherwise publicly discloses the secret, his property right is extinguished.

Although this Court never has squarely addressed the question whether a person can have a property interest in a trade secret, which is admittedly intangible, the Court has found other kinds of intangible interests to be property for purposes of the Fifth Amendment's Taking Clause. That intangible property rights protected by state law are deserving of the protection of the Taking Clause has long been implicit in the thinking of this Court[.]

We therefore hold that to the extent that Monsanto has an interest in its health, safety, and environmental data cognizable as a trade-secret property right under Missouri law, that property right is protected by the Taking Clause of the Fifth Amendment.

Having determined that Monsanto has a property interest in the data it has submitted to EPA, we confront the difficult question whether a "taking" will occur when EPA discloses those data or considers the data in evaluating another application for registration.

As has been admitted on numerous occasions, "this Court has generally 'been unable to develop any "set formula" for determining when "justice and fairness" require that economic injuries caused by public action'" must be deemed a compensable taking. The inquiry into whether a taking has occurred is essentially an "ad hoc, factual" inquiry. The Court, however, has identified several factors that should be taken into account when determining whether a governmental action has gone beyond "regulation" and effects a "taking." Among those factors are: "the character of the governmental action, its economic impact, and its interference with reasonable investment-backed expectations."

We . . . hold that EPA consideration or disclosure of health, safety, and environmental data will constitute a taking if Monsanto submitted the data to EPA between October 22, 1972, and September 30, 1978; the data constituted trade secrets under Missouri law; Monsanto had designated the data as trade secrets at the time of its submission; the use or disclosure conflicts with the explicit assurance of confidentiality or exclusive use contained in the statute during that period; and the operation of the arbitration provision does not adequately compensate for the loss in market value of the data that Monsanto suffers because of EPA's use or disclosure of the trade secrets.

We must next consider whether any taking of private property that may occur by operation of the data-disclosure and data-consideration provisions of FIFRA is a taking for a "public use." We have recently stated that the scope of the "public use" requirement of the Taking Clause is "coterminous with the scope of a sovereign's police powers."

Because the data-disclosure provisions of FIFRA provide for disclosure to the general public, the District Court did not find that those provisions constituted a taking for a private use. Instead, the court found that the data-disclosure provisions served no use. It reasoned that because EPA, before registration, must determine that a product is safe and effective, and because the label on a pesticide, by statute, must set forth the nature, contents, and purpose of the pesticide, the label provided the public with all the assurance it needed that the product is safe and effective. It is enough for us to state that the optimum amount of disclosure to the public is for Congress, not the courts, to decide, and that the statute embodies Congress' judgment on that question. We further observe, however, that public disclosure can provide an effective check on the decision-making processes of EPA and allows members of the public to determine the likelihood of individualized risks peculiar to their use of the product.

We therefore hold that any taking of private property that may occur in connection with EPA's use or disclosure of data submitted to it by Monsanto between October 22, 1972, and September 30, 1978, is a taking for a public use.

We find no constitutional infirmity in the challenged provisions of FIFRA. Operation of the provisions may effect a taking with respect to certain health, safety, and environmental data constituting trade secrets under state law and designated by Monsanto as trade secrets upon submission to EPA between October 22, 1972, and September 30, 1978. But whatever taking may occur is one for a public use, and a Tucker Act remedy is available to provide Monsanto with just compensation. Once a taking has occurred, the proper forum for Monsanto's claim is the Claims Court. Monsanto's challenges to the constitutionality of the arbitration procedure are not yet ripe for review.

****

Note

What competing private and public interests in Monsanto's data are at stake in this case? Although the decision describes a rather unique statutory scheme by which later applicants could benefit from EPA's use and disclosure of the earlier applicant's proprietary data, the case nonetheless is a forceful reminder of the bases for judicial and legislative limits on public access to trade secret data.

Environmental statutes commonly include provisions allowing persons to claim trade secret protection for information that must be submitted to regulatory agencies. Generally such information "shall not be released to any member of the public," California Health & Safety Code § 39660(e)(2), although procedures often are included to allow members of the public to request release of the information and then to require the claimant to obtain a judicial declaration of the information's confidential status. *See, e.g.*, California Health & Safety Code § 44360.[2]

3. Open Meetings

Krause v. Reno, 366 So. 2d 1244 (Fla. App. 1979)

Among the important public aspects to be served by open meetings of governmental bodies are the following: First, there is the citizen input factor. For example, our Supreme Court [has] stated that "[e]very meeting of any board, commission, agency or authority of a municipality should be a marketplace of ideas, so that the governmental agency may have sufficient input from the citizens who are going to be affected by the subsequent action of the municipality." Second, in addition to this need for citizen input, representative government requires that it be responsive to the wishes of the governed, because that is its ultimate source of consent. Third, open meetings produce stability and public confidence in government. Fourth, open meetings reported by the news media insure that our system of government will function as a genuine participatory democracy, i.e., the governed have a right to participate in their government. A fifth interest served by open meetings is the "checking effect" that open meetings have on governmental abuses. Meetings in public facilitate this "checking value." Even if most persons are unable to attend such meetings, they allow the news media to "watchdog"

---

[2] Confidentiality issues related to environmental audits are discussed at Chapter 4(F), *supra*.

the conduct of public officials. Another interest to be served by open meetings is the public can better evaluate public officials and their projects by being privy to the decision-making process. Thereby, for example, the public may vote intelligently on retaining officials, restructuring their offices, and approving or rejecting their projects. Also, public access to governmental meetings enables members of the public to understand more completely the decision-making processes of government and thereby consider future governmental developments and the consequences of those developments for their own lives. Although this list is not all inclusive, we believe that it is persuasive of the several important interests to be served in assaying the Legislative intent and in applying the provisions of our [Government in the] Sunshine Law.

****

Opinion of the Attorney General, State of California (No. 87-1205, March 24, 1988)

The basic question presented herein is whether the Ralph M. Brown Act, Government Code sections 54950 *et seq.*, requires the deliberations of a hearing board of an air pollution control district, after it has conducted a public hearing on a variance, order of abatement, or permit appeal, to be conducted in public.

The Ralph M. Brown Act requires "legislative bodies" of "local agencies" as defined therein to conduct their meetings in sessions open to the public unless expressly excepted in the act.

Thus, section 54953 of the Government Code, the main operative section of the Ralph M. Brown Act, provides:

"All meetings of the legislative body of a local agency shall be open and public, and all persons shall be permitted to attend any meeting of the legislative body of a local agency, *except as otherwise provided in this chapter.*" (Emphasis added.)

Section 54952.2 then defines "legislative body" to include bodies which are delegated any of the authority of a local agency; section 54952.3 then defines "legislative body" to include "advisory" bodies of a local agency. Finally, and most significant to our inquiry, section 54942.5 then defines "legislative body" to include permanent boards or commissions of a local agency. It states:

"As used in this chapter 'legislative body' also includes, *but is not limited to*, planning commissions, library boards, recreation commissions, *and other permanent boards or commissions of a local agency.*" (Emphasis added.)

A hearing board of an air pollution control district would fall within the terms of this last definition of "legislative body." It is a permanent board of a "local agency," that is, the district.

From the foregoing discussion of the Act, it would seem to be clear that a hearing *board* of an air pollution control *district*, being within the definition of a "legislative body," must hold its deliberations with respect to permits, orders of abatement, and variances in public. There is no express exception in the Act to permit closed session on such matters.

A number of arguments have been suggested that hearing boards of air pollution control districts should be excepted from the open meeting requirements of the Act either as a matter of statutory construction or by implication. These arguments are predicated primarily on the premise that the sole reason for the existence of these hearing boards is to act in a quasi-*judicial* or adjudicative capacity. The argument is that the Legislature could not have intended that they fall within the scope of the Act, since they perform no legislative or policy making functions, and are really like courts.

For example, it has been suggested that hearing boards should not be included within the definition of "legislative body" . . . . It is urged that unlike the permanent boards and commissions enumerated therein (planning commissions, library boards, recreation commissions), hearing boards exercise no policy making decisions, but are solely adjudicatory bodies. Accordingly, they were not intended to be included within the phrase "and other permanent boards or commissions of a local agency" . . . .

We see no ambiguity in section 54952.5. It defines "legislative body" to include any permanent board or commission of a "local agency." The functions of the permanent body would therefore be immaterial. Furthermore, as stated in *Rideaux v. Torgrimson* (1939) 12 Cal.3rd 633, 636:

> "When a legislative body enacts a statute which prescribes the meaning of particular terms used by it, that meaning is binding upon the courts."

In short, the Legislature has provided no exception for hearing boards in section 54952.5. Accordingly, any argument that hearing boards should not be included within this definition should be addressed to the Legislature.

[I]t is suggested that to apply the open meeting requirements of the Ralph M. Brown Act to the *deliberations* of hearing boards is the equivalent of requiring a multi-judge court such as the California Supreme Court to conduct its deliberations in public. It is argued that such requirement has a chilling effect upon such deliberations and the free give and take between board members which they believe to be necessary to reach and write a proper decision on the merits of each individual case.

[I]n our view, the fact that hearing boards of air pollution control districts act only in a quasi-judicial capacity does not remove them from the requirements of the Ralph M. Brown Act. The act provides no exception for boards and commissions so acting. Statutes are to be literally applied according to their plain language unless to do so would produce absurd results or would defeat the manifest intention of the Legislature. We discern nothing in the Act manifesting any legislative intent to exclude air pollution control hearing board deliberations from the open meeting requirements of the act. Also, it is our understanding that virtually all (with one major exception) air pollution control hearing boards do follow the open meeting requirements of the Act with respect to their deliberations. They have learned to operate within the Act and follow it. Accordingly, although it may present some difficulties to do so, it cannot be said that it is absurd to require them to do so.

****

Note

Apart from the semantic oddity of defining a purely adjudicatory function as legislative, this Opinion raises a broader question as to the desirability of opening any and all deliberations of an environmental board to the public. Prior to issuance of the Opinion, a broad coalition of attorneys – some who represent industrial air polluters and some who represent environmental groups – argued against applying the Act to hearing board deliberations. Can you surmise some of the bases on which these diverse attorneys reached accord on this question? Note that the issue is whether the board's deliberations must be conducted in public "after it has conducted a public hearing." Note also that the board is statutorily required to embody the results of its deliberations in a written decision which can then be subject to judicial review.

If you were a member of the state legislature, and the argument that hearing board deliberations should not be covered by this Act were addressed to the legislature, as the Attorney General suggests, what would be your response?

D. English as a Barrier

Peter L. Reich, "Greening the Ghetto: A Theory of Environmental Race Discrimination," 41 University of Kansas Law Review 271, 297-298 (1992)

Within NEPA's parameters, some federal agencies occasionally have attempted to remedy an aspect of environmental racism by providing EIS translations to Spanish-speaking populations. For example, in 1980 the United States Department of Energy published a ninety-page EIS summary written in Spanish for a proposed radioactive waste storage facility in New Mexico. Similarly, the United States Department of Housing and Urban Development prepared a draft EIS in Spanish for two proposed housing projects to be built in Puerto Rico. These administrative decisions to translate EIS documents have furnished access to planning for certain minorities who otherwise would have been excluded from the process.

When federal projects are at issue, agencies can use NEPA's authority to remove participation barriers, such as language, experienced by many people of color. This solution is limited, however, in that relatively few projects are reviewed under federal processes. It should also be noted that the above translations were ordered entirely on a discretionary basis; no definitive interpretation of NEPA requires such a procedure.

Beyond the purview of NEPA, there is no existing federal statute or precedent that specifically provides minorities access to environmental decision-making.

****

El Pueblo Para el Aire y Agua Limpio v. County of Kings, (No. 366045, Superior Court, Sacramento County, California) (Ruling on Submitted Matter, December 30, 1991)

In this . . . proceeding, petitioners challenge a decision of the Kings County Board of Supervisors ("board") granting a conditional use permit for the construction and operation of a hazardous waste incinerator by Chemical Waste Management, Inc. ("CWM") at CWM's existing hazardous waste treatment, storage and disposal facility in the Kettleman Hills area of southwest Kings County. The board's decision affirmed determinations by the Kings County Planning Commission that (1) the environmental impact report prepared on the incinerator project adequately complied with the requirements of the California Environmental Quality Act ("CEQA") and (2) the incinerator project was consistent with the Kings County General Plan and Zoning Ordinance. Petitioners contend that these determinations, and the board's grant of a conditional use permit based on the determinations, are invalid.

[T]he Court finds that the Final Subsequent Environmental Impact Report ("FSEIR") on CWM's proposed incinerator project was inadequate as an informational document under CEQA.

The Court finds that the strong emphasis in CEQA on environmental decisionmaking by public officials which involves and informs members of the public would have justified the Spanish translation of an extended summary of the FSEIR, public meeting notices, and public hearing testimony in this case. The residents of Kettleman City, almost 40 percent of whom were monolingual in Spanish, expressed continuous and strong interest in participating in the CEQA review process for the incinerator project at the CWM's Kettleman Hills Facility, just four miles from their homes. Their meaningful involvement in the CEQA review process was effectively precluded by the absence of the Spanish translation.

The Court, however, does not find that the FSEIR was written in a manner incomprehensible to interested laypersons among the public. The text of the FSEIR perhaps contained a significant amount of technical matter which could have been better placed in appendices, but the text was readable. The inadequacies in the analysis, not the readability of the text, constituted the significant deficiency of the FSEIR.

El Pueblo Para el Aire y Agua Limpio v. County of Kings, (No. 366045, Superior Court, Sacramento County, California) (Order, June 22, 1992)

Upon hearing the motions of respondents and real parties in interest for a new trial and considering the arguments of counsel, it appears to the Court that the motions for a new trial should be denied.

Contrary to respondents' assertion in their new trial motion, the Court's ruling of December 30, 1991, did not impose any blanket requirements for the translation of documents from English into Spanish or other languages during the CEQA environmental impact review process. Rather the Court observed that, in the light of the large monolingual Spanish speaking population of Kettleman City interested in the incinerator project at Kettleman Hills, the Spanish translation of an extended FSEIR summary and the hearing proceedings on the FSEIR would have been justified and consistent with the CEQA policy of public inclusion emphasized by the California Supreme Court. The Court declines to transform its observation into a blanket requirement or ruling.

****

Notes

1. Section 5-5(b) of the Presidential Executive Order on environmental justice presented in Chapter 7(D), *infra*, now authorizes federal agencies to "translate crucial public documents, notices, and hearings relating to human health or the environment for limited English speaking populations." Is this an adequate response to the need Professor Reich addresses? Would a Congressional enactment be preferable, and, if so, what should it be?

For examples of state public hazard disclosure statutes, or "right to know laws" for workers or communities, that now require translation of environmental information into languages other than English, *see* New Jersey Statutes Annotated §§ 34:5A-4(c), 34:5A-5(e), 34:5A-11 (Spanish); Oregon Revised Statutes § 654.770 (Spanish, Russian, Thai, Japanese, Chinese, Laotian, Vietnamese, Korean and Cambodian); Pennsylvania Statutes Annotated, title 35, § 7310 (Spanish). What are the arguments for and against this type of legislative mandate on language?

2. In theory, some of the barriers to participation in decisional processes faced by poor and minority communities where little English is spoken, or where illiteracy is high, can be overcome through the assistance of lawyers, especially lawyers who speak languages in addition to English. In the environmental realm, such lawyers ideally also should be familiar with the esoteric, technical "language" of environmental regulation.

In practice, of course, there are not yet very many lawyers who have this ideal breadth of talent and who have made themselves available to these types of communities. One attorney, however, forcefully has argued that in the pursuit of environmental protection for such communities, the profound strengthening of community organizations is far more important than any legal tools.[3]

---

[3] Luke W. Cole, "Empowerment as the Key to Environmental Protection: The Need for Environmental Poverty Law," 19 Ecology Law Quarterly 619 (1992); Luke W. Cole, "The Struggle of Kettleman City: Lessons for the Movement," 5 Maryland Journal of Contemporary Legal Issues 67, 77 (1993) ("'[L]egal approaches are the least favored approaches to solving environmental problems. They are disempowering to community residents because they take the struggle out of the community and put it into the hands of a lawyer."). *See also* Chapter 1(B), note 7, *supra*.

3. A partially analogous access problem is faced by many small businesses across the country, although obviously this problem does not necessarily include the English language obstacle. Small businesses frequently lack the expertise and other resources that would enable them to have effective input into environmental policymaking, and to understand fully all the requirements to which they are subject.[4]

One factor in the recent expansion of environmental law as a component in many lawyers' practice is small businesses' need for legal assistance to compensate for their own limitations. Many environmental agencies also have begun to institute programs specifically designed to assist small businesses in understanding and complying with regulatory requirements, e.g., through the simplification of permit procedures and information reporting forms.[5]

---

[4] *See* Exercise 2 in Chapter 4(B), *supra.* Similar limitations faced by small towns subject to federal environmental regulations have been recognized by the U.S. Environmental Protection Agency. *See* 59 Fed. Reg. 50602 (Oct. 4, 1994) (meeting of EPA's Small Town Environmental Planning Task Force).

[5] *See, e.g..* U.S. Environmental Protection Agency, The Clean Air Act Amendments of 1990: A Guide for Small Businesses (September 1992); Craig A. Moyer *et al.*, Clean Air Act Handbook sec. 5.08 (3d ed. 1993) (describing EPA's ''small business stationary source technical and environmental compliance assistance program'').

Chapter 7
Siting of Polluting Facilities

A. Overview

The term "environmental justice" has been used often and with considerable fanfare in the past few years in connection with disputes over the siting of polluting or risk-creating facilities – particularly hazardous waste facilities – in poor, racial minority neighborhoods. As examined in Chapter 4, "environmental justice" also has been used more broadly to refer to other problems, such as the alleged failure of environmental enforcement and cleanup programs to respond to the needs of poor and minority communities.[1] The term thus now encompasses a variety of perceived breaches of distributive justice in American environmental policy.

Within this broad usage, however, the most dramatic, emotional, and controversial area of "environmental justice" activism has been the siting controversies. When polluting facilities are proposed for disadvantaged communities – most notably communities which are poor and largely African-American, Hispanic, or Native American – serious questions arise as to whether our legal system can produce equitable outcomes in siting decisions, or whether the results virtually always are discriminatory and exploitative.

Only recently, in connection with these siting issues, has "justice" entered significantly into the vocabulary of environmental law for the first time. Recognizing that discussion of justice is common in many other areas of the law, it may seem strange that it has been omitted from environmental law for so long. Perhaps an explanation for this omission is suggested by the readings presented earlier, in Chapter 3(B), *supra*, about the values and priorities that have motivated this field from the outset. Simply stated, the original concern of environmental law was the effect of people's activities on environmental conditions.[2] In contrast, what recent siting controversies have brought

---

[1] *Cf.* Robert D. Bullard, "Environmental Equity: Examining the Evidence of Environmental Racism," Land Use Forum, Winter 1993, at 6 ("This article examines patterns of environmental racism in land use decisions in other states and in California. The focus is primarily on siting decisions, although environmental racism also encompasses many other patterns, such as discriminatory enforcement of environmental regulations and hazardous waste cleanup.")

[2] *See* Richard J. Lazarus, "Pursuing 'Environmental Justice': The Distributional Effects of Environmental Protection" 87 Northwestern University Law Review 787, 854 (1993), where the following is stated:
Environmental protection policy has been almost exclusively concerned with two basic issues during the last several decades: (1) what is an acceptable level of pollution; and (2) what kinds of legal rules would be best suited for reducing pollution to that level. By contrast, policymakers have

to light is that environmental policy has inescapable distributional impacts, i.e., what some people do with environmental resources has great impact on the welfare of other people.[3]

The inequities in living conditions created or exacerbated by decisions on the siting of hazardous waste facilities and other similar types of activities now appear to be too severe to be ignored any longer. Although environmental law fundamentally concentrates on the environmental effects of activities undertaken in pursuit of other societal goals, now the law must evolve to address as well the societal effects of activities undertaken in pursuit of environmental goals. It is this evolution—this recognition in the law that environmental conditions are a crucial aspect of the harsh living conditions of many poor and minority communities—that is raising "environmental justice" to importance.

As noted in Chapter 2, different types of environmental lawyers may tend to be more concerned with distributive, corrective, or procedural justice, depending upon the types of clients they represent over time. For lawyers representing communities claiming

---

paid much less attention to the distributional effects, including the potential for distributional inequities, of environmental protection generally.

Ecological values must recognize and embrace human welfare as an invaluable part of the natural community. Environmentalists should, therefore, strive to redress the basic human needs of those who are wanting as part of their central mission.

See also Joseph M. Petulla, American Environmentalism: Values, Tactics, Priorities 208-209 (1980) ("The question of environmental ethics should not be construed as a problem of rights of nature versus rights of people but at least partially as interest groups competing for wider support over particular issues.").

[3] The most substantial, previous illustrations of the distributional impacts of environmental policy are to be found in an international context, rather than within domestic American environmental policy. As early as the 1972 United Nations Conference on the Human Environment (Stockholm Conference), and again in the 1992 United Nations Conference on Environment and Development (Rio Conference), various Third World nations emphasized the adverse effects they suffer from the environmental policies and resource use patterns of the industrialized nations. Analogous arguments regarding the hardships suffered by poorer communities in the United States have not achieved comparable visibility until now. *See* A. Dan Tarlock, "Environmental Protection: The Potential Misfit Between Equity and Efficiency," 63 Colorado Law Review 871, 872 (1992) ("While the issue of developing versus developed areas, or North versus South equity, is at the heart of global environmental politics, similar issues arise within the United States and other developed countries.") *See also* Xavier Carlos Vasquez, "The North American Free Trade Agreement and Environmental Racism," 34 Harvard International Law Journal 357 (1993).

As examples of international recognition of these concerns, *see, e.g.,* Stockholm Conference Action Plan for the Human Environment, Recommendation 103(a): "[T]he burdens of the environmental policies of the industrialized countries should not be transferred, either directly or indirectly to the developing countries. As a general rule, no country should solve or disregard its environmental problems at the expense of other countries."; Rio Declaration on Environment and Development, Principle 7, which states, "In view of the different contributions to global environmental degradation, States have common but differentiated responsibilities. The developed countries acknowledge the responsibility that they bear in the international pursuit of sustainable development in view of the pressures their societies place on the global environment and of the technologies and financial resources they command."; *id.* at Principle 14: "States should effectively cooperate to discourage or prevent the relocation and transfer to other States of any activities and substances that cause severe environmental degradation or are found to be harmful to human health."

More particularized statements of this sort can be found in Agenda 21 adopted by the Rio Conference. *See, e.g.,* Paragraph 20.4: "There is international concern that part of the international movement of hazardous wastes is being carried out in contravention of existing national legislation and international instruments to the detriment of the environment and public health of all countries, particularly developing countries." Additional provisions of the Rio Declaration and the Stockholm Declaration are quoted in Chapter 3(C), *supra.*

to be adversely affected by facility siting, the problems of environmental justice are predominantly problems of distributive fairness in the allocation of environmental risks and burdens among different communities. Additionally, as suggested in the materials on access in Chapter 6, procedural justice issues also often arise for communities claiming environmental injustice. With multiple and overlapping justice claims raised by communities' lawyers, and contending claims for fair treatment urged by other parties as well, the siting controversies, more so than any other type of environmental dispute, bring together all of the principal types of justice claims examined in this book. This extraordinary complexity may help to explain the dramatic, and often apparently intractable, nature of these cases.

Although "environmental justice" appears to be emerging as the dominant label for these disputes, other phrases occasionally are used interchangeably. "Environmental equity" thus seems to share the same meanings as "environmental justice," suggesting the broad objectives of fairness.[4] "Environmental racism" and "environmental race discrimination" also often are used to describe this area of concern, although obviously their connotation is an underlying problem, rather than a solution.[5]

The first section of this chapter will explore environmental racism and its relationship to facility siting. The next portion will examine the principal legal tools and strategies that thus far appear to have some utility in addressing these difficult problems of facility siting. Finally, recent developments in Presidential and Congressional responses to environmental injustice will be presented.

B. Racism and Siting

At the heart of the environmental justice objection to facility siting is the charge that American practices for locating polluting and environmentally dangerous facilities demonstrate racial discrimination against people who are poor and members of racial minorities. In examining this charge, this section will first look at the history of the "environmental justice movement," the recent explosion of legal, political, governmental, grassroots, and scholarly activity. Next we will examine some of the data that have been marshaled with regard to discrimination in environmental risks and burdens, including some analyses that dispute major findings on which the movement is founded.

---

[4] Some community activists have objected to use of the term "environmental equity" as a synonym for "environmental justice." They argue that "equity" suggests that the overall problem of hazardous pollution is to be shared among communities, while "justice" in this context connotes the elimination of such pollution from all communities. *See, e.g.*, Marianne Lavelle, "Residents Want 'Justice,' The EPA Offers 'Equity'," The National Law Journal, September 21, 1992, at S12.

[5] "One shorthand expression for such claims is 'environmental racism,' but 'environmental justice' (or 'equity') appears to have emerged as the more politically attractive expression, presumably because its connotation is more positive and, at the same time, less divisive." Richard J. Lazarus, "Pursuing 'Environmental Justice': The Distributional Effects of Environmental Protection" 87 Northwestern University Law Review 787, 790 (1993).

Finally, recent attempts to assign clear definitions to racism in this context, and to identify some causes of siting patterns, will be explored.

1. Historical Background

Green Power Foundation, Final Report: Urban Environmental Improvement Project—Los Angeles—Phase II (November 15, 1972)

Within the last few years ecological concerns have evolved into *total* environmental awareness. However, more times than not, this environmental outrage has only resulted in attempts to rescue oil-soaked birds, preserve wild rivers, or save endangered redwood trees. However, these are not the primary and only environmental problems—the quality of life in U. S. cities has progressively grown less healthy and more stressful. Non-white Americans, who typically inhabit the concrete jungles in these cities, are more likely to be preoccupied with attempts to exist—a decaying environment is taken for granted. The U. S. Environmental Protection Agency (EPA) has initiated action programs designed to find ways of ameliorating the environmental decay that plagues our cities today. High on its list of priorities is a commitment to involve the youth of America in its environmental protection programs.

EPA has stressed youthful participation in environmental improvement because today's youth will inherit tomorrow's environment. In 1971, the EPA initiated Summer Programs to Renew the Environment (SPARE), a nation-wide summer and continuing youth education and employment program.

Green Power Foundation has conducted two successful SPARE-like pilot programs: (1) 1971 - Phase I, A Survey of Inner City Residents; and (2) 1972 - Phase II, Urban Environmental Improvement Planning and Implementation Project, a follow-up with student action teams to determine the effectiveness of addressing the environmental concerns brought out in Phase I. The Phase I pilot project was designed to ascertain the expressed needs and attitudes of inner-city residents regarding their environment.

The students developed a questionnaire to obtain survey data on attitudes and priorities of environmental problems confronting residents of South Central Los Angeles. For the first time ever, inner-city residents were polled to ascertain their attitudes and urban environmental priorities of concern.

The attitudes of inner-city residents toward their urban environment, based on a survey of 4,557 inner-city residents, can be summarized as follows:

1. Residents of the inner-city are generally aware of the magnitude and kind of environmental problems in their areas. (Only 8% of the residents interviewed were not aware of serious problems).
2. The most serious environmental problem in the inner-city survey area was found to be "wandering cats and dogs", with air pollution rated as the second most serious problem. (12.8% and 12% of the responses).
3. Inner-city residents strongly believe that a dirty environment has deleterious effects on their children. (Highest positive response to survey questions—81.6%).

4. Inner-city residents strongly believe that more resources should be allocated to solving environmental problems. (Second highest response to survey questions—80.6%).
5. The general attitude of inner-city residents surveyed was a lack of faith that anything will be done about their environmental problems. This attitude is associated with a history of inaction and inability of public agencies to deal effectively with the manifested problems of the inner-city. For example, there is an obvious need for the city to enforce animal regulations and to enforce existing regulations regarding trash and solid waste, etc., which is not being met in the survey area.

****

Note

This 1972 Report by a Los Angeles community organization confirms, as we already have noted in Chapter 3(B), *supra*, that very early in the development of modern environmental policy, there was some attention given to the relationship between environmental quality and the welfare of poor and minority communities.[6]

Similarly, a recent survey of fifteen studies on "the social distribution of environmental hazards" included the following observations:

First, an inspection of the publication dates of these studies reveals that information about environmental inequity has been available for some time. Rather than being a recent discovery, documentation of environmental injustices stretches back two decades, almost to Earth Day—an event viewed by many as a major turning point in public awareness about environmental issues. Evidently, it has taken some time for public awareness to catch up to the issues of environmental injustice. It is also interesting to note that most of the studies that have been conducted in this period have focused on the distribution of air pollution.

Bunyan Bryant and Paul Mohai, "Environmental Racism: Reviewing the Evidence," in Race and the Incidence of Environmental Hazards 165 (Bunyan Bryant and Paul Mohai, eds., 1992). *See also* James H. Colopy, "The Road Less Traveled: Pursuing Environmental Justice Through Title VI of the Civil Rights Act of 1964," 13 Stanford Environmental Law Journal 125, 182 (1994) ("The [EPA] made some progress in the late 1970s, publishing a brochure entitled "Our Common Cause," in which civil rights leaders wrote of the importance of the environment to minority communities, and funding environmental work by civil rights advocates.")

****

---

[6] Further evidence of this attention can be found in *First National Bank v. Richardson*, 494 F.2d 1369 (7th Cir. 1973), which is quoted in Chapter 7(C)(4), *infra*.

Robert Suro, "Pollution Weary Minorities Try Civil Rights Tack," New York Times, January 11, 1993

With little coordination and with no well-known national leaders, the environmental justice movement has developed out of many individual local protests, usually focused on a single nearby problem. No one really knows the movement's size, but in October 1991 about 500 representatives of community groups met in Washington for "The First National People of Color Environmental Summit."

The movement in the United States has counterparts in many developing nations, like Costa Rica, India and Indonesia, where grass-roots campaigners have led the opposition to some environmental hazards. Organizers in the United States and those in third world countries face arguments that pollution is economic necessity.

Robert D. Bullard, a sociologist at the University of California at Riverside, is widely credited with conducting the first extensive research that linked an environmental hazard to the race of those exposed to it. In a 1979 study in Houston, he showed that since the 1920's all the city-owned landfills and six of the eight garbage incinerators had been in black neighborhoods even though Houston was once an overwhelmingly white city.

The first solid evidence of inequities on a national scale emerged from a study published in 1987 by the United Church of Christ's Commission for Racial Justice, which found that race, even more than poverty, was the shared characteristic of communities exposed to toxic wastes.

****

Robert D. Bullard, "Environmental Blackmail in Minority Communities," in Race and the Incidence of Environmental Hazards 85-86, 90-91 (Bunyan Bryant & Paul Mohai, eds. 1992)

Poor and minority residents had the most to gain in the passage of environmental regulations such as the Clean Air Act since they lived closest to the worst sources of the pollution. These communities, however, continue to be burdened with a disproportionately large share of industrial pollution problems, even after the passage of all the regulations. Uneven enforcement of environmental and land-use regulations is a contributor to this problem.

Zoning, deed restrictions, and other "protectionist" devices have failed to effectively segregate industrial uses from residential uses in many black and lower income communities. The various social classes, with or without land use controls, are "unequally able to protect their environmental interests." Rich neighborhoods are able to leverage their economic and political clout into fending off unwanted uses (even public housing for the poor) while residents of poor neighborhoods have to put up with all kinds of unwanted neighbors, including noxious facilities.

Public opposition has been more vocal in middle and upper income groups on the issue of noxious facility siting. The Not In My Back Yard (NIMBY) syndrome has been the usual reaction in these communities. As affluent communities became more active in opposing a certain facility, the siting effort shifted toward a more powerless community. Opposition groups often called for the facilities to be sited "somewhere else." "Somewhere Else, USA" often ends up being located in poor, powerless, minority communities. It is this unequal sharing of benefits and burden that has engendered feelings of unfair treatment among poor and minority communities.

Facility siting in the United States is largely reflective of the long pattern of disparate treatment of black communities. There is a "direct historical connection between the exploitation of the land and the exploitation of people, especially black people." Polluting industries have exploited the pro-growth and pro-jobs sentiment exhibited among the poor, working class, and minority communities. Industries such as paper mills, waste disposal and treatment facilities, heavy metals operations, and chemical plants, searching for operating space, found minority communities to be a logical choice for their expansion. These communities and their leaders were seen as having a Third World view of development. That is, "any development is better than no development at all." Moreover, many residents in these communities were suspicious of environmentalists, a sentiment that aligned them with the pro-growth advocates.

The 1980s have seen a shift in the way black communities react to the jobs-environment issue. This shift has revolved around the issue of equity. Blacks have begun to challenge the legitimacy of environmental blackmail and the notion of trade-offs. They are now asking: Are the costs borne by the black community imposed to spare the larger community? Can environmental inequities (resulting from industrial facility siting decisions) be compensated? What are "acceptable" risks? Concern about equity is at the heart of black people's reaction to industrial facility siting where there is an inherent imbalance between localized costs and dispersed benefits. Few residents want garbage dumps and landfills in their backyards. The price of siting noxious facilities has skyrocketed in recent years as a result of more stringent federal regulations and the growing militancy among the poor, working class, and minority communities. Compensation appears to hold little promise in mitigating locational conflict and environmental disputes in these communities.

The civil rights movement has its roots in the southern United States. Southern racism deprived blacks of "political rights, economic opportunity, social justice, and human dignity." The new environmental-equity movement is also centered in the South, a region where marked ecological disparities exist between black and white communities. The 1980s have seen the emergence of a small cadre of blacks who equate environmental discrimination with a civil rights issue. An alliance has been forged between organized labor, blacks, and environmental groups, as exhibited by the 1983 Urban Environment Conference workshops held in New Orleans. Environmental and civil rights issues were presented as compatible agenda items by the conference organizers.

A growing number of grassroots organizations and their leaders have begun to adopt confrontational strategies (e.g., protests, neighborhood demonstrations, picketing, political pressure, litigation, etc.) to reduce and eliminate environmental stressors. The national black political leadership has also demonstrated a willingness to take a strong pro-environment stance. The League of Conservation Voters, for example, assigned the Congressional Black Caucus high marks for having one of the best pro-environment voting records.

Toxic waste disposal has generated protests in many communities across the country. The first national environmental protest by blacks came in 1982 after the mostly black Warren County, North Carolina was selected as the burial site for 32,000 cubic yards of soil contaminated with the highly toxic PCBs (polychlorinated biphenyls). The soil was illegally dumped along the roadways in fourteen North Carolina counties in 1978. Black civil rights activists, political leaders, and local residents marched in protest demonstrations against the construction of the PCB landfill in their community. Why was Warren County selected as the landfill site? The decision made more political sense than environmental sense.

Although the protests were unsuccessful in halting the landfill construction, they marked the first time blacks mobilized a nationally broad-based group to protest environmental inequities. The protests prompted Congressman Walter E. Fauntroy (Representative from the District of Columbia), who had been active in the demonstrations, to initiate the U. S. General Accounting Office (1983) study of hazardous waste landfill siting in the South.[7] The GAO study observed a strong relationship between the siting of offsite hazardous landfills and race of surrounding communities. Three of the four offsite hazardous waste landfills in EPA's Region IV were located in black communities, while blacks made up only twenty percent of the region's population.

****

Notes

1. Professor Bullard ascribes the NIMBY syndrome to "middle and upper income groups." As will be seen in other readings in this chapter, environmental justice activists usually distinguish more affluent groups' NIMBY efforts from the efforts of poor and minority communities to keep undesirable land uses out of their areas. The latter efforts are presented as something other than manifestations of the NIMBY position.[8] Often they are described as part of a broader pollution prevention agenda and as intended to prevent *any* communities from having to bear the burdens and risks of facilities such as hazardous waste treatment and disposal sites.[9] As you examine the readings in this chapter, consider what specific steps might be taken by communities in these siting disputes to promote that broader agenda. Do you find evidence that such steps have

---

[7] [Ed.] General Accounting Office, Siting of Hazardous Waste Landfills and their Correlation with Racial and Economic Status of Surrounding Communities (1983).

[8] *But see* A. Dan Tarlock, "City Versus Countryside: Environmental Equity in Context," 21 Fordham Urban Law Journal 461, 465 (1994) ("[T]he movement asserts that disadvantaged communities should adopt a 'Not in My Backyard' (NIMBY) strategy.").

[9] *See* Nicholas Freudenberg *et al.*, "Not in Our Backyards: The Grassroots Environmental Movement," in America Environmentalism: The U.S. Environmental Movement, 1970-1990 (Riley E. Dunlap *et al.*, eds. 1992), at 27, 35 ("Critics of NIMBY groups also fail to acknowledge that many local groups move beyond simple nay-saying to support socially constructive alternatives that express a NIABY [not in anyone's back yard] philosophy. Thus, many groups opposing the construction of garbage incinerators become advocates for recycling and waste reduction measures such as packaging controls.").

Further discussion of pollution prevention strategies is presented in Chapter 3(D), *supra*.

been pursued in any of the siting controversies thus far? Are there examples of a community not only resisting the siting of a new waste treatment facility in its midst, but also striving to prevent the facility's location elsewhere or to reduce the risks associated with the continued transportation of the wastes to an existing facility? If there is no evidence of this or similar steps, does that mean that the environmental justice claim is merely a new label for NIMBY as it is now being asserted by poor and minority communities? Even if environmental justice claims in the siting context were simply the belated embracing of a NIMBY position by disadvantaged communities, does that necessarily diminish their moral force?

2. In a recent commentary on nine siting controversies, Professor Bullard made the following observations on community leadership:

It is clear that the local grassroots activists in the impacted communities provided the essential leadership in dealing with the disputes. The typical grassroots leader was a woman. For example, women led the fight in seven of the nine cases examined. Only the West Dallas Coalition for Environmental Justice and Richmond's West County Toxics Coalition were headed by men.

Women activists were quick to express their concern about the threat to their family, home, and community. The typical organizer found leadership thrust upon her by immediate circumstances with little warning or prior training for the job. Lack of experience, however, did not prove an insurmountable barrier to successful organizing. The manner in which the local issue was framed appears to have influenced the type of leadership that emerged. Local activists immediately turned their energies to what they defined as environmental discrimination, for discrimination is a fact of life in all of these communities. Most people of color face it daily.

The quest for environmental justice thus extends the quest for basic civil rights. Actions taken by grassroots activists to reduce environmental inequities are consistent with the struggle to end the other forms of social injustice found throughout our society— in housing, education, employment, health care, criminal justice, and politics.

The mainstream environmental groups do not have a long history of working with African-American, Latino, Asian, Pacific Islander, and Native-American groups. For the most part, they have failed to adequately address environmental problems that disproportionately impact people of color. Despite some exceptions, the national groups have failed to sufficiently make the connection between key environmental and social justice issues.

Robert D. Bullard, "Anatomy of Environmental Racism and the Environmental Justice Movement," in Confronting Environmental Racism: Voices from the Grassroots 30 (Robert D. Bullard, ed., 1993).

2. Data and Debate

As the preceding historical material indicates, some of the principal developments in the environmental justice movement have been studies presenting data that demonstrate distributional inequities in the siting of polluting or risk-creating facilities. Some of those studies will be excerpted here, along with analyses that question their methods or implications. These readings also supplement the historical background in the preceding section, and they anticipate the discussion in later sections about the causes of inequities and strategies for redressing them.

Environmental racism, like any other charge of exploitation of poor, minority communities, is a highly charged issue. Nonetheless, amidst the passions and political reactions this realm of controversy ignites, the attorney who is involved in these matters must try to develop a solid grasp of the relevant facts. It is difficult to imagine an attorney making a worthwhile, honest contribution either to environmental quality, or to social equity, without having a clear sense of what relevant facts are known and what facts are in question. The readings that follow present some of the evidence.

****

Commission for Racial Justice (United Church of Christ), Toxic Wastes and Race in the United States: A National Report on the Racial and Socio-Economic Characteristics of Communities with Hazardous Waste Sites xi-xv, 13 (1987)

Issues surrounding the siting of hazardous waste facilities in racial and ethnic communities gained national prominence in 1982. The Commission for Racial Justice joined ranks with residents of predominantly Black and poor Warren County, North Carolina in opposing the establishment of a polychlorinated biphenyl (PCB) disposal landfill. This opposition culminated in a nonviolent civil disobedience campaign and more than 500 arrests. As a result of the protests in Warren County, the [General Accounting Office] studied the racial and socio-economic status of communities surrounding four landfills in southeastern United States. It found that Blacks comprised the majority of the population in three of the four communities studied.

Previous to the Warren County demonstrations, racial and ethnic communities had been marginally involved with issues of hazardous wastes. One reason for this can be traced to the nature of the environmental movement which has historically been white middle and upper-class in its orientation. This does not mean, however, that racial and ethnic communities do not care about the quality of their environment and its effect on their lives. Throughout the course of the Commission for Racial Justice's involvement with issues of hazardous wastes and environmental pollution, we have found numerous grassroots racial and ethnic groups actively seeking to deal with this problem in their communities.

Racial and ethnic communities have been and continue to be beset by poverty, unemployment and problems related to poor housing, education and health. These communities cannot afford the luxury of being primarily concerned about the quality of their environment when confronted by a plethora of pressing problems related to their day-to-day survival. Within this context, racial and ethnic communities become particularly vulnerable to those who advocate the siting of a hazardous waste facility as an avenue for employment and economic development. Thus, proposals that economic incentives be offered to mitigate local opposition to the establishment of new hazardous waste facilities raise disturbing social policy questions.

Having observed these developments, the United Church of Christ Commission for Racial Justice decided, in 1986, to conduct extensive research on the relationship between the location of sites containing hazardous wastes and the racial and socio-economic characteristics of persons living in close proximity to those sites. The Commission for Racial Justice employed Public Data Access, Inc., a New York-based research firm, to assist in these investigations. It was hoped that these studies would lead, for the first time, to a comprehensive national analysis of the relationship between hazardous wastes and racial and ethnic communities.

"Hazardous wastes" is the term used by the EPA to define by-products of industrial production which present particularly troublesome health and environmental problems. Newly generated hazardous wastes must be managed in an approved "facility", which is defined by the EPA as any land and structures thereon which are used for treating, storing or disposing of hazardous wastes (TSD facility). Such facilities may include landfills, surface impoundments or incinerators. A "commercial" facility is defined as any facility (public or private) which accepts hazardous wastes from a third party for a fee or other remuneration.

"Uncontrolled toxic waste sites" refer to closed and abandoned sites on the EPA's list of sites which pose a present and potential threat to human health and the environment. The problem of human exposure to uncontrolled hazardous wastes is national in its scope. By 1985, the EPA had inventoried approximately 20,000 uncontrolled sites containing hazardous wastes across the nation. The potential health problems associated with the existence of these sites is highlighted by the fact that approximately 75 percent of U.S. cities derive their water supplies, in total or in part, from groundwater.

MAJOR FINDINGS

This report presents findings from two cross-sectional studies on demographic patterns associated with (1) commercial hazardous waste facilities and (2) uncontrolled toxic waste sites. The first was an analytical study which revealed a striking relationship between the location of commercial hazardous waste facilities and race. The second was a descriptive study which documented the widespread presence of uncontrolled toxic waste sites in racial and ethnic communities throughout the United States. Among the many findings that emerged from these studies, the following are most important:

Demographic Characteristics of Communities with Commercial Hazardous Waste Facilities
— Race proved to be the most significant among variables tested in association with the location of commercial hazardous waste facilities. This represented a consistent national pattern.
— Communities with the greatest number of commercial hazardous waste facilities had the highest composition of racial and ethnic residents. In communities with two or more facilities or one of the nation's five largest landfills, the average minority percentage of the population[10] was more than three times that of communities without facilities (38 percent vs. 12 percent).

[10] In this report, "minority percentage of the population" was used as a measure of "race".

– In communities with one commercial hazardous waste facility, the average minority percentage of the population was twice the average minority percentage of the population in communities without such facilities (24 percent vs. 12 percent).

– Although socio-economic status appeared to play an important role in the location of commercial hazardous waste facilities, race still proved to be more significant. This remained true after the study controlled for urbanization and regional differences. Incomes and home values were substantially lower when communities with commercial facilities were compared to communities in the surrounding counties without facilities.

– Three out of the five largest commercial hazardous waste landfills in the United States were located in predominantly Black or Hispanic communities. These three landfills accounted for 40 percent of the total estimated commercial landfill capacity in the nation.

Demographic Characteristics of Communities with Uncontrolled Toxic Waste Sites
– Three out of every five Black and Hispanic Americans lived in communities with uncontrolled toxic waste sites.

– More than 15 million Blacks lived in communities with one or more uncontrolled toxic waste sites.

– More than 8 million Hispanics lived in communities with one or more uncontrolled toxic waste sites.

– Blacks were heavily over-represented in the populations of metropolitan areas with the largest number of uncontrolled toxic waste sites. These areas include:

Memphis, TN	(173 sites)	Cleveland, OH	(106 sites)
St. Louis, MO	(160 sites)	Chicago, IL	(103 sites)
Houston, TX	(152 sites)	Atlanta, GA	(91 sites)

– Los Angeles, California had more Hispanics living in communities with uncontrolled toxic waste sites than any other metropolitan area in the United States.
– Approximately half of all Asian/Pacific Islanders and American Indians lived in communities with uncontrolled toxic waste sites.
– Overall, the presence of uncontrolled toxic waste sites was highly pervasive. More than half of the total population in the United States resided in communities with uncontrolled toxic waste sites.

MAJOR CONCLUSIONS AND RECOMMENDATIONS

The findings of the analytical study on the location of commercial hazardous waste facilities suggest the existence of clear patterns which show that communities with greater minority percentages of the population are more likely to be the sites of such facilities. The possibility that these patterns resulted by chance is virtually impossible, strongly suggesting that some underlying factor or factors, which are related to race played a role in the location of commercial hazardous waste facilities. Therefore, the Commission for Racial Justice concludes that, indeed, race has been a factor in the location of commercial hazardous waste facilities in the United States.

The findings of the descriptive study on the location of uncontrolled toxic waste sites suggest an inordinate concentration of such sites in Black and Hispanic communities, particularly in urban areas. This situation reveals that the issue of race is an important factor in describing the problem of uncontrolled toxic waste sites. We, therefore, conclude that the cleanup of uncontrolled toxic waste sites in Black and Hispanic communities in the United States should be given the highest possible priority.

These findings expose a serious void in present government programs addressing racial and ethnic concerns in this area. This report, therefore, strongly urges the formation of necessary offices and task forces by federal, state and local governments to fill this void. Among the many recommendations of this report we call special attention to the following:

– We urge the President of the United States to issue an executive order mandating federal agencies to consider the impact of current policies and regulations on racial and ethnic communities.

– We urge the formation of an Office of Hazardous Wastes and Racial and Ethnic Affairs by the U.S. Environmental Protection Agency. This office should insure that racial and ethnic concerns regarding hazardous wastes, such as the cleanup of uncontrolled sites, are adequately addressed. In addition, we urge the EPA to establish a National Advisory Council on Racial and Ethnic Concerns.

– We urge state governments to evaluate and make appropriate revisions in their criteria for the siting of new hazardous waste facilities to adequately take into account the racial and socioeconomic characteristics of potential host communities.

RESULTS

This section summarizes the major findings of both studies: the analysis of race and the location of commercial hazardous waste facilities and the descriptive study on the racial composition of communities with uncontrolled toxic waste sites. The first study found that the group of residential ZIP code areas with the highest number of commercial hazardous waste facilities also had the highest mean percentage of residents who belong to a racial and ethnic group. Conversely those residential ZIP codes with no waste facilities had a lower proportion of racial and ethnic residents.

Specifically, in communities with one operating commercial hazardous waste facility the mean minority percentage of the population was approximately twice that of communities without facilities (24 percent vs. 12 percent). In communities with two or more operating commercial hazardous waste facilities or one of the five largest landfills, the mean minority percentage of the population was more than three times that of communities without facilities (38 percent vs. 12 percent).

The analysis also revealed that mean household income and the mean value of owner-occupied homes were not as significant as the mean minority percentage of the population in differentiating residential ZIP codes with lesser numbers of hazardous waste facilities versus those with greater numbers and the largest landfills. After controlling for regional differences and urbanization, the mean value of owner-occupied homes in a community was a significant discriminator but less so than the minority percentage of the population.

In summary, the results of the discriminant analysis tests revealed that the minority percentage of the population in relation to the presence of commercial hazardous waste facilities was statistically very significant. The percentage of community residents that belong to a racial and ethnic group was a stronger predictor of the level of commercial hazardous waste activity than was household income, the value of homes, the number of uncontrolled toxic waste sites or the estimated amount of hazardous wastes generated by industry.

The descriptive study, which focused on closed or uncontrolled toxic waste sites, found their presence in American communities to be highly pervasive. This study found that more than half of the population in the United States lived in residential ZIP code areas with one or more uncontrolled toxic waste sites. The study also found that three out of every five Black and Hispanic Americans lived in communities with uncontrolled toxic waste sites. This figure represents more than 15 million Blacks and 8 million Hispanics. Approximately 2 million Asian/ Pacific Islanders and 700,000 American Indians lived in such communities.

****

Robert D. Bullard, ''Anatomy of Environmental Racism and the Environmental Justice Movement,'' in Confronting Environmental Racism: Voices from the Grassroots 17-19 (Robert D. Bullard, ed., 1993)

Whether by conscious design or institutional neglect, communities of color in urban ghettos, in rural ''poverty pockets,'' or on economically impoverished Native-American reservations face some of the worst environmental devastation in the nation. Clearly, racial discrimination was not legislated out of existence in the 1960s. While some significant progress was made during this decade, people of color continue to struggle for equal treatment in many areas, including environmental justice. Agencies at all levels of government, including the federal EPA, have done a poor job protecting people of color from the ravages of pollution and industrial encroachment. It has thus been an up-hill battle convincing white judges, juries, government officials, and policymakers that racism exists in environmental protection, enforcement, and policy formulation.

The most polluted urban communities are those with crumbling infrastructure, ongoing economic disinvestment, deteriorating housing, inadequate schools, chronic unemployment, a high poverty rate, and an overloaded health-care system. Riot-torn South Central Los Angeles typifies this urban neglect. It is not surprising that the ''dirtiest'' zip code in California belongs to the mostly African-American and Latino neighborhood in that part of the city. In the Los Angeles basin, over 71 percent of the African-Americans and 50 percent of the Latinos live in areas with the most polluted air, while only 34 percent of the white population does. This pattern exists nationally as well.

Income alone does not account for these above-average percentages. Housing segregation and development patterns play a key role in determining where people live. Moreover, urban development and the ''spatial configuration'' of communities flow from the forces and relationships of industrial production which, in turn, are influenced and subsidized by government policy. There is widespread agreement that vestiges of race-based decisionmaking still influence housing, education, employment, and criminal justice. The same is true for municipal services such as garbage pickup and disposal, neighborhood sanitation, fire and police protection, and library services. Institutional racism influences decisions on local land use, enforcement of environmental regulations, industrial facility siting, management of economic vulnerability, and the paths of freeways and highways.

People skeptical of the assertion that poor people and people of color are targeted for waste-disposal sites should consider the report the Cerrell Associates provided the California Waste Management Board. In their 1984 report, *Political Difficulties Facing Waste-to-Energy Conversion Plant Siting*, they offered a detailed profile of those neighborhoods most likely to organize effective resistance against incinerators. The policy conclusion based on this analysis is clear. As the report states:

> All socioeconomic groupings tend to resent the nearby siting of major facilities, but middle and upper socioeconomic strata possess better resources to effectuate their opposition. Middle and higher socioeconomic strata neighborhoods should not fall within the one-mile and five-mile radius of the proposed site.

Where then will incinerators or other polluting facilities be sited? For Cerrell Associates, the answer is low-income, disempowered neighborhoods with a high concentration of nonvoters. The ideal site, according [to] their report, has nothing to do with environmental soundness but everything to do with lack of social power. Communities of color in California are far more likely to fit this profile than are their white counterparts.

Those still skeptical of the existence of environmental racism should also consider the fact that zoning boards and planning commissions are typically stacked with white developers. Generally, the decisions of these bodies reflect the special interests of the individuals who sit on these boards. People of color have been systematically excluded from these decisionmaking boards, commissions, and governmental agencies (or allowed only token representation). Grassroots leaders are now demanding a shared role in all the decisions that shape their communities. They are challenging the intended or unintended racist assumptions underlying environmental and industrial policies.

****

Christopher Boerner *et al.*, Environmental Justice? 4-6 (1994)

The first major criticism of the present research centers on the definition of the term "community." Defining minority communities as those areas where the percentage of nonwhite residents exceeds that of the entire population means that a community may be considered "minority" even if the vast majority of its residents are white. Based on this methodology, for example, Staten Island—home of the nation's largest landfill—is considered a minority community even though over 80 percent of its residents are white. In fact, Staten Island is the "whitest" of New York City's five boroughs.

A second, but related, problem is that these studies ignore population densities. Merely citing the proportion of minority or low-income residents in a given host community does not provide information about how many people are actually exposed to environmental harms. For example, given that blacks presently comprise approximately 16 percent of the nation's population, a host community of 1,000 residents, 20 percent of whom are black, would be considered "minority," while a host community of 6,000 residents, 15 percent of whom are black, would not. By overlooking population density, the studies fail to point out that more blacks (900 versus 200) would be exposed to the pollution in the second, "non-minority" community, than in the first.

In addition to the problems associated with proportionality and population density, the environmental justice studies . . . often define the affected area in geographic terms that are too broad. Much of the prior research is based on ZIP-code areas, which are frequently large units established by the U.S. Postal Service. As a result, the data likely suffer from what statisticians call "aggregation errors." That is to say, the studies reach conclusions from the ZIP-code data which would not be valid if a smaller, more consistent geographic unit were examined. A recent study released by the Social and Demographic Research Institute at the University of Massachusetts, Amherst (UMass) confirms that an analysis of census tracts — small geographic units with relatively fixed boundaries — yields strikingly different results.[11]

The UMass study compared the social and demographic characteristics of census tracts that contain commercial TSDFs with those tracts that do not have TSDFs. Contrary to conventional wisdom, the UMass researchers found that the percentage of minorities living in neighborhoods with commercial facilities is no greater than in areas without such facilities. Indeed, in the 25 largest metropolitan areas studied, commercial hazardous waste facilities are slightly more likely to be in industrial neighborhoods with a *lower* percentage of minorities and a *higher* percentage of white working-class families. According to Douglas L. Anderton, director of the UMass project, "We looked at smaller neighborhood areas and found that facilities are more often located in census tracts that are white working-class industrialized neighborhoods. Even other census tracts nearest to those with facilities had no higher percentage of minorities." The results of the UMass study — the most comprehensive analysis of environmental justice to date — cast serious doubt on much of the [earlier] research.

A third flaw in the existing environmental justice studies is that they imply rather than explicitly state the actual risk presented by commercial TSDFs. While the research attempts to disclose the prevalence of commercial waste plants in poor and minority communities, there is no corresponding information about the dangers associated with

---

[11] Douglas Anderton, *et al.*, "Hazardous Waste Facilities: 'Environmental Equity' Issues in Metropolitan Areas," (Amherst: Social and Demographic Research Institute, University of Massachusetts and Northeast Regional Environmental Public Health Center) published in Evaluation Review, Vol. 18, No. 2, April 1994, pp. 123-140.

living near such facilities. The regulatory requirements regarding the building and operation of industrial and waste facilities in the United States are among the most stringent of any industrialized country in the world. These requirements, along with the voluntary efforts of industry, significantly reduce the noxious emissions of commercial waste plants and other facilities.

Moreover, health risks are a function of actual exposure, not simply proximity to a waste facility. The environmental justice advocates' claims of negative health effects are not substantiated by scientific studies. In fact, many of the legislative proposals to combat environmental inequities may result in greater harm to minority and poor residents than the emissions from noxious facilities themselves. By reducing the incentives for businesses to locate in poor and minority areas, these measures may exacerbate local problems of poverty and unemployment – conditions far more unhealthy than the minute risks associated with waste disposal facilities and industrial plants.

Finally, existing research on environmental justice fails to establish that discriminatory siting and permitting practices caused present environmental disparities. While the studies match the location of industrial and waste facilities with the current socioeconomic and race characteristics of the surrounding neighborhoods, they do not consider community conditions *when the facilities were sited*. Furthermore, they fail to explore alternate or additional explanations for higher concentrations of minority and low-income citizens near undesirable facilities. Thus, none of the studies prove that the siting process actually caused the disproportionate burden that poor and minority communities purportedly now bear. [T]hese gaps leave open the possibility that other factors, such as the dynamics of the housing market, may lead minorities and the poor to move into areas of high industrial activity.

****

Benjamin A. Goldman *et al.*, Toxic Wastes and Race Revisited: An Update of the 1987 Report on the Racial and Socioeconomic Characteristics of Communities with Hazardous Waste Sites I, 13-18 (1994)

Despite growing national attention to the issue of "environmental justice," people of color today are even more likely than whites to live in communities with commercial hazardous waste facilities than they were a decade ago. The disproportionate environmental impacts first identified and documented in the 1987 report *Toxic Wastes and Race in the United States* have grown more severe.

Using data updated to 1993 from the 1990 U. S. Census and using ZIP codes as the units of comparison, this report finds a continued disturbing correlation between the location of hazardous waste facilities and communities where people of color live.

- Between 1980 and 1993, the concentration of people of color living in ZIP codes with commercial hazardous waste facilities increased from 25 percent to almost 31 percent of the average population around the facilities.
- In 1993, people of color were 47 percent more likely than whites to live near a commercial hazardous waste facility.

– As in 1980, the percentage of people of color in 1993 remains three times higher in areas with the highest concentration of commercial hazardous waste facilities than in areas without commercial waste facilities.

This report analyzes 530 commercial (or "off-site") hazardous waste treatment, storage and disposal facilities (TSDFs) in operation as of the early 1990s. As in the 1987 report, it does not include Superfund sites, facilities closed prior to the 1990s, on-site (non-commercial) hazardous waste facilities or municipal solid waste facilities in analyzing commercial TSDFs.

Changes from 1980 to 1993 could be due to a number of factors, including the migration, birth, or death of individuals, and the relocation, start-up, or closure of toxic waste facilities. While this analysis does not determine which of these factors may be most responsible for the significant changes, it demonstrates that the racial gap between communities with commercial toxic waste sites and those without has grown significantly. Different factors may be at work in different locations, requiring site-specific research, analysis, and action.

Varied public policy responses are required across the country to combat the complex causes of environmental injustice. Effective solutions need to include toxics use reduction, community revitalization, and community participation in decision making.

Numerous studies have been published since the 1987 *Toxic Wastes and Race in the United States* report examining various environmental disparities by race and income. A recent review of the empirical literature found that 63 out of 64 studies documented various environmental disparities by race or income, including the location of noxious facilities, toxic releases and exposures, ambient levels of air pollution, and environmental health effects (the exception was a study funded by the largest waste management firm, WMX Technologies Inc.).[12]

Existing research provides mixed evidence of the causes of demographic change in communities with waste facilities. A 1994 study by Professor Vicki Been of New York University, for example, looked at changes over time in selected communities with hazardous or solid waste facilities and found different factors were working in different cases. This study reexamined the results of two influential analyses that used 1980 census data and that were published in 1983, using census data from before and after the facilities in question were first sited.

Professor Been found that the Southeastern waste sites studied by the U.S. General Accounting Office were all in communities that originally had both high levels of poverty and predominantly African American populations (using only 1980 census data, the U.S. GAO found just 3 of the 4 sites were predominantly African American). She did

---

[12] [Ed.] The reference is to the University of Massachusetts study, which "was supported by a grant from Waste Management Incorporated, as sponsored by the Institute for Chemical Waste Management, to the Northeast Regional Environmental Public Health Center, University of Massachusetts." Douglas L. Anderton *et al.*, "Hazardous Waste Facilities: 'Environmental Equity' Issues in Metropolitan Areas," Evaluation Review, Volume 18, Number 2, at 123 (April 1994).

not find, however, that these communities became poorer or increased in African American percent of the population after the waste facilities were sited. Professor Been found that the Houston waste sites studied earlier by Professor Robert D. Bullard were originally in disproportionately African American communities, but they did not originally have disproportionately lower incomes. In this case, the percentages of African Americans rose and incomes fell after the solid waste facilities were sited. While different trends were observed in each case, Professor Been concluded that both evidenced a "disproportionate effect upon African Americans."

A study conducted in 1993 by Professor James T. Hamilton of Duke University found that counties with commercial facilities that planned reductions in hazardous waste capacity were significantly more white than those that planned to maintain or increase their capacity. These findings about capacity reductions suggest that closures may also be more likely in white communities, which would leave a disproportionate number of operating facilities in minority areas.

An award-winning 1992 *National Law Journal* investigation found that EPA is slower to clean up waste sites in minority communities, is less likely to remove abandoned wastes, and consistently levies lower fines on polluters in minority communities, averaging as little as a fifth of the fines in white communities for violations of the federal hazardous waste law (in contrast, no significant disparity in such fines was found for poor versus high-income communities). Stricter hazardous waste enforcement in white communities could contribute to waste handlers' locating, maintaining, or expanding operations more frequently in minority areas, while closing or scaling back operations in white communities where regulatory costs tend to be higher.

Sociologists at the University of Massachusetts at Amherst (UMass-Amherst) recently released an analysis of a data set quite similar to the one used here. Using census tract data for 1980 and 1990, these researchers reported evidence of economic decline in communities with commercial hazardous waste facilities, but no evidence of "white flight" from these areas. By claiming "there is no consistent, statistically significant pattern of racial or ethnic discrimination in the distribution of commercial TSDFs [hazardous waste treatment, storage, and disposal facilities]," this and previous work of the UMass-Amherst researchers challenge the basic findings of the 1987 *Toxic Wastes and Race* report.

The contrary findings of the UMass-Amherst work could be due to three important methodological design decisions these researchers have made, all of which are different from the design of this study. First, they did not use the entire U.S. as their comparison group, but rather only metropolitan areas or rural counties with commercial hazardous waste sites. Their rationale for omitting most areas of the country from their analysis is that they assume all areas that are currently without operating waste facilities "are not feasible sites for TSDFs." The effect of this decision, however, is to increase significantly the percent [of] people of color in their control areas, which reduces the likelihood [of] finding any statistically significant racial disparities.

Second, the UMass-Amherst researchers did not examine disparities for all people of color as a group, but rather only separately for blacks and Hispanics. This decision leaves out eleven percent of the people of color population in the U. S., including all Asian and Native Americans. Moreover, if people of color are more likely to be neighbors in the areas that host waste sites, then this decision would also reduce the likelihood of finding any statistically significant racial disparities.

Third, they did not use ZIP code areas as their geographic unit of analysis, but rather U.S. Census tracts, which may on average be smaller. Numerous other studies have also used census tracts as the geographic unit of analysis; the bulk of these studies, however, did find significant disproportionate impacts by race. When the UMass-Amherst authors combined census tracts to create larger local areas, they too found racial disparities – even more significant disparities than those reported in the original 1987 report. Their results suggest that there may be a complex pattern of white enclaves within black areas with waste facilities. Since they also found that the white enclaves had higher levels of industrial employment, their findings suggest that there may be an imbalance between the distribution of beneficial employment effects (only in the white enclaves) and potentially adverse environmental effects (in both the white enclaves and surrounding black areas) of commercial hazardous waste sites and associated industries. This imbalance may further compound the perceptions of environmental injustice associated with these facilities.

It is interesting to note that even with these significant differences in research design, the UMass-Amherst results may be reinterpreted similarly to the results of this study. The black percent of the population in areas with commercial waste sites increased 2.5 times faster than in their comparison areas (up 18% in TSDF tracts versus 7% in non-TSDF tracts). The authors failed to note this result or test its statistical significance. They were limited in their ability to examine these changes over time, however, because the U.S. Census Bureau did not prepare rural tract data prior to 1990. As a consequence, the authors omitted rural sites, which comprise more than 10 percent of all commercial hazardous waste facilities, from their 1980 base year.

The last study that is relevant to the examination of changes in waste site distributions over time is the original 1987 *Toxic Wastes and Race* report itself. In addition to examining operating commercial hazardous waste facilities, this study examined the distribution of older, inactive hazardous waste sites. The racial disparities surrounding these older closed sites, which are far more prevalent than operating ones (over 30,000 compared with over 500), were not as pronounced as those found for the newer, operating facilities. No further research has yet been published that explores why there appear to be greater racial disparities for communities with the newer operating facilities than for those with the older closed sites. However, the combination of these earlier results with the changes from 1980 to 1993 documented here suggests that the trends over time of increasing racial disparities may apply more broadly to the universe of closed and on-site toxic waste facilities. More research would be needed to confirm or disprove this hypothesis.

The commercial waste management industry represents only a fraction of the toxic hazards posed by all of industry (it manages less than 3 percent of the toxic wastes generated in the U.S.). No one has examined, for example, whether the patterns of disproportionate impact that have been found in this industry are greater or less than those that may be found in any other industry. The trends demonstrated in this study raise the question of whether other industries imitate the pattern of disproportionate impact in the commercial hazardous waste management industry.

Since the 1970s, it has generally become more difficult to site new hazardous waste management facilities. This trend is due in part to greater public awareness of the hazards associated with toxic wastes, as well as stricter laws regarding hazardous waste management. While this study provides an initial breakdown of toxic waste facility siting in communities of color by start year of the facility, further research should be conducted to determine if there is a link between increased public knowledge of risk, increased difficulty in siting hazardous facilities and increased disparities by race and income. As more communities work to block siting, those communities with less political and economic power may be forced to shoulder more of the burden.

Since the original *Toxic Wastes and Race* report was released by the United Church of Christ in 1987, the issue of environmental injustice in toxic waste facility siting has received growing attention. This 1994 study is the first to examine and find significant national changes in environmental disparities that have occurred since environmental justice became a national issue. The findings in this report suggest that growing awareness of these issues has not yet had the effect of reducing racial disparities in the distribution of toxic waste sites. The opposite may in fact be occurring.

This report has not determined the root causes of this pattern. No matter what the causes, the distribution of these facilities shows how some of the most hazardous inefficiencies of our economy can also pose significant social inequities. Approximately 84 percent of toxic waste generators rely on the services of the hazardous waste management business sector to handle some or all of their most dangerous wastes. If public policies can help improve production practices throughout the much larger universe of hazardous waste generators, then the disproportionate environmental impacts observed here would eventually become history. Toxic use reduction must be the foundation of any effective policy response to this issue.[13] This involves planning for the elimination of certain production practices that rely on toxic inputs, increasing the use of other technologies that use non-toxic substitutes, and converting the human and capital resources that are necessary for this transition.

Other types of public policies could be used to leverage the present demands for commercial hazardous waste management services toward accomplishing these economic transitions. Firms that are granted permits to use or operate commercial waste facilities

---

[13] [Ed.] *See generally* Sanford J. Lewis *et al.*, From Poison to Prevention: A White Paper on Replacing Hazardous Waste Facility Siting with Toxics Reduction (1989); National Toxics Campaign, Fighting Toxics: A Manual for Protecting Your Family, Community, and Workplace (Gary Cohen and John O'Connor, eds. 1990); Luke W. Cole, "Empowerment as the Key to Environmental Protection: The Need for Environmental Poverty Law," 19 Ecology Law Quarterly 619, 645 (1992) ("Grassroots activists around the country, by stopping the siting of toxic waste disposal facilities in their communities, have begun to force industry to move from pollution *control* to pollution *prevention*. Put simply, because so few waste disposal sites exist, and because it is so difficult to establish new sites, the price of toxic waste disposal has risen to the point where companies are seriously working to replace toxic inputs to their manufacturing processes in order to minimize the production of toxic waste.").

could be required to meet toxic use reduction performance goals, or provide certain beneficial services or resources that mitigate the negative impacts that such facilities can have on host communities.

Effective toxic use reduction policies also need to employ a variety of incentives and penalties to facilitate the needed changes in our economy. Within the environmental justice context, a key component of such public policy must be the pro-active development of environmentally sustainable economic opportunities within the very communities that are now suffering from disproportionate environmental impacts. This involves investments in infrastructure, education and training, and small business development. Without this approach, communities with the least wherewithal will inevitably be forced by necessity to trade off environmental health for economic subsistence.

Lasting solutions will require the active, full participation of affected citizens along with government and industry. This means involving affected parties from the outset in the formation, implementation, and evaluation of policy responses. Accomplishing effective public participation in communities at risk will require changing the ways in which governments and businesses have traditionally interacted with people in these locations — with special consideration and resources devoted to disadvantaged populations that face disproportionate risks. These problems are too complex to leave them simply to the technical experts. Appropriate solutions will necessarily differ from one community to the next, reflecting the varied local conditions and needs of communities. These needs will be addressed only if the policy making process is driven by successful citizen participation at all levels of government.

Finally, public policies designed to combat disproportionate environmental impacts must be informed about the complexity of historical forces that have yielded the observed inequities. If, for example, legislative changes help well-organized communities shut down undesirable facilities, the result may be increased racial disparities as the only facilities that remain in operation will be in relatively disempowered areas. If right-to-know laws provide equal access to toxics data, this information will likely be used more aggressively by better equipped and better educated communities, again yielding increased disparities unless specific technical resources and training are targeted to less advantaged areas. If programs are created to compensate communities for accepting toxic wastes with monetary benefits, then unwanted facilities are likely to be further channeled to the most economically distressed locales. These concerns should not be interpreted, however, as an argument not to implement such policies. Instead, the communities which are less-organized politically, and have less formal education and employment opportunities will require additional resources if they are truly to benefit from and be empowered by well-intentioned legislation of the types described above.

****

Notes

1. Faced with these conflicting studies, it is surely difficult for the student of environmental law to reach firm conclusions about the extent of the distributional injustice associated with siting patterns nationally. On the one hand, there is an almost intuitive

sense – backed by common observations – that the charge of maldistribution in environmental burdens and risks is valid.[14] On the other hand, an objective and detailed look at the evidence may raise some questions about the politically popular sentiment of widespread injustice in this realm. In short, the student – like the environmental lawyer in practice – is challenged to understand the evidence as honestly as possible, while maintaining personal sensitivity to the broader realities of poverty and racial discrimination in the United States.

2. Even if the data were to convincingly demonstrate no racially discriminatory effects in the siting of facilities, should the legal system nonetheless respond to the widespread public belief that such effects exist? In other words, if many people believe there is a problem, is that enough of a basis for corrective measures to be developed at the legislative or executive branch levels? Are there any ways in which the judiciary properly can respond to such public perceptions?

3. Ultimately how important are national or regional data regarding environmental inequity in the work of an environmental lawyer who is addressing a particular siting controversy? What are the strategic benefits and risks for the lawyer and client in linking any one such controversy to the broader "movement"? What are the benefits and risks of not doing so?

3. Definitions and Causes

Benjamin F. Chavis, Jr., "Foreward", in Confronting Environmental Racism: Voices from the Grassroots 3 (Robert D. Bullard, ed., 1993)

Environmental racism is racial discrimination in environmental policymaking. It is racial discrimination in the enforcement of regulations and laws. It is racial discrimination in the deliberate targeting of communities of color for toxic waste disposal and siting of polluting industries. It is racial discrimination in the official sanctioning of the life-threatening presence of poisons and pollutants in communities of color. And, it is racial discrimination in the history of excluding people of color from the mainstream environmental groups, decisionmaking boards, commissions, and regulatory bodies.

****

---

[14] In an article by Professor Tarlock on the relationship between "ecosystem integrity" and claims of poor and minority communities for equity, he candidly stated his premise "that there is *some undetermined degree* of legitimacy to these claims . . . ." A. Dan Tarlock, "Environmental Protection: The Potential Misfit between Equity and Efficiency," 63 University of Colorado Law Review 871, 875 (1992).

Robert D. Bullard, "Environmental Equity: Examining the Evidence of Environmental Racism," Land Use Forum, Winter 1993, at 6.

The term "environmental racism" encompasses any policy, practice, or directive that, *intentionally or unintentionally,* differentially impacts or disadvantages individuals, groups, or communities based on race or color. It also refers to exclusionary and restrictive practices that limit participation by people of color in decision-making boards, commissions, and staffs.

****

Gerald Torres, "Introduction: Understanding Environmental Racism," 63 University of Colorado Law Review 839-841 (1992)

Obviously, the term is divided into two parts, but environmental clearly modifies racism. Thus in order to make sense of the term one must have a clear idea of what it means to call a particular activity racist. Racism is one of those terms in contemporary political usage that is highly charged and which has an apparent meaning. The meaning of the term is clouded to the extent that it gets broadly applied to a variety of activities and outcomes. But racism has been and should be a term of special opprobrium. We risk having the term lose its condemnatory force by using it too often or inappropriately. By calling something racist when another term might suffice risks subjecting the word to a kind of verbal inflation.

The term racism draws its contemporary moral strength by being clearly identified with the history of the structural oppression of African-American and other people of color in this society. Thus both individual acts as well as official acts may be racist, but not every activity that is analyzable according to its racial distinctiveness may in fact be racist. I count as racism those activities which support or justify the superiority of one racial group over another. When seeking to determine whether an activity is racist, the one characteristic that must be present is one of domination and subordination. The action need not necessarily be one of intention, but it may be both intentional and dominating.

In analyzing environmental policies and activities from the perspective of their subordinating impact on racial groups we are led inexorably to examine the distributional impacts of environmental rules. We can examine both the substantive distributional impact of those rules in practice and the substantive blindness in the production of rules that lead to racially subordinating activities. In short, when we label an environmental practice as an example of environmental racism we are saying that the predictable distributional impact of that decision contributes to the structure of racial subordination and domination that has similarly marked many of our public policies in this country. We might also be saying that excluding considerations of racial impact in constructing the substantive environmental rules contributes to the subordination of identifiable racial groups. In many cases, this subordinating impact will be the result of an unconscious process. Regardless of how unconscious the process may be, however, if the perception of the affected class is that the impact is fundamentally racially targeted then we must assume that the substantive effect is racist unless a better or different justification can be put forward.

This means that environmental regulations, like all other actions of the regulatory state, have a potential racial impact and the willful ignorance of that impact may itself be racist even if the intention behind the rule had no racial animus at all. Environmental regulations, like other regulations, gain no immunity by claiming color-blindness where a demonstrable impact on subordinated racial groups exists.

[R]ejecting the color-blindness approach in order to take racial impact into account is not racist. Instead, at this stage in the historical development of our country taking into account the racially distributional impacts of a particular regulation may be required in order to avoid perpetuating a racially identifiable set of harms. Self-awareness of the racial dimension of environmental policy is especially important to the extent that the United States' environmental regulations and regulatory processes are taken to be the model for the rest of the world. Racism is not a phenomenon that is restricted to the United States, rather it is a phenomenon that is endemic to human society across the globe. Once a racially disparate impact is made clear, pleading ignorance is no defense.

****

Bunyan Bryant and Paul Mohai, "Environmental Racism: Reviewing the Evidence," in Race and the Incidence of Environmental Hazards 163-64, 169 (Bunyan Bryant and Paul Mohai, eds., 1992)

The United Church of Christ report concluded that it is "virtually impossible" that the nation's commercial hazardous waste facilities are distributed disproportionately in minority communities merely by chance, and that underlying factors related to race, therefore, in all likelihood play a role in the location of these facilities. Among others these factors include: 1) the availability of cheap land, often located in minority communities and neighborhoods; 2) the lack of local opposition to the facility, often resulting from minorities' lack of organization and political resources as well as their need for jobs; and 3) the lack of mobility of minorities resulting from poverty and housing discrimination that traps them in neighborhoods where hazardous waste facilities are located. The United Church of Christ report noted that these mechanisms and resulting inequitable outcomes represent institutionalized forms of racism. When the report was released, Dr. Benjamin F. Chavis, Jr., termed the racial biases in the location of commercial hazardous waste facilities as "environmental racism."

The striking findings and the scope of the United Church of Christ study suggest that environmental racism is not confined to hazardous waste alone. A major objective of our investigation was, therefore, to document the existence of other studies which have used systematic data to examine the social distribution of pollution and to determine whether the evidence from these studies, taken together, demonstrates a consistent pattern of environmental racism.

A question that is often raised is whether the racial bias in the distribution of environmental hazards is simply a function of poverty. That is, rather than race per se, is it not poverty that affects the distribution of environmental hazards? And are not minorities disproportionately impacted simply because they are disproportionately poor? Classical economic theory would predict that poverty plays a role. Because of limited income and wealth, poor people do not have the financial means to buy out of polluted neighborhoods and into environmentally more desirable ones. Also, land values tend to be cheaper in poor neighborhoods and are thus attractive to polluting industries that seek to reduce the costs of doing business. However, housing discrimination further restricts the mobility of minorities. Also, because noxious sites are unwanted (the "NIMBY" syndrome) and because industries tend to take the path of least resistance, communities with little political clout are often targeted for such facilities. These communities tend to be where residents are unaware of the policy decisions affecting them and are unorganized and lack resources for taking political action; such resources include time, money, contacts, knowledge of the political system, and others. Minority communities are at a disadvantage not only in terms of availability of resources but also because of underrepresentation on governing bodies when location decisions are made. Underrepresentation translates into limited access to policy makers and lack of advocates for minority interests. Taken together, these factors suggest that race has an additional impact on the distribution of environmental hazards, independent of income.

In summary, review of the 15 studies which have examined the distribution of environmental hazards by income and race indicates both a class and racial bias. Furthermore, that the racial bias is not simply a function of poverty alone also appears to be born out by the data. All but one of the 11 studies which have examined the distribution of environmental hazards by race have found a significant bias. In addition, in five of the eight studies where it was possible to assess the relative importance of race with income, racial biases have been found to be more significant. Noteworthy also is the fact that all three studies which have been national in scope and which have provided both income and race information have found race to be more importantly related to the distribution of environmental hazards than income. Taken together, these findings thus appear to support the assertion of those who have argued that race has an additional effect on the distribution of environmental hazards that is independent of class.

****

Note

1. What do you believe is gained by labeling siting patterns as "environmental racism"? Is anything lost by doing so?

2. For what purposes might it be important to distinguish whether disproportionate siting of polluting facilities in disadvantaged communities is the result of intentional choices rather than a reflection of disregard for the characteristics of those communities?

For what purposes might it be important to distinguish conclusively whether race is a variable separate from poverty in the intentional or inadvertent maldistribution of these facilities?

As the readings in Chapter 7(C), *infra*, demonstrate, these distinctions clearly can have great significance in litigation. What bearing could each of these distinctions have on the formulation of legislative and regulatory policy aiming at more equitable siting outcomes? Consider how these distinctions are treated in the materials on Presidential and Congressional responses presented in Chapter 7(D), *supra*.

****

Robert D. Bullard, Dumping in Dixie: Race, Class, and Environmental Quality 11-12 (1990)

Environmental elitism has been grouped into three categories: (1) *compositional elitism* implies that environmentalists come from privileged class strata, (2) *ideological elitism* implies that environmental reforms are a subterfuge for distributing the benefits to environmentalists and costs to nonenvironmentalists, and (3) *impact elitism* implies that environmental reforms have regressive distributional impacts.

Impact elitism has been the major sore point between environmentalists and advocates for social justice who see some reform proposals creating, exacerbating, and sustaining social inequities. Conflict centered largely on the "jobs versus environment" argument. Imbedded in this argument are three competing advocacy groups[:] (1) *environmentalists* are concerned about leisure and recreation, wildlife and wilderness preservation, resource conservation, pollution abatement, and industry regulation, (2) *social justice advocates'* major concerns include basic civil rights, social equity, expanded opportunity, economic mobility, and institutional discrimination, and (3) *economic boosters* have as their chief concerns maximizing profits, industrial expansion, economic stability, laissez-faire operation, and deregulation.

Economic boosters and pro-growth advocates convinced minority leaders that environmental regulations were bad for business, even when locational decisions had adverse impacts on the less advantaged. Pro-growth advocates used a number of strategies to advance their goals, including public relations campaigns, lobbying public officials, evoking police powers of government, paying off or co-opting dissidents, and granting small concessions when plans could be modified. Environmental reform proposals were presented as prescriptions for plant closures, layoffs, and economic dislocation. [Commentators] referred to this practice as "job blackmail."

Pro-growth advocates have claimed the workplace is an arena in which unavoidable trade-offs must be made between jobs and hazards: If workers want to keep their jobs, they must work under conditions that may be hazardous to them, their families and their community. Black workers are especially vulnerable to job blackmail because of the threat of unemployment and their concentration in certain types of occupations. The black workforce remains overrepresented in low-paying, low-skill, high-risk blue collar and service occupations where there is a more than an adequate supply of replacement labor. Black workers are twice as likely to be unemployed as their white counterparts. Fear of unemployment acts as a potent incentive for many blacks to stay in and accept jobs they know are health threatening.

****

Richard J. Lazarus, "Pursuing 'Environmental Justice': The Distributional Effects of Environmental Protection," 87 Northwestern University Law Review 787, 806-08, 810-12 (1993)

The structural roots of environmental inequities are very likely the same as those that produce other forms of racially disproportionate impacts. In this regard, environmental protection is yet another expression of a more widespread phenomenon.

The most obvious and common sources are racist attitudes—whether in blatant, thinly guised, or unconscious forms—that pervade decision-making. Historically, racial minorities have been persistent victims of racial discrimination in this country. Although de jure discrimination is now forbidden by law, racist attitudes, both consciously and unconsciously held, are plainly widespread. These range from hostility toward racial minorities, to false stereotypical judgments about members of that class. People routinely make stereotypical judgments about others based on racial identity. While such judgments may appear less threatening than those based on outright racial hostility, their adverse impact may in fact be more potent because of their pervasiveness and masked nature, which makes them so difficult to identify and root out.

Therefore, it is not at all unlikely—and, indeed, it may be probable—that racist attitudes and false stereotypes have influenced various decisions relating to environmental protection. Certainly there is no reason to suppose that environmental protection is somehow immune from actions based on societal attitudes that, while widely condemned, are nevertheless prevalent. For example, the use of environmental quality to support racially exclusionary zoning practices would seem to confirm that suspicion.

In any event, powerful vestiges of generations of racist policies plainly persist, and these vestiges are self-perpetuating. As a result of racist laws and attitudes extending back to slavery itself, racial minorities today possess significantly less power both in the marketplace and in the political fora, particularly at the national level. This absence of economic and political clout makes it much more probable that racial minorities will receive an unfavorably disproportionate share of the benefits (less) and burdens (more) of living in society, including those associated with environmental protection. For example, the absence of economic resources compounds the threat of distributional inequities associated with environmental protection. Because those with fewer economic resources are disproportionately affected adversely by across-the-board price increases, such individuals are also more likely to suffer greater economic harm when prices rise because of environmental protection. The economic plight of many minority communities also confines [their] members as a practical matter to the less healthy residential areas which are, for that reason, less expensive to live in. This confinement also creates the potential for what some have dubbed "environmental blackmail," as the community finds it more difficult to oppose the siting of a facility that, notwithstanding significant environmental risks, offers the possibility of immediate short-term economic relief.

Lawmakers inevitably seek the path of least political resistance when allocating the burdens of environmental protection. In deciding both from where and to whom environmental risks should be reallocated in the treatment and prevention of pollution, lawmakers are necessarily more responsive to the demands of constituents who possess the greatest political influence. This phenomenon is evident in the siting of other undesirable public projects and private undertakings, ranging from highways to prisons. There is no obvious theoretical reason why the same forces should not be at work when the object of the project or undertaking is pollution control.[15]

There exist, moreover, factors more endemic to environmental law itself that may exacerbate distributional inequities likely present in the context of any public welfare law. These factors suggest more than the disturbing, yet somewhat irresistible thesis, that the distributional dimension of environmental protection policy likely suffers from the same inequities that persist generally in society. They suggest the far more troubling, and even less appealing, proposition that the problems of distributional inequity may in fact be more pervasive in the environmental protection arena than they are in other areas of traditional concern to civil rights organizations, such as education, employment, and housing.

Indeed, it is the absence of that minority involvement so prevalent in the more classic areas of civil rights concern that may render the distributional problem worse for environmental protection. Minority interests have traditionally had little voice in the various points of influence that strike the distributional balances necessary to get environmental protection laws enacted, regulations promulgated, and enforcement actions initiated. The interest groups historically active in the environmental protection area include a variety of mainstream environmental organizations representing a spectrum of interests (conservation, recreation, hunting, wildlife protection, resource protection, human health), as well as a variety of commercial and industrial concerns. Until very recently, if at all, the implications for racial minorities of environmental protection laws have not been a focal point of concern for any of these organizations.

****

---

[15] [Ed.] For a discussion of the development of a Los Angeles citizens group formed to oppose the siting of a succession of projects affecting their community – a state prison, a pipeline, and then a hazardous waste incinerator, *see* Gabriel Gutierrez, "Mothers of East Los Angeles Strike Back," in Unequal Protection: Environmental Justice and Communities of Color 220 (Robert D. Bullard, ed. 1994).

Note

If siting decisions are based on intentional targeting of racial minority areas, then it would seem logical, as Lazarus asserts, that distributional inequity in environmental impacts would be at least as pervasive as inequity in areas such as education, employment, and housing. Similarly, as he also observes, the historic non-participation of minority groups in environmental policymaking then may well have allowed environmental inequities that are even more severe than in those other realms. Are Lazarus's views still persuasive if, as noted in the Torres statement on environmental racism, the distribution of environmental burdens "contributes to the structure of racial subordination and domination" as a result of unconscious or "color-blind" attitudes, rather than intentional discrimination?

****

Vicki Been, "Locally Undesirable Land Uses in Minority Neighborhoods: Disproportionate Siting or Market Dynamics?" 103 Yale Law Journal 1383, 1384-92, 1406 (1994)

The environmental justice movement contends that people of color and the poor are exposed to greater environmental risks than are whites and wealthier individuals. The movement charges that this disparity is due in part to racism and classism in the siting of environmental risks, the promulgation of environmental laws and regulations, the enforcement of environmental laws, and the attention given to the cleanup of polluted areas. To support the first charge—that the siting of waste dumps, polluting factories, and other locally undesirable land uses (LULUs) has been racist and classist—advocates for environmental justice have cited more than a dozen studies analyzing the relationship between neighborhoods' socioeconomic characteristics and the number of LULUs they host. The studies demonstrate that those neighborhoods in which LULUs are located have, on average, a higher percentage of racial minorities and are poorer than non-host communities.[16] That research does not, however, establish that the host communities

---

[16] The literature seems to assume that a siting pattern is disproportionate whenever the percentage of people of color in a host community is higher than the percentage of people of color in the nation's population or in the population of non-host communities. This measure of proportionality is simplistic. First, it ignores the density of population within a neighborhood. Assume, for example, that a siting decision maker is faced with two communities, one of which has 5000 people, 12% of whom are people of color, while the other has 1000 people, 20% of whom are people of color. Assume also that the percentage of people of color in the nation is 12%. Under the measure of proportionality generally used in the literature, the LULU would be disproportionately sited if it were placed in the second community, even though that choice would expose fewer people of color to the LULU than would the other site. A better measure of proportionality would take into account the number of people affected by a siting, rather than just focusing on the percentage of the affected population that is composed of people of color. Second, this measure of proportionality can be misleading if studies do not provide information about how far the distribution of the population within the host neighborhoods deviates from thenational distribution. By describing a community as "minority" or "poor" whenever the percentage of people of color or poor in the community exceeds that of the population as a whole, a study using this measure of proportionality could classify a LULU as disproportionately sited even if it is located in a predominantly white neighborhood in which the population variance from the national distribution is statistically insignificant.

were disproportionately minority or poor at the time the sites were selected. Most of the studies compare the *current* socioeconomic characteristics of communities that host various LULUs to those of communities that do not host such LULUs. This approach leaves open the possibility that the sites for LULUs were chosen fairly, but that subsequent events produced the current disproportion in the distribution of LULUs. In other words, the research fails to prove environmental justice advocates' claim that the disproportionate burden poor and minority communities now bear in hosting LULUs is the result of racism and classism in the *siting process* itself.

In addition, the research fails to explore an alternative or additional explanation for the proven correlation between the current demographics of communities and the likelihood that they host LULUs. Regardless of whether the LULUs originally were sited fairly, it could well be that neighborhoods surrounding LULUs became poorer and became home to a greater percentage of people of color over the years following the sitings. Such factors as poverty, housing discrimination, and the location of jobs, transportation, and other public services may have led the poor and racial minorities to "come to the nuisance" – to move to neighborhoods that host LULUs – because those neighborhoods offered the cheapest available housing. Despite the plausibility of that scenario, none of the existing research on environmental justice has examined how the siting of undesirable land uses has subsequently affected the socioeconomic characteristics of host communities. Because the research fails to prove that the siting process causes any of the disproportionate burden the poor and minorities now bear, and because the research has ignored the possibility that market dynamics may have played some role in the distribution of that burden, policymakers now have no way of knowing whether the siting process is "broke" and needs fixing. Nor can they know whether even an ideal siting system that ensured a perfectly fair initial distribution of LULUs would result in any long-term benefit to the poor or to people of color.

[T]he existing research . . . is insufficient to determine whether the siting process placed LULUs in neighborhoods that were disproportionately minority or poor at the time the facility was opened, whether the siting of the facility subsequently drove host neighborhoods to become home to a larger percentage of people of color or the poor than other communities, or whether both of these phenomena contributed to the current distribution of LULUs. [M]arket dynamics may play a significant role in creating the disparity between the racial composition of host communities and that of non-host communities. In [one study], LULUs initially were sited somewhat disproportionately in poor communities and communities of color. After the sitings, the levels of poverty and percentages of African-Americans in the host neighborhoods increased, and the property values in these neighborhoods declined. Accordingly, the study suggests that while siting decisions do disproportionately affect minorities and the poor, market dynamics also play a very significant role in creating the uneven distribution of the burdens LULUs impose. Even if siting processes can be improved, therefore, market forces are likely to create a pattern in which LULUs become surrounded by people of color or the poor, and consequently come to impose a disproportionate burden upon those groups. [Another], smaller study, on the other hand, finds a correlation between neighborhood demographics and initial siting decisions, but finds no evidence that market dynamics are leading the poor or people of color to "come to the nuisance."

The siting of a LULU can influence the characteristics of the surrounding neighborhood in two ways. First, an undesirable land use may cause those who can afford to move to become dissatisfied and leave the neighborhood. Second, by making the neighborhood less desirable, the LULU may decrease the value of the neighborhood's property, making the housing more available to lower income households and less attractive to higher income households. The end result of both influences is likely to be that the neighborhood becomes poorer than it was before the siting of the LULU.

The neighborhood also is likely to become home to more people of color. Racial discrimination in the sale and rental of housing relegates people of color (especially African-Americans) to the least desirable neighborhoods, regardless of their income level. Moreover, once a neighborhood becomes a community of color, racial discrimination in the promulgation and enforcement of zoning and environmental protection laws, the provision of municipal services, and the lending practices of banks may cause neighborhood quality to decline further. That additional decline, in turn, will induce those who can leave the neighborhood — the least poor and those least subject to discrimination — to do so.

The dynamics of the housing market therefore are likely to cause the poor and people of color to move to or remain in the neighborhoods in which LULUs are located, regardless of the demographics of the communities when the LULUs were first sited. As long as the market allows the existing distribution of wealth to allocate goods and services, it would be surprising indeed if, over the long run, LULUs did not impose a disproportionate burden upon the poor. And as long as the market discriminates on the basis of race, it would be remarkable if LULUs did not impose a disproportionate burden upon the poor.

By failing to address how LULUs have affected the demographics of their host communities, the current research has ignored the possibility that the correlation between the location of LULUs and the socioeconomic characteristics of neighborhoods may be a function of aspects of our free market system other than, or in addition to, the siting process. It is crucial to examine that possibility. Both the justice of the distribution of LULUs and the remedy for any injustice may differ if market dynamics play a significant role in the distribution.

If the siting process is primarily responsible for the correlation between the location of LULUs and the demographics of host neighborhoods, the process may be unjust under current constitutional doctrine, at least as to people of color. Siting processes that result in the selection of host neighborhoods that are disproportionately poor (but not disproportionately composed of people of color) would not be unconstitutional because the Supreme Court has been reluctant to recognize poverty as a suspect classification.[17] A siting process motivated by racial prejudice, however, would be unconstitutional. A

---

[17] *San Antonio Indep. Sch. Dist. v. Rodriguez,* 411 U.S. 1 (1973). Under various theories of fairness, e.g., John Rawls' Difference Principle, however, such discrimination against the poor would be unfair and would justify changes in the siting process. John Rawls, A Theory of Justice 75-83 (1971).

process that disproportionately affects people of color also would be unfair under some statutory schemes and some constitutional theories of discrimination.

On the other hand, if the disproportionate distribution of LULUs results from market forces which drive the poor, regardless of their race, to live in neighborhoods that offer cheaper housing because they host LULUs, then the fairness of the distribution becomes a question about the fairness of our market economy. Some might argue that the disproportionate burden is part and parcel of a free market economy that is, overall, fairer than alternative schemes, and that the costs of regulating the market to reduce the disproportionate burden outweigh the benefits of doing so. Others might argue that those moving to a host neighborhood are compensated through the market for the disproportionate burden they bear by lower housing costs, and therefore that the situation is just. Similarly, some might contend that while the poor suffer lower quality neighborhoods, they also suffer lower quality food, housing, and medical care, and that the systemic problem of poverty is better addressed through income redistribution programs than through changes in siting processes.

Even if decisionmakers were to agree that it is unfair to allow post-siting market dynamics to create disproportionate environmental risk for the poor or minorities, the remedy for that injustice would have to be much more fundamental than the remedy for unjust siting *decisions*. Indeed, if market forces are the primary cause of the correlation between the presence of LULUs and the current socioeconomic characteristics of a neighborhood, even a siting process radically revised to ensure that LULUs are distributed equally among all neighborhoods may have only a short-term effect. The areas surrounding LULUs distributed equitably will become less desirable neighborhoods, and thus may soon be left to people of color or the poor, recreating the pattern of inequitable siting. Accordingly, if a disproportionate burden results from or is exacerbated by market dynamics, an effective remedy might require such reforms as stricter enforcement of laws against housing discrimination, more serious efforts to achieve residential integration, changes in the processes of siting low and moderate income housing, changes in programs designed to aid the poor in securing decent housing, greater regulatory protection for those neighborhoods that are chosen to host LULUs, and changes in production and consumption processes to reduce the number of LULUs needed.

Information about the role market dynamics play in the distribution of LULUs would promote a better understanding of the nature of the problem of environmental injustice and help point the way to appropriate solutions for the problem. Nonetheless, market dynamics have been largely ignored by the current research on environmental justice.

Significant evidence suggests that LULUs are disproportionately located in neighborhoods that are now home to more of the nation's people of color and poor than other neighborhoods. Efforts to address that disparity are hampered, however, by the lack of data about which came first – the people of color and poor or the LULU. If the neighborhoods were disproportionately populated by people of color or the poor at the time the siting decisions were made, a reasonable inference can be drawn that the siting process had a disproportionate effect upon the poor and people of color. In that case, changes in the siting process may be required.

On the other hand, if, after the LULU was built, the neighborhoods in which LULUs were sited became increasingly poor, or became home to an increasing percentage of people of color, the cure for the problem of disproportionate siting is likely to be much more complicated and difficult. The distribution of LULUs would then look more like a confluence of the forces of housing discrimination, poverty, and free market economics. Remedies would have to take those forces into account.

****

Notes

1. Starting this analysis from the possibility that initial siting decisions were fair, Professor Been explores the independent role of subsequent housing market dynamics and their racially discriminatory effects. In doing so, however, she does not seek to refute the possibility that siting processes are indeed skewed at the outset to discriminate against people of color or against poor people. Consider whether the following statement is making the same points as Been or different ones.

> Poor people and minorities do not attract polluters. Low-cost land does, and for the same reasons that it attracts poor people. In many industrial regions, including most of those now condemned as physical evidence of "environmental racism" (the South Side of Chicago, for example) minorities were given their first access to the American Dream. Employers motivated by the capitalist urge to make a profit (and regardless of their personal racism or lack thereof) hired the best workers they could find at the lowest wage they could pay. Regardless of our current attitudes, this often worked to the advantage of the economically disadvantaged, especially minorities, giving them their first opportunity to enter the industrial workplace. In addition, workers preferred to live close to their place of employment, for obvious reasons. Thus, they moved to the general vicinity of the pollution sources. This resulted in one of the largest internal migrations in American history as rural-born African Americans moved to industrial urban areas. Even with the pollution and the low wage jobs, their lives were greatly improved. How ironic that the very economic forces that eventually spawned the civil rights movement would be condemned as environmental racism today.

Testimony of Kent Jeffreys, Director of Environmental Studies for the Competitive Enterprise Institute, before the House Committee on the Judiciary, Subcommittee on Civil and Constitutional Rights, March 3, 1993.

2. In view of the strongly pejorative and emotional character of a charge of racism, it should not be surprising that scholars and activists have wrestled with various possible meanings of the term and interpretations of the data. It also should not be surprising

that some veteran attorneys for environmental groups have resisted the accusation that their work has improperly ignored or exacerbated the plight of poor and minority Americans.[18] Consider the following comments of one such lawyer:

> Recognition of the pluralistic nature of our political system is essential and the coupling of environmental advocacy with that of racial and social justice raises the questions of whose concepts of racial and social justice must be accepted. I do not want to restrict my associates in environmental advocacy to those who agree with me on issues of racial or social justice. Environmental advocacy, therefore, justifies and indeed requires coalitions of people and groups with different views of what constitutes racial and social justice, much the same as advocacy of racial and social justice, however defined, requires coalitions which may include advocates of road systems to carry logging trucks into most wilderness areas. This may be one aspect of the very "pluralism" which is the antithesis of racism.

David Sive, " An Environmentalist's View of Environmental Racism," Newsletter of the ABA Standing Committee on Environmental Law, Volume 12, No. 1, pp. 5-6 (1992-93).

3. In Chapter 1 we considered the relationship between a lawyer's personal values and his or her duty to the client. We asked whether a choice simply to provide vigorous and honest representation to any client within the adversary process, regardless of one's own appraisal of the environmental values at stake, was morally sufficient. The environmental justice movement may suggest a double-barreled, negative answer to that question: Not only would it be irresponsible to undertake environmental law work without consideration of underlying environmental values, but the immorality of such work would be further aggravated by failure to consider the effects of the work on the welfare of poor and minority communities.

Sive's statement seems to suggest a middle ground – that an environmental lawyer should work to promote environmental values, but need not take on simultaneous responsibility for correcting other social evils as well. In that view, it would be enough for an attorney to pursue environmental protection objectives, without also trying to resolve broader social inequities. This view seems informed by, and perhaps comforted by, the following type of observation:

> The distributional inequities that appear to exist in environmental protection are undoubtedly the product of broader social forces. To be sure, features endemic to the ways in which environmental protection laws have historically been fashioned may have exacerbated the problem in the environmental context. But the origins

---

[18] "The environmental movement of the 1970s finds much of its structural roots and moral inspiration in the civil rights movement that preceded it. Hence, for many in the environmental community, the notion that the two social movements could be at odds was very likely too personally obnoxious to be believed or even tolerated." Richard J. Lazarus, "Pursuing 'Environmental Justice': The Distributional Effects of Environmental Protection," 87 Northwestern University Law Review 787, 789 (1993).

of the resulting distributional disparities do not begin, nor will they end, with reforming either the structure of environmental protection decisionmaking or the substance of environmental law itself.

Richard J. Lazarus, "Pursuing 'Environmental Justice': The Distributional Effects of Environmental Protection," 87 Northwestern University Law Review 787, 825 (1993).

Which of these three positions – neutral advocacy, broad advocacy for both environmental protection and distributive justice, or narrower environmental protection advocacy – do you believe best states the environmental attorney's responsibility to society?

Is there also a fourth possibility, analogous to the common medical maxim "First do no harm."[19] Would it be sufficient for the environmental lawyer, whether embracing neutral advocacy or narrower environmental protection advocacy, to make an additional commitment to "do no harm," i.e., purposely to avoid aggravating any existing maldistribution of environmental or economic disadvantages? With your answer to this question in mind, reconsider Problem (e) in Chapter 1(B)(1), *supra*.

4. If you were asked to represent an electric utility company in its efforts to have a relatively pristine river dammed for electric energy production purposes, would you let your own concern for preservation of the river, and for the related animal and plant life, affect your decision? Would your decision by affected by evidence that construction of the dam would raise energy prices for consumers generally and would have an especially severe impact on low-income consumers?[20]

Conversely, if you were asked to represent a local environmental group opposing the dam, would your decision be influenced by evidence that construction of the dam actually would decrease energy costs for poor consumers? Would your decision be affected by the likelihood that if you are successful in blocking the construction of the dam on this river, the project nonetheless is quite likely to be constructed on an equally pristine river in a different part of the state?

C. Legal Tools and Strategies

1. Linkage to Concepts of Justice

This section examines legal tools and strategies that may have some effectiveness in resolving inequities in facility siting. Ideally any attempt at rectifying such inequities

---

[19] *See* The Medical Works of Hippocrates 35 (John Chadwick *et al.*, trans. 1950) ("Practise two things in your dealing with disease: either help or do not harm the patient."); Respectfully Quoted 163 (Suzy Platt ed. 1989) ("'To do no harm' is echoed in two places in the Hippocratic Oath . . . .").

[20] *See generally* Kenneth A. Manaster, "Energy Equity for the Poor: The Search for Fairness in Federal Energy Assistance Policy," 7 Harvard Environmental Law Review 371 (1983) ("The greatest hardships from increased energy costs fall on poor people and on those who live on fixed incomes, such as retired persons.").

should be based upon a clear understanding of the concept of justice that is to be achieved in a given instance. Without such understanding, it would seem to be impossible to determine whether a just outcome has been reached. Alternatively, of course, even in the absence of clear articulation of pertinent concepts of justice, it could be argued that the environmental disadvantages already suffered by poor and minority communities are so indisputably great and unwarranted that *any* reduction or avoidance of added environmental burdens for them must be presumed to contribute to a more just distribution of such burdens. Would you agree with that alternative argument as a basis for the development of new siting policies and procedures?

As the next reading indicates, one legal scholar recently has responded in depth to the lack of focused efforts by environmental justice advocates and legislators to articulate such concepts.

****

Vicki Been, "What's Fairness Got To Do With It? Environmental Justice and the Siting of Locally Undesirable Land Uses," 78 Cornell Law Review 1001, 1006, 1008-09, 1084-85 (1993)

The various legislative solutions to the problem of disproportionate siting reflect different concepts about why disproportionate siting is wrong, and about what would constitute "fair" siting. The differences are not surprising. Calls for environmental justice are essentially calls for "equality" and . . . "equality in the end is a rhetorical device that tends to persuade precisely by virtue of 'cloak[ing] strongly divergent ideas over which people do in fact disagree.'" Advocates of environmental justice have wisely chosen to advance general concepts of equality, rather than endanger their coalition by attempting to specify the precise content of "justice," "equity" or "fairness."

This article takes a hard look at the content of the goal of environmental justice. It explores what various conceptions of equality would look like if translated into concrete siting programs. Attempts to specify what "virtue words" such as fairness, justice, and equity mean often unmask many vices: this project is no exception. In the context of siting, all the leading theories of fairness encounter significant philosophical and pragmatic objections.

[This article] advances seven theoretical arguments about why disproportionate siting is unfair, and explores what fairness would mean under each of those theories. First, fair siting could mean that LULUs are evenly apportioned among all neighborhoods. Second, fair siting might mean that neighborhoods in which a LULU is not sited must compensate the host community for its damages. Third, fairness could require "progressive siting," in which wealthier neighborhoods receive a greater number of LULUs, or pay a greater share of a host community's damages, than poor or minority neighborhoods. Fourth, fairness could demand that all communities receive an equal number of vetoes that they could use to bid against other communities for the privilege of excluding a LULU. Fifth, fair siting might require that those who benefit from a LULU bear its cost. Sixth, fairness could simply require that the siting process involve no intentional discrimination against people of color. Seventh, fair siting could require a process that shows "equal concern and respect" for all neighborhoods.

[D]ifferent theories of fairness should lead to radically different siting programs, so that one cannot adequately evaluate a fair siting proposal without first identifying its underlying conception of fairness.

[U]nless the notion of fair siting is tied to a specific theory of fairness, it is impossible to determine what fair siting will look like in practice or to determine how effective proposals to ensure fair siting will be.

[H]ard looks at seemingly incontestible concepts lead to better solutions than even the most enthusiastic agreement with vacuous slogans.

****

Been's article examines the seven suggested approaches in great detail, linking them to a broad range of concepts of justice, including virtually all of the those presented in Chapter 2, *supra*.[21] For example, equal apportionment corresponds to the first egalitarian formula of distributive justice presented by Bowie, i.e., "For any commodity *x*, the just method of distribution is to divide *x* equally." Similarly, the compensation approach inclines toward Bowie's second egalitarian formula, whereby "the just distribution of income is the equal distribution," even though "individual commodities may be distributed unequally."[22] Been also observes, "Under general notions of compensatory justice, a neighborhood would be considered fully compensated if it believes itself no worse off from the compensated siting than from no siting." *Id.* at 1041.

Been also links the progressive siting approach to "backward-looking" "compensatory justice," which we have encompassed within the corrective justice heading. She thus offers the following as one rationale for requiring advantaged neighborhoods to bear more of the burden of LULUs than poor and minority areas: "advantaged neighborhoods should bear more of the LULU burden in order to redress or remedy past discrimination against poor and minority neighborhoods." *Id.* at 1047. Another possible, "forward-looking" rationale she considers is based on the Rawls concept of distributive justice, whereby progressive siting would be just so long as it yielded "the greatest benefit, or the least burden, to the least advantaged." *Id.* at 1048. Turning to what Chapter 2 categorizes as procedural justice, particularly as expressed in the Hart excerpt

---

[21] An additional approach that Been acknowledges in passing is utilitarianism, which she observes is generally associated in the siting context "with the assumption that fairness concerns are satisfied if the site chosen for a LULU is the scientifically and technologically best site possible. This application of utilitarianism assumes that the designation of the technologically best site is a value-free, apolitical process, and that all appropriate measures of utility are included in the technological siting criteria. Neither assumption bears any relationship to the reality of the siting process." Vicki Been, "What's Fairness Got To Do With It? Environmental Justice and the Siting of Locally Undesirable Land Uses," 78 Cornell Law Review 1001, at 1027 n. 133 (1993).

[22] "Compensation schemes are academics' favorite solutions to siting problems." *Id.* at 1040.

there, Been notes, "The most obvious theory of fairness as process would assert that a distribution is fair as long as it results from a process that was agreed upon in advance by all those potentially affected." *Id.* at 1060. She also identifies procedural justice among the bases for some of the other approaches she examines, such as the avoidance of intentional discrimination and the treatment of all neighborhoods with equal concern and respect. *Id.* at 1060-64.

Pursuing this type of linkage between specific meanings of justice and approaches to siting, consider how the various concepts introduced in Chapter 2 might be promoted by the tools and strategies presented in the following materials. For example, using two more of the formulas presented by Bowie, do siting practices harm "certain values to which [all people] have an equal right," or do those practices infringe upon everyone's "equal right to a minimum standard of living"? What are those values or the specific components of that right? Which of the legal tools examined here best protect them?

****

2. The Need for Legal Action

The following readings relate to the need for legal action to be taken with respect to the siting problems. In some of these statements, it appears to be assumed that no real solution is possible without strong regulatory measures being instituted and legally enforceable rights being delineated. Other positions address economic or other nonlegal approaches that wholly or partially might redress the perceived injustices without legal tools being brought to bear.[23]

****

Robert D. Bullard, "Environmentalism with Justice," in Confronting Environmental Racism: Voices from the Grassroots 203 (Robert D. Bullard, ed., 1993)

[T]he environmental justice framework attempts to uncover the underlying assumptions that contribute to and produce unequal protection. This framework brings to the surface the blunt questions of "who gets what, why, and how much." To be specific, the environmental justice framework:

- incorporates the principle of the right of all individuals to be protected from environmental degradation:

---

[23] It has been forcefully argued that waste facility siting decisions are "political and economic," rather than legal; that grassroots activism, rather than law, is the effective response to environmental racism; and that, therefore, environmental justice legal strategy must be "firmly grounded in, and secondary to, a community-based political organizing strategy." Luke W. Cole, "Remedies for Environmental Racism: A View from the Field," 90 Michigan Law Review 1991, 1996-1997 (1992). *See also* Luke W. Cole, "Empowerment as the Key to Environmental Protection: The Need for Environmental Poverty Law," 19 Ecology Law Quarterly 619 (1992).

- adopts a public health model of prevention (that eliminates the threat before harm occurs) as the preferred strategy;
- shifts the burden of proof to polluters/ dischargers who do harm, discriminate, or who do not give equal protection to racial and ethnic minorities, and other "protected" classes; and
- redresses disproportionate impact through "targeted" action and resources.

****

Vicki Been, "What's Fairness Got To Do With It? Environmental Justice and the Siting of Locally Undesirable Land Uses," 78 Cornell Law Review 1001, 1006, 1015 (1993)

[T]he evidence . . . is more than sufficient to require legislatures to address the fairness of the distribution of LULUs. The question of how to site LULUs fairly is important regardless of whether siting decisions in the past were discriminatory in either intent or effect. Whatever their race or class, the residents of any area chosen today to host a LULU legitimately may ask, "Why us?" The government must find a satisfactory answer, or else society will find itself in the stalemate that planners refer to as the "build absolutely nothing anywhere near anybody" (BANANA) dilemma.

****

Christopher Boerner et al., Environmental Justice? 7-10, 18-19 (1994)

The crux of environmental justice concerns is that particular communities (chiefly those composed of people of color and the poor) have been forced to bear disproportionately the external costs of industrial processes. It follows, then, that one way of achieving environmental equity is to ensure that these costs are borne proportionately by all who reap the benefits of these processes. Policymakers have essentially three options for accomplishing this: eliminate all external costs of industrial processes; allocate the external costs evenly through the political system; or fairly compensate the individuals who bear these costs.

Option One: Waste Elimination – The "BANANA" Principle

Many environmental justice advocates appear to desire above all else the complete elimination of pollution, so that *no* community has to bear the external costs of industrial processes. The following statements by prominent environmental justice advocates indicate that, indeed, total waste elimination is their ultimate goal:

We're not saying to take the incinerators and the toxic waste dumps out of our communities and put them in white communities – we're saying they should not be in anybody's community. (Rev. Ben Chavis, executive director of the National Association for the Advancement of Colored People and executive director of the Commission for Racial Justice of the United Church of Christ)

A model environmental justice framework . . . incorporates the principle of the "right" of *all* individuals to be protected from environmental degradation [and] adopts a public health model of prevention (elimination of the threat before harm occurs as the preferred strategy . . . (Dr. Robert Bullard, director of research at the Center for Afro-American Studies, UCLA [sic]; author of *Invisible Houston* and *Dumping in Dixie)*

Environmental Justice demands the cessation of the production of all toxins, hazardous wastes, and radioactive materials . . . . (The Sixth Principle of Environmental Justice adopted by the First People of Color Environmental Leadership Summit, October 27, 1991)

"Environmental Justice" means we'd like to see no community impacted. If you say the word "equity" it sounds that if we all share the problem, it's OK. (Charles Lee, director of the Special Project on Toxic Injustice of the United Church of Christ)

Clearly, the real cry of these environmental justice advocates goes beyond the familiar "NIMBY," or "not in my backyard." These activists are instead crying "BANANA" – "build absolutely nothing anywhere near anything" or, as one activist insisted, "NOPE" – "not on planet earth." Eliminating pollution would, of course, eradicate the problem of disproportionately distributed pollution, which is at the heart of the environmental justice issue. However, a moment of reflection on the BANANA principle, or a policy of complete waste elimination, reveals that such a policy is ultimately not feasible. Manufacturers simply cannot reduce pollution indefinitely without eliminating many valuable products and processes that Americans take for granted. In most cases, phasing out particular products is much more costly to society than accepting and treating the pollution required to create those products.

Option Two: Allocate External Costs Politically

Because some pollution is inevitable in modern society, policymakers may decide that the best way to ensure environmental justice is to have the government determine which communities must host undesirable facilities. Of course, a purely political solution in which those in power simply decide where polluting and waste facilities should be located is probably not in the best interest of minorities and the economically disadvantaged, as these groups are typically underrepresented in the government. Most of those who advocate a political solution to environmental inequity argue instead for the establishment of nebulous legal and regulatory mechanisms that would force those in power to allocate pollution "fairly."

Unfortunately, it is difficult to pinpoint exactly what those legal and regulatory mechanisms are. For the most part, environmental justice advocates have refrained from proposing concrete political remedies for environmental inequities. While activists often suggest creating various offices, councils, and task forces, they rarely detail how these entities should influence the pollution allocation process. Though they advocate increased community involvement in siting decisions, they have yet to propose specific policies delineating how public participation is to be improved. Instead, environmental justice advocates have primarily sought to advance general concepts of equality, not wishing to endanger their coalition by specifying the precise methods of achieving "justice," "equity," and "fairness."

The few legal and regulatory mechanisms that have been suggested to remedy disparity in the allocation of pollution essentially boil down to two devices: (1) regulations which would directly limit or prohibit future industrial siting in minority and disadvantaged communities; and 2) penalties against presently active polluting and waste facilities that disproportionately impact minorities. The threat of such penalties, of course, would motivate facility owners to relocate or site future developments in non-minority neighborhoods.

Option Three: Compensate Individuals Who Bear External Costs

A third possible solution to the environmental justice problem attempts to eliminate the primary environmental injustice by "diffusing" the concentrated external costs associated with a polluting or waste facility and compensating those individuals disproportionately impacted by the facility. There are primarily two methods of accomplishing both cost-diffusion and residential compensation. If the beneficiaries of a facility are somewhat well-defined (e.g., the residents of a multi-county region which shares a waste disposal facility), the government may use tax revenue from those citizens to compensate the host community. Alternatively, the undesirable facility could directly compensate local residents, reflecting the cost of doing so in the prices charged to those who utilize the facility's services. Under both schemes, the external costs of the facility are dispersed so that all who share its benefits also bear a portion of its costs. The fundamental difference between the two scenarios is that, in the former case, beneficiaries bear these costs wearing their taxpayer hat, while in the latter, they do so as consumers.

Economists refer to the procedure embodied in the second scheme as the "internalization" of external costs. Under such an approach, facility owners view the adverse local impact of their plant as part of their operating costs and charge prices sufficiently high to cover these costs—using the added revenue to compensate local residents. As a result, pollution costs are no longer borne solely by those "outside" of the production process, but are, instead, equitably dispersed among those utilizing the facility's services. Due to offsetting benefits, residents of the host communities are, on balance, no worse off than they would be without the facilities.

The specific nature of these "offsetting benefits" may vary and should remain in the purview of the potential host community and the prospective developer. Some possible forms of compensation include direct payments to affected landowners, "host fees" which are paid into a community's general revenue fund and may be used to finance a variety of public projects or to lower property taxes, grants for improving local health-care delivery and education, and the provision of parks and other recreational amenities.

The compensation package offered Brooksville, Mississippi, for example, included direct payments to the community's general revenue fund, financing for roadway construction and maintenance, the establishment of various civic and research centers, and an agreement to provide the community with significant employment opportunities. In a less elaborate compensation agreement, Modern Landfill Inc. offered each citizen of Lewiston, New York $960 annually for a 20-year period for the right to expand a landfill.

With respect to the environmental justice issue, compensating individuals for bearing external costs entails at least two significant advantages. Most importantly, compensation approaches are "just." Encouraging those who benefit from a facility to provide compensation to host communities alleviates the fundamental injustice in the status quo and achieves a fairer distribution of environmental burdens and benefits. Unlike the proposed political remedies for environmental inequities, which merely attempt to alter the socio-economic and racial makeup of adversely affected communities, compensation assures that *no community* (regardless of race and income status) bears more than its fair share of environmental costs.

Of course, many may argue that it is immoral to "pay" individuals to expose themselves to health risks. These critics, however, should keep in mind the regulatory environment in which compensation agreements are negotiated. As discussed earlier, present environmental standards are designed to guarantee a base level of environmental protection in which the exposure risks associated with polluting and waste facilities are quite minor. For example, the risk of developing cancer from living at the fence line of a properly constructed solid waste landfill is estimated to be one in a million. To put this in perspective, that's 30 times greater than the chance of being struck by lightning.

While many environmental justice advocates recite anecdotes of health problems in communities adjacent to licensed facilities and claim that present regulations are inadequate, they can produce no scientific data tying these alleged health problems to pollution exposure. However, should such a relationship be established, the appropriate policy response would be to raise the inadequate environmental standards, not to prevent individuals and facility owners from negotiating compensation agreements. As long as environmental regulations guarantee minimal risk, there should be no moral difficulties with compensating individuals for voluntarily accepting the nuisances associated with waste and polluting facilities.

****

Robert D. Bullard, Dumping in Dixie: Race, Class, and Environmental Quality 90-91, 95 (1992)

The application of economic trade-offs in mitigating siting disputes and environmental conflict continues to generate a wide range of discussion. This is especially true for poor communities that are beset with rising unemployment, extreme poverty, a shrinking tax base, and decaying business infrastructure. Compensation, economic incentives, and monetary inducements have been proposed, for example, as an alternative strategy to minimize citizen opposition to hazardous-waste facility siting. The endorsement of trade-offs usually emanates from city leaders rather than from local citizens.

How does compensation operate? Communities that agree to host hazardous-waste and other noxious facilities are promised compensation in an amount such that the perceived benefits outweigh the risks. The economic inducements are supposed to serve as equalizers to redress the imbalance. There are, however, risks and potential inequities associated with a policy of compensation. Moreover, the moral question surrounding compensation has not been adequately addressed. That is, should society pay those who are less fortunate to accept risks that others can afford to escape? Obviously, compensation taken to the extreme can only exacerbate existing environmental inequities. The Commission for Racial Justice cautions us on the use of compensation in environmental disputes: "To advance such a theory [compensation] in the absence of the consideration of the racial and socioeconomic characteristics of host communities and existing forms of institutionalized racism leaves room for potential discrimination."

No doubt, compensation will continue to be used as a lure in the facility siting war, particularly in controversial siting proposals. Some communities are more amenable to accepting economic trade-offs, while others will aggressively resist such proposals. Compensation is not a panacea for mitigating public opposition and resistance to facilities that are perceived by local citizens to be a risk to their health and safety, community image, and economic investment (property values).

****

Notes

1. What concepts of justice underlie the respective views of Boerner and Bullard?

2. A number of assumptions appear to be inherent in the respective positions of Boerner and Bullard with respect to the compensation approach. For example, Boerner explicitly grounds his view on the assumption that "environmental regulations guarantee minimal risk." Would Bullard agree with that assumption? Would you? If you disagree with it, what is the evidentiary basis for your disagreement?

If in fact risk is "minimal," what injury is there to compensate for at all? Is compensation then only a symbolic or political gesture? Is it simply a means of acknowledging the voluntary acceptance of "the nuisances associated with waste and polluting facilities?"

****

3. State Siting Statutes

In response to the growing need for hazardous waste treatment and disposal facilities around the nation, many states have enacted legislation to facilitate the siting and construction of such facilities. One important aspect of these state statutes is their attempt to confront the common likelihood of local opposition to placement of waste facilities within a particular community. As the following materials and cases illustrate, the states have taken a variety of approaches to this complex legislative task.

In examining these state efforts, consider the range of statutory objectives—both environmental and nonenvironmental—being pursued. Consider also whether statutes such as these are helpful or harmful to poor and minority communities attempts' to secure fairer treatment in siting decisions. In other words, who benefits and who suffers from statutory attempts to override local community control of siting in order to promote statewide or national objectives?

****

Rachel D. Godsil, "Remedying Environmental Racism," 90 Michigan Law Review 394, 403-08 (1991)

States have set up hazardous waste management programs either to overcome local hostility or bypass local opposition. States tend to take one of three general approaches to this problem: super review, site designation, and local control. Some states have also statutorily mandated the incentives approach, compelling developers to compensate local communities that host hazardous waste facilities.

1. Super Review: The Most Common Approach

Under the super review approach, a hazardous waste facility developer chooses a prospective site and applies for a permit with the authorizing agency, typically a state EPA or Department of Natural Resources. That agency will review the application and evaluate the environmental impact. Once the application satisfies the state's criteria, it is presented to a special administrative body appointed to quell the fears of the affected community.

States' environmental impact criteria differ, as do the complexity of their applications. Indiana demands that developers apply for a "certificate of environmental compatibility." An Indiana application must delineate the hydrogeological characteristics of the site, the proposed monitoring program, an environmental assessment, and an engineering plan. In Wisconsin, the developer waits until the Department of Natural Resources determines the site suitable—based on, among other things, topography, soils, geology and hydrogeology—before specifying details of the construction and monitoring plan. States also consider "soft criteria"—the effect of the site upon the community, as opposed to the effect on the environment. Michigan's statute requires, for example, an assessment of the impact of a site on the scenic, historic, and recreational aspects of an area.

If the proposed site meets the state's criteria, the application will be passed on to a special siting board. The special siting boards are usually made up of experts (geologists, chemical engineers, academics and state agency directors) and local representatives. The local representatives are temporary, representing districts proposed for facilities. The methods of choosing local representatives vary from state to state. In Iowa, the local representatives are chosen by the city council and county board of supervisors, while in New York they are chosen by the governor. Ohio and Connecticut do not have local representatives on the board, but instead hold public hearings to encourage local participation.

The super review approach attempts to add legitimacy to the siting process through the creation of special siting boards. The siting board is supposed to encourage informed debate and to create an opportunity for local community members to voice their concerns to experts rather than engage in reflexive opposition. All states that use this method, however, also have preemption clauses: if the board fails to eliminate local opposition, it can ignore the opposition. An aim of the super review approach is to minimize the issue of political expediency and emphasize environmental safety.

The super review method, however, fails to prevent discriminatory siting. Private developers still choose the sites. These developers have a cost incentive to choose sites with lower land values, which are typically inhabited by the poor, most often by poor minorities. Moreover, even if states preempt local land-use statutes, those opposing the site may pursue other methods to block the sites. Opponents of a facility can litigate, use their informal connections in state government to prevent the operation of a preemption statute, or resort to civil disobedience. Once developers realize that the super review approach will not fully assuage the NIMBY syndrome, they will continue to designate siting areas in poor, minority communities in order to prevent siting delays and save the expense of a protracted fight.

2. Site Designation

Under the site designation approach, rather than responding to the developer's selection, the state creates an inventory of possible sites. In three states, Massachusetts, Maryland, and Minnesota, an agency or board designates sites around the state for future hazardous waste facilities. Arizona designated one future site by statute, but otherwise follows a permit review process.

The Maryland plan requires the City of Baltimore, each county and each unincorporated municipality, to submit a list of suitable sites to the Maryland Environmental Service. The Service then evaluates the sites and compiles an inventory list. Maryland uses the super review approach concurrently. Developers must obtain a certificate of public necessity from the Hazardous Waste Facilities Siting Board, whose government-appointed members represent diverse public and private interests and hail from different regions of the state.

Minnesota created a Waste Management Board, which designates candidate sites for construction of disposal facilities, no two of which can be in a single county. The Board solicits proposals from potential developers and operators rather than local governments. After developing a list of potential sites, the Board asks local governments, metropolitan governments, and regional development commissions for comments. Minnesota's plan then provides for local ''project review committees'' for each candidate site, to encourage communication between local communities and state regulatory authorities, and to appease local concerns. The Board makes a final selection following an evaluation of the site and with the benefit of local participation.

This method offers more promise to ameliorate environmental racism than does the super review approach because the state, unlike [a] developer, is not motivated by profit. It therefore will be less likely to designate potential sites solely on the basis of the lowest land values. By taking a more comprehensive view of the sites, the state could ensure that no single area becomes overburdened.

The site designation approach is hardly infallible, however. For example, the Maryland plan, in which counties are required to designate *suitable* sites, may create an impetus for counties to select *unsuitable* sites, hoping to dissuade the Environmental Service from putting the county's sites on its inventory. [One commentator] suggests other syndromes which may prevent this method from successfully furthering equity – "Not In My Term Of Office" (NIMTOF) and "Not In My Election Year" (NIMEY): politicians from communities with political clout may lobby the agency to remove their district from the list. In addition, the community may litigate against the facility or otherwise try to delay the siting. The prospect of such delays may lead a harried agency to choose the community least able to sustain the NIMBY syndrome – the poor and minority community – rather than battle a more influential community.

3. Local Control

Only two states, California and Florida, continue to adhere to the local control approach. Under this approach, local land use regulations are not preempted by a state hazardous waste management plan. In other words, a locale can create strict land use regulations to block any hazardous waste site.

In California, local ordinances cannot be preempted by the state hazardous waste management plan – the state can never force a city to accept a hazardous waste site. The California statute states that "[n]o provision of this chapter shall limit the authority of any state or local agency in the enforcement or administration of any provision of law which it is specifically permitted or required to enforce and administer." The Florida statute is not absolute. If the Department of Environmental Regulation has issued a permit to a developer, but a local government determines a developer's plans to construct a hazardous waste facility conflict with its local rules, the developer may petition the governor and the cabinet for a variance. They will grant a variance only if the developer can establish, by clear and convincing evidence, that the facility will not have a "significant adverse impact" on the regional environment or economy.

This approach does nothing to allay the NIMBY syndrome. Indeed, the local approach condones it. Any locale can statutorily exclude hazardous waste facilities. When it becomes necessary to site such a facility, the state will have to find methods to coax a community to accept the facility. Minority communities tend to be more susceptible to states' coaxing mechanisms – the most typical being the incentives approach.

4. The Incentives Approach

Some states have begun to require compensation to host communities in an effort to eliminate local opposition.[24] The general notion is that developers or state taxpayers should compensate the community targeted for a hazardous waste facility because only that community incurs the costs of the facility while the entire state enjoys the benefits. Theoretically, the developer will be required to compensate the community for the social costs of the facility. This compensation, if it actually reflects the costs, may eliminate opposition to the facility and ensure that the facility will be built only if the benefits of building the facility outweigh the costs – finally internalized by the developer.

---

[24] [Ed.] Further discussion of the statutory approach based on compensation can be found at Kelly Michele Colquette *et al.*, "Environmental Racism: The Causes, Consequences, and Commendations," 5 Tulane Environmental Law Journal 153, 170-174 (1991).

In response, one commentator claims that the social costs of hazardous waste facilities have not proved compensable; instead, "offers of compensation have occasionally increased local opposition" when opponents of a proposed facility have perceived compensation as a bribe. Moreover, many civil rights activists reject the incentives approach as extortion and compensation as "blood money." Civil rights advocates recognize that the compensation may appeal to local politicians representing minority communities in dire need of revenues for basic services, but argue that wealthy communities should not be allowed to pay the disadvantaged to accept risks that the affluent can afford to escape.

****

Stablex Corporation v. Town of Hooksett, 122 N.H. 1091, 456 A.2d 94 (1982)

This is an appeal by the plaintiff, Stablex Corporation, from an adverse decision of the Superior Court disposing of its joint petition: (1) seeking a declaratory judgment, and (2) appealing a decision of the Town of Hooksett's Planning Board. For the reasons that follow, we reverse.

Since 1980, Stablex has been in the process of attempting to obtain State and local approval of its plan to construct a hazardous waste disposal facility in Hooksett. In its petition for declaratory judgment, Stablex challenged the legality of certain ordinances adopted by the Town of Hooksett, which required that any proposed hazardous waste facility be subject to a popular vote and therefore a potential local veto. Stablex claimed that such ordinances were barred by preemptive State and federal legislation relating to hazardous waste facilities. In the appeal portion of the petition, Stablex challenged the legality of a February 2, 1981, decision by the Hooksett Planning Board, in which Stablex's application for site-plan approval was denied.

FACTS

Since 1980, Stablex Corporation has held an option on land in Hooksett that is zoned industrial pursuant to the following provision of the Hooksett Zoning Ordinance:

"VII:B. *Permitted Uses.*

All types of manufacturing, processing, fabrication, assembly, freight, handling, warehousing and similar operations, including administration and research, provided such operations are so operated and noises, glare, heat, fumes, odors, and similar conditions are so controlled that they will not be obnoxious or injurious to adjoining property.

At approximately the time that it purchased its option on the land, Stablex approached town officials to make them aware of its interest in building a hazardous waste disposal facility on the site for the treatment, neutralization, and disposal of inorganic hazardous wastes.

Since 1979, anyone seeking to construct or operate a hazardous waste treatment facility in this State has had to secure prior State approval of the project under a complex regulatory scheme which is discussed below. Stablex began the process required for State approval in September 1980 by filing an application with the State to construct and operate a waste treatment facility. At the same time it submitted a duplicate copy of the application to the town for review by its planning board.

The State has not yet completed its review of Stablex's application. A series of public hearings and meetings conducted by the Hooksett Planning Board in 1980 and 1981, however, resulted in two significant actions by the town affecting Stablex's proposal.

First, on December 19, 1980, the town's board of selectmen presented, and a special town meeting adopted, a set of town ordinances alleged to have been enacted under the provisions of RSA 31:39 [New Hampshire Revised Statutes Annotated]. These ordinances provide in relevant part:

"BY-LAWS RESPECTING THE COLLECTION, PROCESSING, REMOVAL AND DISPOSAL OF HAZARDOUS WASTE MATERIAL – ARTICLE I
1. No privately owned or privately operated dump, storage place, or other facility primarily used for the collecting, receiving, processing, reprocessing, treatment, recovery, storage, disposal, or burying of hazardous waste shall be maintained within the Town of Hooksett, except by prior permission of the voters of the Town obtained in an annual or special town meeting.

ARTICLE III
1. No building shall be erected nor any land used for the primary purpose of collecting, receiving, processing, reprocessing, treating, recovering, or separating hazardous waste, except by prior permission of the voters of the Town obtained at an annual or special town meeting."

These ordinances clearly provided that notwithstanding State approval of a proposed hazardous waste facility, local approval in the form of a popular referendum, was required in order for such a facility to be built in the town.

Second, on February 2, 1981, the Hooksett Planning Board voted to deny Stablex's application for site-plan approval, basing its decision on two sections, articles I (preamble) and III F of the Hooksett Zoning Ordinance. The planning board took the position that insufficient information had been submitted to permit it to determine whether the proposed plant would be injurious to "the comfort, peace, enjoyment, health and safety of the community."

Stablex maintains that the town had no authority to enact ordinances requiring local popular approval of a hazardous waste facility because State and federal legislation enacted in 1979 and 1981 had clearly preempted this area of regulation. It follows that the actions of the Hooksett Planning Board would also be invalid if the claim of State and federal preemption prevails. Finally, Stablex argues that the town's actions, even if not barred by State preemption, nonetheless deprived it of its vested rights in property without due process of law. We need not address this argument in light of our holding that State legislation preempted the area of hazardous waste regulation.

The Regulatory Framework

The disposal of hazardous wastes has become a problem of enormous significance at both the State and national level. The uncontrolled disposal of such wastes is recognized as posing a most serious threat to public health and safety. In response to this threat, the Speaker of the New Hampshire House released a four-volume report in 1980 discussing hazardous waste problems on a State and national level as well as some existing and proposed legislative responses to those problems. This report notes that the United States Environmental Protection Agency (EPA) has estimated that approximately fifty-seven million metric tons of hazardous wastes are generated each year in the United States. The EPA estimates that ninety percent of these wastes are disposed of improperly. New Hampshire generates an estimated sixteen million gallons of hazardous chemical wastes each year.

Our State lacks any approved hazardous waste disposal facility. There are, however, eight known sites in New Hampshire where hazardous wastes have been illegally disposed of, the most notorious of which are located in Nashua, Epping, Kingston, and Raymond. Cleanup costs for these sites alone are estimated to be in the millions of dollars. State and federal hazardous waste legislation was thus enacted against a background that can only be termed a State and national emergency.

The Federal Regulations

In 1976, the United States Congress enacted Public Law 94-580, the Resource Conservation and Recovery Act of 1976 (RCRA), 42 U.S.C. §§ 6901-6987, which authorizes the EPA to promulgate national rules and regulations governing the identification, generation, storage, treatment, and disposal of hazardous wastes. Section 6925 of RCRA requires the administrator of the EPA to promulgate regulations pursuant to which any person owning or operating a hazardous waste treatment facility must acquire a permit. Such permits are to be issued only after a facility has satisfied the strict standards set forth in section 6924.

A fundamental assumption of the RCRA is that the individual States would continue to improve their own existing programs as well as develop new programs in conformity with the federal standards.

The 1979 New Hampshire Legislation

In 1979, the New Hampshire legislature enacted the State's first hazardous waste management program. *See* Laws 1979, ch. 347. Chapter 347 established an administrative body, the Bureau of Solid Waste Management, to which all permit applications had to be submitted, and which was empowered to administer the comprehensive State program. The bureau was granted rule-making authority, which it used to develop and promulgate the New Hampshire Hazardous Waste Rules, which became effective on June 3, 1981.

The 1981 Recodifications

In 1981, our legislature repealed the 1979 hazardous waste legislation, and recodified those sections as RSA chapter 147-A. RSA chapter 147-A re-establishes the Bureau of Solid Waste Management, giving it not only substantially the same powers it had under the original statute, but, along with the attorney general's office, some additional investigatory and enforcement powers. The provisions of RSA 147-A:4 II require that each application for a permit must be accompanied by a fee of up to $1,000 to be used to finance an exhaustive review by the bureau's technical staff. The bureau's Hazardous Waste Rule section 1905.08 contains an exhaustive list of the technical standards governing the review process, standards which are designed to ensure the protection of human health and the environment. RSA 147-A:5 requires that an applicant wishing to build a hazardous waste treatment facility provide satisfactory evidence of its financial responsibility, so the bureau may be assured that the facility will comply with the appropriate environmental standards and protect the public health and safety. RSA chapter 147-A further provides for strict liability for operators and increases the penalties for operator violations.

The General Court also enacted three new statutory chapters in 1981, RSA chapters 147-B, 147-C, and 147-D.

RSA chapter 147-B provides for a hazardous waste cleanup fund to deal with past illegal dumping activities in this State.

RSA chapter 147-C provides for municipal hazardous waste facility review committees. This statute mandates that the bureau notify the governing body of the town in which a proposed hazardous waste facility is to be located. The town's governing body is then required to appoint a municipal review committee. RSA chapter 147-C thus mirrors the bureau's Hazardous Waste Rule section 1905.09(h), which also provides for a municipal review committee. While contemplating duties for the committee that are similar to those prescribed by the bureau's rule, RSA chapter 147-C goes further by making appointment of such a committee mandatory. The bureau's rule had simply made appointment of the committee a discretionary matter.

The review committee is the body deemed to ''[r]epresent the town in the public hearing process relating to the facility's permit application.'' The committee is provided access to all information that is given to the bureau, except for materials that are considered trade secrets. The committee is charged with studying the effect that the proposed facility will have on the health and welfare of the people in the community, on its environment, and economy. Based on its study, the committee must ''[s]ubmit a report to the bureau . . . containing the committee's recommendations regarding the proposed disposal facility, including a recommendation as to whether or not the site certificate should be granted.''

Finally, RSA 147-C:7 provides for an appeal by the committee to the commissioner of health and welfare if ''the committee determines that the bureau proposes to issue a permit to a disposal facility which, in the judgment of the committee, does not adequately protect the health and safety of the residents of the town . . . .'' The commissioner is required to hear this committee appeal on an expedited basis and must issue a decision within fifteen days.

RSA chapter 147-D authorizes a town to levy fees on any hazardous waste facility located within its borders. It is against this backdrop of comprehensive regulation that the Town of Hooksett asserts that its powers of ''home rule'' have not been preempted by State or federal legislation regulating hazardous wastes.

The Town of Hooksett's Preemption and Home Rule Claims

In support of its position, the Town of Hooksett advances what is essentially a three-part argument. First, it claims that cities and towns in this State have longstanding powers of home rule enabling them to enact zoning ordinances and regulations for the protection of the health, safety, and welfare of their citizens. The town maintains specifically, that cities and towns have long possessed the authority under the police powers enumerated in RSA 31:39 and its predecessors, to regulate the disposal of garbage and other waste materials. Finally, the town argues that section 293:1 of the 1977 session laws, which amended former RSA 147:26-a, constituted an express acknowledgment that municipalities could regulate commercial and industrial wastes. The town thus contends it has the *affirmative* power to enact the popular consent ordinances challenged here.

Alternatively, the town argues that while these long-standing powers *could* have been preempted by the State legislature, they were not so preempted by the hazardous waste legislation at issue in this case. The town claims in this context that RSA chapters 147-A, 147-B, 147-C, and 147-D, at worst, are silent as to the preemption of home rule powers. The town argues, therefore, that if the statutes are silent, we must hold that powers previously delegated to municipalities under other statutes have not been impliedly repealed because of the disfavor we accord the doctrine of repeal of statutes by implication. The town suggests that this legislative silence on the question is of particular significance because the legislative history reveals that the subject of "home rule" was very much on the minds of legislators during the 1979 and 1981 legislative sessions. The town compares this legislative silence with what it claims is a clear subordination of home rule and an express preemption of the solid waste management field in a statute also adopted in 1981.

Finally, the town argues that far from being "silent" on the issue of *home rule*, the hazardous waste legislation in fact expressly provides for it. In support of this argument, the Town points to two provisions of the 1981 hazardous waste legislation. The town first relies on RSA chapter 147-C which, as noted before, establishes a municipal hazardous waste review committee. RSA 147-C:6 provides for a limitation on the committee's power, which the town claims amounts to an *express* preservation of home rule. This section states:

> "*Committee's Powers.* This chapter shall not be deemed to permit the committee to preempt the powers of any local board or other local authority relative to the regulation of zoning and planning."

The town further relies upon RSA chapter 147-D, which allows a city or town in which a facility is located to levy fees on the facility. The legislature described such fees as being intended as a "positive incentive to foster the siting of these facilities." The town insists that this fee-enabling legislation makes sense only if the towns are understood as retaining the *option* of *rejecting* such facilities. In other words, the town argues that an "incentive" is only meaningful where choice exists. Thus, the town claims that the legislature in RSA chapter 147-D, has expressly preserved home rule powers of municipalities in hazardous waste regulation.

There is No Tradition of Home Rule in the Regulation of Hazardous Wastes

We have no quarrel with the Town of Hooksett's claim that the legislature has delegated extensive zoning and regulatory powers to the cities and towns, enabling them to provide for and protect the public health and welfare. We do *not* agree, however, that the cities and towns in this State have been given concurrent affirmative authority to regulate the disposal of hazardous wastes by virtue of the statutory provisions the town cites. To the contrary, we find that until the legislature in 1979 enacted hazardous waste legislation, the problem of hazardous waste had never been explicitly addressed in this State.

The Field of Hazardous Waste Regulation has been Preempted by the State

We conclude that the State hazardous waste statute, RSA 147:48 through :57 and its successor, RSA chapters 147-A through -D arose from the legislature's serious concern over the lack of a comprehensive statewide program to deal with the growing problem of hazardous waste disposal. We find that the legislature, responding to the options offered by the federal government in the Resource Conservation and Recovery Act of 1976, devised a comprehensive and detailed program of statewide regulation, which on its face must be viewed as preempting any local actions having the intent or the effect of frustrating it. We have consistently held that where the State has enacted a comprehensive regulatory scheme, no local actions or ordinances will be permitted to contravene it.

The town argues strenuously that RSA 147-C:6 contains an express limitation on the powers of the municipal review committee. We hold that this provision means what it says, namely, that nothing in "this chapter" which created the *municipal review committee* shall be deemed to permit *that* committee to preempt local powers of zoning and planning. Nowhere in RSA 147-C:6 or any other part of the hazardous waste legislation is there an indication that the legislature intended this to be an overall limitation on the powers of the Bureau of Solid Waste Management which, in RSA chapter 147-A, has been given the sole authority to act with finality on permit applications.

The town's claim is further weakened by other language in the chapter it has cited. RSA 147-C:4 I(d) provides that the municipal review committee shall submit a report to the bureau containing its "*recommendations* regarding the proposed disposal facility, including a *recommendation* as to whether or not the site certificate should be granted." (Emphasis added.) The statute goes on to provide for a right of appeal should the committee disagree with the bureau's decision to grant a site permit. This language hardly supports the claim that the powers of any entity other than the committee itself are being limited, or that any entity other than the bureau has the authority to approve or disapprove a site-permit application.

As noted before, the Town of Hooksett also claims that the entire structure of RSA chapter 147-D, in which the legislature authorized the collection of fees from hazardous waste facilities, makes sense only if the cities and towns are understood to have retained an ultimate veto over the siting of such facilities. We do not find this argument to be persuasive. The declaration of purpose of RSA chapter 147-D itself states that the reason for the fee-imposing power conferred by the statute is to provide a positive incentive which should not be used as an exclusionary taxation mechanism. Creation of the means for municipalities to derive revenue from hazardous waste disposal facilities appears to have been intended merely as an affirmative incentive for cities and towns to cooperate in locating such facilities within their borders. The converse is not implied, namely that towns have the power to refuse such facilities, particularly in light of the legislature's admonition that such fees should not be used in an attempt to exclude such facilities.

The Scope of State Preemption.

The State program embodied in RSA chapters 147-A, 147-B, 147-C, and 147-D represents a comprehensive plan intended to be implemented on a statewide basis. As such, it completely preempts the field of hazardous waste legislation in this State. We have stated repeatedly that "[t]owns may not regulate a field that the State has preempted." The Town of Hooksett's popular consent ordinances are therefore invalid. It necessarily follows that the Town of Hooksett Planning Board has no powers with respect to the approval or disapproval of Stablex's application for a site permit to construct a hazardous waste facility on the land on which it has an option in Hooksett. Any local regulations relating to such matters as traffic and roads, landscaping and building specifications, snow, garbage, and sewage removal, signs, and other related subjects, to which any industrial facility would be subjected and which are administered in good faith and without exclusionary effect, may validly be applied to a facility approved by the State bureau.

Reversed.

****

City of Shelton v. Commissioner of the Department of Environmental Protection, 193 Conn. 506, 479 A.2d 208 (1984)

The plaintiff, the city of Shelton, brought three separate actions seeking to prevent the CRRA [Connecticut Resources Recovery Authority] from implementing its plan to operate a forty-two acre regional landfill in Shelton on a site where a smaller private landfill had previously been operated. In the first case, . . . the city took an administrative appeal from the decision of the Deputy Commissioner of Environmental Protection, John Anderson, granting the CRRA a solid waste disposal permit for the proposed expanded landfill. In this administrative appeal the city claimed that the CRRA was a state agency and hence was not entitled to proceed without filing an environmental impact evaluation (EIE) as required by General Statutes § 22a-1b. In the second case, . . . the city sought to enjoin the defendant CRRA from operating the landfill on the grounds that the proposed expansion of the landfill violated the city's zoning regulations and that the CRRA had failed to obtain the city's consent as required by General Statutes § 22a-276. In the third case, . . . the city sought a declaratory judgment against the defendant Stanley Pac, the Commissioner of Environmental Protection, and others that its local zoning regulations prevented the CRRA from expanding the landfill, notwithstanding the granting of the permit by the Department of Environmental Protection

(DEP). After a consolidated trial of the three cases, the trial court sustained the city's administrative appeal, granted the requested injunction and ruled, in the declaratory judgment action, that the Shelton zoning regulations prohibited the CRRA's use of the DEP permit to expand the horizontal area of the landfill that had previously covered a portion of the site. The defendants have appealed from the judgments in all three cases.

During the dependency of this appeal, the General Assembly enacted legislation directed at the specific dispute now before us. Public Acts 1984, No. 84-331 provides in § 1 that the CRRA "shall not be construed to be a department, institution or agency of the state." The act provides further in § 2 that "[n]otwithstanding the provisions of subsection (c) of section 22a-208 of the general statutes . . . concerning the right of any local body to regulate, through zoning, land usage for solid waste disposal and section 22a-276 of the general statutes, the Connecticut resources recovery authority may use and operate as a solid waste disposal area, pursuant to a [DEP] permit. . .any real property owned by said authority on or before the effective date of this act, any portion of which has been operated as a solid waste disposal area. . . ."

[W]e hold that in light of the enactment of Public Acts 1984, No. 84-331, the judgments of the trial court must be set aside and the cases remanded with direction to dismiss the administrative appeal and to render judgment for the defendants in the remaining cases.

As we recently stated, "[a] local ordinance is preempted by a state statute whenever the legislature has demonstrated an intent to occupy the entire field of regulation on the matter; or, as here, whenever the local ordinance irreconcilably conflicts with the statute." "Whether an ordinance conflicts with a statute or statutes can only be determined by reviewing the policy and purposes behind the statute and measuring the degree to which the ordinance frustrates the achievement of the state's objectives."

In 1973 the legislature created the CRRA as part of a comprehensive program whose purpose was to address the growing statewide problems of solid waste disposal. The legislature . . . declared the policy of the state "that solid waste disposal and resources recovery facilities and projects are to be implemented either by the state of Connecticut or under state auspices . . . ." The CRRA was created to make and implement statewide solid waste management plans[,] subject to the authority of the Commissioner of Environmental Protection to issue permits for any solid waste disposal facility.

These statutes evidence a legislative intent to commit the difficult regional problems of solid waste disposal to regional and statewide solution. The legislature would reasonably have determined that only a decision-making body with a mandate to consider the needs of more than one community could adequately balance the competing concerns of various localities within the state. Local zoning regulations, such as Shelton's, which operate to exclude the facilities that the CRRA has found necessary, and the DEP has found environmentally acceptable, frustrate the explicit purposes of the state statutes and are therefore preempted.

****

Notes

1. Does either *Stablex* or *Shelton* contain any indication of the racial character or income levels of the local community opposing the waste facility?[25] Would such factors have any impact on the court's analysis in either case?

2. Could such factors properly be considered by the state legislature if it enacted legislation specifically aimed at a siting controversy, as occurred in *Shelton*? Is resort to the political arena, including the legislature, the probable effect of state siting laws that override local opposition?

3. In *Bourque v. Dettore*, 589 A.2d 815 (Rhode Island 1991), a state statute granted to a majority of neighboring landowners a blanket veto over any application for a local license to construct a household appliance ("white goods") recycling facility. The statute was silent as to the grounds on which the neighbors' objections could be based. Nonetheless, the court upheld the statute against a variety of constitutional challenges.[26] Among the various rationales for its conclusion, the court stated:

> [T]he Legislature deemed it necessary to provide the residents of local cities and towns with the power to regulate, among other things, storehouses and dealerships engaged in the recycling of white goods. The Legislature clearly intended to circumscribe activities by landowners that potentially could have adverse effects on neighboring land-owners. . . . Consequently we believe that such matters certainly bear a substantial relation to the public health, safety, and decency of the community and, therefore, may properly be the subject of state or municipal regulations under the police power — even if conditioned on the objection of neighboring landowners.
> *Id.* at 820.

Is this analysis an adequate justification for the NIMBY position? Is *Bourque* consistent with the courts' approaches in *Stablex* and *Shelton*? What factual differences among these cases might justify their respective outcomes? Should the *Bourque* case be decided

---

[25] Did you make any personal assumptions about either or both of these factors as you read each case, or were they absent from your thinking? *Cf.* John T. Noonan, Jr., Persons and Masks of the Law 6 (1976) ("Rules, not persons, are the ordinary subject matter of legal study. . . . Little or no attention is given to the persons in whose minds and in whose interaction the rules have lived — to the persons whose difficulties have occasioned the articulation of the rule . . . .")

If you did make such assumptions, were there any factual bases for them?

For another example of a siting controversy that was resolved, *inter alia*, on the basis of preemption of a local ordinance, and with no discussion of the racial or economic character of the community, *see Warren County v. State of North Carolina*, 528 F. Supp. 276 (E.D.N.C. 1981). Ironically, this dispute became what is often referred to as the first environmental justice protest. *See* Chapter 7(B)-(C), *supra*. Another decision involving this same site similarly contained no such discussion, although the court acknowledged the stakes for the community in the most general way. *Twitty v. State of North Carolina*, 527 F. Supp. 778, 783 (E.D.N.C. 1981). The court said, "The Court appreciates and understands the concern of plaintiffs and other citizens of Warren County concerning the disposition of the hazardous chemical wastes. All North Carolinians and, indeed, all Americans are likewise concerned. That very concern brought about the [preemptive] enactments of Congress which govern the disposition of this case."

[26] Which of the constitutional concerns addressed in Chapter 5, *supra*, would seem to be appropriate to raise against this statute?

differently if the neighbors' veto power were created solely by a municipal ordinance rather than by a state statute?

4. What are the basic components of a state siting statute that you believe would strike a just balance between (a) statewide environmental concerns (for example, regarding needs for hazardous waste treatment facilities, household appliance recycling facilities, or solid waste landfills), (b) virtually all local communities' inclination to avoid being the location of polluting or risky facilities, and (c) the distinctive concerns of poor and minority communities?

4. Litigation Theories

In the past few years during which the environmental justice movement has grown, a variety of theories have been raised in litigation as possible grounds for relief from allegedly unjust siting decisions. Some of these theories have been based upon environmental statutes, but constitutional provisions and civil rights statutes also have received attention. This section will examine some of the most prominent of these varied approaches.[27]

a. *Environmental Statutes*

Among the many types of plaintiffs bringing cases under environmental statutes over the past couple of decades, organizations representing the interests of poor and minority neighborhoods occasionally have been found. Particularly with respect to disputes over the construction of highways and other public works projects, communities have relied on environmental statutes to raise objections that now would be seen as falling within the environmental justice rubric. Some of these statutory theories will be examined here, with an eye toward assessing their ultimate value in redressing distributional inequities.[28]

****

First National Bank v. Richardson, 494 F.2d 1369, 1377-78 (7th Cir. 1973)

The Congressional declaration of national environmental policy expressed in NEPA [National Environmental Policy Act] is as broad as the mind can conceive. After speaking of the "overall welfare and development of man," Congress declared that

---

[27] Comments on the application of common law theories, such as nuisance doctrine, can be found at Naikang Tsao, "Ameliorating Environmental Racism: A Citizens' Guide to Combatting the Discriminatory Siting of Toxic Waste Dumps," 67 New York University Law Review 366, 382-394 (1992); Walter Willard, "Environmental Racism: The Merging of Civil Rights and Environmental Activism," 19 Southern University Law Review 77, 86-89 (1992).

[28] An environmental poverty lawyer has ranked various legal theories in a hierarchy, with environmental statutes as the most preferred for use in environmental justice siting cases, the Civil Rights Act of 1964 next in order, and Equal Protection claims in the final position. Luke W. Cole, "Environmental Justice Litigation: Another Stone in David's Sling," 21 Fordham Urban Law Journal 523, 526 (1994).

See also Colin Crawford, "Strategies for Environmental Justice: Rethinking CERCLA Medical Monitoring Lawsuits," 74 Boston University Law Review 267 (1994).

"[I]t is the continuing policy of the Federal Government . . . to use all practicable means and measures, including financial and technical assistance, in a manner calculated to foster and promote the general welfare, to create and maintain conditions under which man and nature can exist in productive harmony, and fulfill the social, economic, and other requirements of present and future generations of Americans." 42 U.S.C.A. § 4331(a).

Of necessity, NEPA must be construed to include protection of the quality of life for city residents particularly in view of "the profound influences of population growth, high-density urbanization, [and] industrial expansion . . . " (42 U.S.C.A. § 4331(a)). Unfortunately, the environmental problems of the city are not as readily identifiable as clean air and clean water. The Council on Environmental Quality has noted:[29]

"Life in the inner city embraces a range of environmental problems, some starkly evident, some disguised, some acknowledged as environmental, some wearing other labels . . . . [In the inner city] many of our most severe environmental problems interact with social and economic conditions which the Nation is also seeking to improve. The traditional environmental objectives of clean air and water and preservation of national parks and wilderness are not the central concerns of most inner city poor. They focus instead on more immediate economic and social interest. . . . [T]here is growing evidence that among the urban poor—those with the most to gain from environmental improvement—are some who have decided to embrace environmentalism in their own distinct way. Their use of the term environment is broader than the traditional definition. Their concept embraces not only more parks, but better housing; not only cleaner air and water, but rat extermination. The variety of environmental problems of the inner city and the absence of simple answers to these problems make it particularly important that efforts to overcome them be tailored to the needs and priorities of each locality."

These considerations mandate a balancing and weighing of multiple factors in order to determine the cumulative and absolute efforts of the project.

****

Note

The language of the Seventh Circuit and the Council on Environmental Quality represents an extremely expansive view of NEPA's scope in terms of what aspects of modern living conditions are encompassed within the "environment." Although there is no major judicial decision yet that directly extends NEPA to an environmental inequity problem, or to alleged exacerbation of racial discrimination or poverty,[30] there are a

---

[29] 2 Council on Environmental Quality Ann. Rep. 189-91 (August 1971).

[30] Skepticism about the utility of NEPA and environmental impact statements in promoting siting fairness is expressed at Vicki Been, "What's Fairness Got To Do With It? Environmental Justice and the Siting of Locally Undesirable Land Uses,". 78 Cornell Law Review 1001, 1066-1068 (1993); Peter L. Reich, "Greening the Ghetto: A Theory of Environmental Race Discrimination," 41 Kansas Law Review 271, 298 (1992). Professor Reich is more sanguine, however, about the utility of state statutes that are modeled on NEPA. *Id.* at 305-313.

few decisions that arguably provide a foundation for such an extension, as the following materials suggest.

For example, students of NEPA usually give some attention to the per curiam opinion of the Supreme Court in *Strycker's Bay Neighborhood Council, Inc. v. Karlen*, 444 U.S. 223 (1980), because of its negative statements on the availability of substantive judicial review of federal agency decisions subject to NEPA. Looking at that case in terms of the possible breadth of NEPA's scope, however, it may be recalled that one of the concerns in that dispute over siting of a low-income housing project, at least as described by the Court of Appeals, was "environmental factors, such as crowding low-income housing into a concentrated area." *Id.* at 227. Although the Supreme Court rejected the Court of Appeals' treatment of the "concentration" factor, it does not appear that the Supreme Court ruled this factor to be beyond NEPA's domain.[31]

Consider also how Executive Order 12898 and the accompanying Presidential Memorandum, presented in Chapter 7(D), *infra*, may contribute to enlarging NEPA's scope. Note also that the NEPA regulations of the Council on Environmental Quality presently include within the statutory coverage "cultural, economic, social, or health" effects, "whether direct, indirect, or cumulative." 40 C.F.R. sec. 1508.8. The regulations also declare, however, "that economic or social effects are not intended by themselves to require preparation of an environmental impact statement." 40 C.F.R. sec. 1508.14.[32]

****

Keith v. Volpe, 858 F.2d 467 (9th Cir. 1988)

This action began on February 16, 1972, when Ralph W. Keith and other individuals living in the path of the proposed Century Freeway, together with the Los Angeles Chapter of the National Association for the Advancement of Colored People (NAACP), the Sierra Club, the Environmental Defense Fund, and the Freeway Fighters filed an environmental and civil rights complaint in district court against various state and federal agencies and officials. The complaint sought injunctive relief to halt construction of the freeway until the defendants complied with state and federal environmental, civil rights, and housing laws to provide replacement housing for displaced residents without discrimination against minority and poor persons.

On July 7, 1972, the district court issued a preliminary injunction prohibiting further work on the freeway until federal and state officials complied with environmental and relocation assistance statutes. *Keith v. Volpe*, 352 F. Supp. 1324 (C.D. Cal. 1972), *aff'd en banc sub nom., Keith v. California Highway Commission*, 506 F.2d 696 (9th Cir. 1974), *cert. denied*, 420 U.S. 908 (1975).

---

[31] Further discussion of this type of neighborhood impact under NEPA can be found at Gerald Torres, "Environmental Burdens and Democratic Justice," 21 Fordham Urban Law Journal 431, 446-447 (1994).

[32] These regulations are discussed at *Citizens Committee Against Interstate Route 675 v. Lewis*, 542 F. Supp. 496, 533-535 (S.D. Ohio 1982).

After years of negotiations, the parties entered into a consent decree, which the district court approved on September 22, 1981. The court then dissolved the preliminary injunction, thus permitting further work on the freeway project pursuant to the decree's provisions. The decree remains in effect.

One of the purposes of the consent decree was "to provide for the housing needs of those living in the area of the proposed path of the freeway." Specifically, the decree required the defendants to provide displacees with 3700 units of replenishment housing under its "Housing Plan." Under the Plan's terms, 55 percent of all replacement units would be affordable to low-income households and 25 percent would be affordable to moderate-income households.

****

Note

One of the District Court's grounds for enjoining the Century Freeway in 1972 was the federal government's failure to prepare an environmental impact statement under NEPA, and an environmental impact report under the California Environmental Quality Act, particularly with reference to air pollution impacts. 352 F. Supp. at 1330-38. Additional grounds included requirements of the Federal-Aid Highway Act, and the later Uniform Relocation Assistance and Real Property Acquisition Policies Act, mandating consideration of the freeway's "economic and social effects" in order to "insure that a few individuals do not suffer disproportionate injuries as a result of programs designed for the benefit of the public as a whole." *Id.* at 1338, 1341-42. Somewhat similar approaches were pursued, with varying results, by poor and minority communities in *Lathan v. Volpe*, 455 F.2d 1111 (9th Cir. 1971); *Monroe County Conservation Council, Inc. v. Adams*, 566 F.2d 419, 426 (2d Cir. 1977) ("In sum, according to the EIS, "[n]o major change is foreseen in neighborhood character, cohesiveness and stability, nor are there any known minority groups affected by the [highway] project."); and *Coalition of Concerned Citizens against I-670 v. Damian*, 608 F. Supp. 110 (S.D. Ohio 1984).

A much more recent instance in which a poor, minority community relied upon highway statutes—in addition to NEPA, civil rights, and other statutory environmental grounds—to address adverse environmental and social effects of a federal project is the complaint in *Clean Air Alternative Coalition, Inc. v. U.S. Department of Transportation*, which is discussed in Chapter 7(C)(4)(c), *infra*. A more particularized use of a single environmental statute is illustrated in the next reading.

****

In the Matter of Genesee Power Station Limited Partnership, PSD Appeal Nos. 93-1 through 93-7, United States Environmental Protection Agency, 1993 PSD LEXIS 3, October 22, 1993

Before the Environmental Appeals Board, United States Environmental Protection Agency
Opinion of the Board by Judge McCallum:[33]

The Environmental Appeals Board has received nine petitions seeking review of a Prevention of Significant Deterioration (PSD) permit issued to Genesee Power Station Limited Partnership (Genesee) for construction of a 35-megawatt steam/electric power plant designed to burn several types of wood waste. The PSD permit was prepared under an EPA delegation by the staff of the Air Quality Division of the Michigan Department of Natural Resources (MDNR) and issued by the Michigan Air Pollution Control Commission (Commission). As requested by the board, the Commission through MDNR filed a response to six of the petitions. For the reasons set forth below, with respect to one issue raised by the American Lung Association of Michigan, we are remanding the permit to the Commission so that it may reconsider its determination of the best available control technology for lead emissions. With respect to all other issues raised in the petitions, we are denying review.

Genesee proposes to install and operate a 35-megawatt steam/electric power plant designed to burn several types of wood waste including demolition debris, pallets, dunnage, construction waste, tree trimmings, landclearing/inforest and sawmill residue. The plant, which will use a spreader system to burn the fuel, will be located northeast of Flint, Michigan in an industrial park.

New major stationary sources of air pollution, such as the proposed Genesee facility, are required under the Clean Air Act to obtain an air pollution permit before commencing construction. If the facility is in an area where one or more national ambient air quality standards (NAAQS) are not being violated (attainment and unclassified areas), the permit is referred to as prevention of significant deterioration of air quality (PSD) permit. CAA § 165, 42 U.S.C. 7475.

The PSD permit under consideration here imposes emissions limitations for the following four criteria pollutants: PM-10, carbon monoxide, nitrogen oxides, and lead. The permit does not impose an emissions limitations for sulfur dioxide, because that pollutant is not expected to be emitted in sufficient quantities to trigger the PSD requirements. The PSD permit also does not impose an emissions limitation for ozone, because the proposed site is in an area that is nonattainment for that pollutant.

[33] Pursuant to an order dated October 22, 1993, the Board is deleting portions of its September 8th Order Denying Review in part and Remanding in Part. This revised opinion reflects those deletions and minor rhetorical changes necessitated by such deletions. This opinion replaces and supersedes, nunc pro tunc, the September 8th opinion. Neither the language deleted from the September 8th opinion nor the fact that such language was deleted has any precedential value in this or any other case.

Genesee submitted an initial PSD permit application on June 8, 1992, and the application was deemed complete on October 1, 1992. The public comment period for the draft permit lasted 42 days, and two public hearings were held, one on October 27, 1992, and the other on December 1, 1992. The service of the notice of the issuance of the final permit decision was dated December 7, 1992. The Board has received petitions for review from the following groups and individuals: American Lung Association of Michigan (ALAM); Flint Branch of the NAACP; Society of Afro-American People; Flint/Genesee Neighborhood Association; Linda Elston and Betty Strong; Genesee County Medical Society; Violet Worthington; Cherie N. Misner; and Sister Marjorie Polys.

Richard Dicks, Executive Director of the Society of Afro-American People in Michigan, argues that the Commission's issuance of the PSD permit represents an instance of "governmental environmental racism," because the facility will be located near the predominantly African American Flint/Genesee neighborhood. According to Mr. Dicks, this environmental racism is evidenced by the manner in which the public hearings were held. Specifically, Mr. Dicks charges that;

> This conclusion [of environmental racism] is supported by the obvious promotion by the DNR for this project. And the inability for people of color and other residents of the economically deprived area to attend, or be involved in the hearings properly, is a civil rights concern.

Mr. Dicks also notes that, as the residents of the Flint/Genesee neighborhood waited for their chance to speak at the December 1, 1992 public hearing, the Commission was considering a permit application for a different facility to be located in Marquette County, Michigan. According to Mr. Dicks, the Commission denied that permit because the white residents of the surrounding community did not want the incinerator to be built:

> Five or six white residents from Marquette, Michigan who addressed the commission just before us. Live in a rural farm area that was not populated. They told the Commission that they did not want an incinerator built near their property because it might affect their farm animals.

> At this time one of the commissioners immediately stated that "if the people don't want this in their community we shouldn't put it there, because I sure wouldn't want it in my community." The commission then voted not to issue the permit to build the incinerator and the five or six people from Marquette left.

Mr. Dicks contrasts this treatment with the treatment received by the residents of the Flint/Genesee neighborhood, who expressed strong opposition to the location of the proposed Genesee power plant at the hearing, but failed to persuade the Commission to deny the permit. Mr. Dicks also notes that: "The commissioner that took such a strong stance for the people from Marquette, who said that they just didn't want a[n] incinerator in their community—well he said nothing in support of our plea."

In its response to comments, MDNR declined to respond to comments raising the environmental racism issue on the ground that "they are beyond the scope of Air Quality's rules and regulations." In its Response to the Petitions, MDNR only mentions the environmental racism issue in passing. It lists the issue along with several other issues and states that it is denying review of such issues because they are "vague and/ or unsubstantiated" or "not subject to federal or state air quality rules and regulations," or because petitioners have failed to provide supporting evidence. MDNR does not specify which reason or reasons apply to the environmental racism argument.

We read Mr. Dick's petition as arguing that the Commission acted with a racially discriminatory intent when it granted the Genesee permit. As evidence of this intent, Mr. Dicks cites the disparate treatment received by the African American opponents of the Genesee facility at the December 1, 1992 meeting: While the Commission was swayed to deny the Marquette permit by the opposition of white Marquette residents, the Commission was not swayed to deny the Genesee permit by the opposition of the African American Flint/Genesee residents.

Assuming without deciding that Mr. Dicks' environmental racism argument is within the scope of the Commission's authority to consider under applicable air quality rules and regulations (for Mr. Dicks does not challenge any of the emissions limitations prescribed for the facility near the Flint/Genesee neighborhood), we conclude that the Commission's action was proper in that there is no basis in the record for concluding that it acted with a racially discriminatory intent.[34]

Mr. Dicks' argument is based on the assumption that the Commission denied the Marquette County permit because the white Marquette County residents had come to oppose it. Mr. Dicks supports his contention with a remark allegedly made by of one of the Commissioners, i.e. "[I]f the people don't want this in their community we shouldn't put it there, because I sure wouldn't want it in my community." Mr. Dicks' contention, however, is not borne out by the minutes of the December 1, 1992 hearing. Those minutes indicate that the Commission denied the Marquette permit not because of the opposition of the white Marquette County residents, but (i) local zoning approval for the facility had been denied, (ii) the facility's proximity to a wetland would violate the federal Wild and Scenic Rivers Act, and (iii) the facility would not comply with state law. These are legitimate, nondiscriminatory reasons for denying a permit. They suggest that the opposition of local white residents was not the basis for the Commission's decision. The minutes, therefore, negate Mr. Dicks' assumption to the contrary. Accordingly, we can find no support for Mr. Dicks' claim of disparate treatment, and a thorough search of the record has revealed no other evidence that the Commission was acting with a racially discriminatory intent when it granted the Genesee permit. Review of Mr. Dicks' petition is therefore denied.

---

[34] In his petition, Mr. Dicks does not invoke the Equal Protection clause of the U.S. Constitution. Accordingly, we do not reach the issue of whether Mr. Dicks has made out an Equal Protection claim cognizable under the Constitution, even assuming we would have authority to review such a claim. We note, however, that to make out a claim under the Equal Protection clause of the Constitution, it would be necessary to show that the Commission chose or somehow encouraged the choice of the proposed site of the Genesee facility with an intent to discriminate against the African American residents of the Flint/ Genesee neighborhood.

The residents of the Flint/Genesee neighborhood, however, should not feel that the Genesee facility permit gives Genesee a license to threaten their health and safety. The record demonstrates that emissions allowed under the permit will meet all applicable air quality regulations, which are specifically established to protect human health. For example, emissions allowed under the permit will not cause a violation of the federal primary National Ambient Air Quality Standards (NAAQS), which for covered pollutants specify the level of air quality that EPA has determined will protect the public health, "allowing an adequate margin of safety." The permit also requires that emissions meet State health-based restrictions on toxic emissions. In fact, with respect to some of the pollutants that have been the subject of most concern, the predicted ambient impact of emissions will be far below levels that have been determined to protect human health. Also, . . . the permit is being remanded so that the Commission may consider whether fuel cleaning should be required to reduce lead emissions even further. Thus, emissions allowed under the PSD permit will not be permitted to exceed, and in certain instances will be far below, applicable air quality standards adopted to protect human health and welfare.

****

Notes

1. As indicated in the first footnote of the *Genesee Power* decision, the October 22, 1993 Order was a revision of an earlier opinion of the Environmental Appeals Board issued on September 8, 1993. This prompt revision was issued in response to a Motion for Clarification filed by the EPA Office of the General Counsel on behalf of certain EPA staff units. The earlier opinion had reached the same result in the case, but had included additional grounds for rejecting the environmental racism objection and another claim.

With regard to the environmental racism issue, the Appeals Board originally had included a statement that the siting decision regarding the power plant "is a local land use or zoning decision." *In the Matter of Genesee Power Station Limited Partnership*, PSD Appeal Nos. 93-1–93-7, U.S. Environmental Protection Agency, 1993 PSD LEXIS 1, September 8, 1993, at *19. The Board then relied upon Section 131 of the Clean Air Act, a little-noticed provision that declares that the Act does not infringe upon or transfer any local land use powers. The Board found that this provision limited the state air pollution Commission's ability, while "acting in its capacity as a PSD permit-issuing authority under a federal delegation," to consider any factors other than "whether the facility at the proposed site would meet federal air quality requirements." *Id.* at *20. The Board concluded that a broader exercise of power by the Board, such as consideration of community opposition to the proposed location of the Genesee facility, would violate Section 131.

In the October revision, the Board changed its position on this question and deleted the Section 131 discussion entirely. Instead, as quoted above, the Board "[assumed] without deciding that Mr. Dicks' environmental racism argument is within the scope of the Commission's authority to consider under applicable air quality rules and regulations."

Why would the EPA staff disagree with the Board's original conclusion on this additional ground for denying the environmental racism claim? Note that the permit holder, Genesee Power Station Limited Partnership, persuaded the Board to respond to the EPA motion simply by deleting the alternative ground for its original ruling without examining the issue any further on the merits. The Partnership urged that the issues raised by EPA's request "are of national importance and should be decided with the full benefit of the adversary process but are not so presented here, for the issues raised do not, as [Office of the General Counsel] acknowledges, affect the outcome of the case." *Id.* at *2. *See also* "Judges Say Racism Can't be Weighed in CAA New Source Call," Inside EPA, September 17, 1993, at 1 (describing the original *Genesee Power* ruling as "a major decision that some say confounds EPA Administrator Carol Browner's environmental justice initiative").

2. After examining the new Executive Order on environmental justice presented in Chapter 7(D), *infra*, consider whether the outcome of *Genesee Power* might have been different had that Order already been issued and implemented.

3. In some environmental justice siting litigation based on environmental statutes, settlements have been reached that involve more than just some mitigation of the adverse environmental impacts at the heart of the suit. In such settlements, there may also be agreements for the provision of collateral benefits to the affected community, such as health clinics, increased hiring of local residents at the facility in question, and financial aid to nonprofit organizations within the community. If you represented a community plaintiff in settlement discussions involving such possible benefits, what justifications would you offer for bringing these broader social and economic factors into an environmental lawsuit?

b. *Equal Protection Doctrine*

In contrast with the use of environmental statutes as vehicles for attacks on siting inequities, the materials in this section and the next focus on attempts to redress these inequities through legal theories directly aimed at social injustice. Attempts to rely upon the constitutional guarantee of equal protection of the laws will be presented first.[35] The subsequent section will present more recent thinking about the utility of Title VI of the Civil Rights Act of 1964.

****

---

[35] Other uses of equal protection doctrine in environmental law are presented in Chapter 5(B)(1), *supra*.

Peter L. Reich, "Greening the Ghetto: A Theory of Environmental
Race Discrimination," 41 University of Kansas Law Review 271, 287-91 (1992)

Racially disparate hazard siting is essentially an issue of the maldistribution of environmental costs and benefits: minorities pay the costs of industrial production—pollution—while society in general accrues the benefits—consumer goods, employment, and revenue. For purposes of discussion, I will refer to the jurisprudential concept militating against such unfair apportionment of costs, benefits, or entitlements as the "equality principle." In American law, problems of inequality are traditionally analyzed under the rubric of equal protection, which has served as a unifying ideal of citizenship to bring aliens and other previously excluded groups into the civic culture. Equal protection remedies are available at the federal level through the Fifth and Fourteenth Amendments[36] and in many states under their own constitutions. The equality principle is also manifested in federal and state civil rights laws barring discrimination in education, employment, housing, and voting. Applying the principle to environmental racism, people of color should be protected from disproportionate hazardous exposure just as they are protected from inferior employment, housing, or other realms traditionally subject to equal protection analysis and statutory antidiscrimination bans.

The exclusionary nature of the planning process is related to disparate siting because adverse environmental impacts are most likely to be imposed on an unrepresented community, particularly when language is a barrier to its involvement. The legal concept addressing the need for public participation in administrative decisionmaking, including environmental decisionmaking, will be referred to as the "access principle." Administrative law scholars have emphasized that popular input into agency rulemaking and adjudication can counteract influential interests, provide overlooked data, and open the process to the scrutiny of all affected individuals. In the environmental decisionmaking context, the value of such public involvement is manifested in the impact statement requirement of the National Environmental Policy Act (NEPA) and in the often broader provisions of state environmental policy acts (SEPAs). Implementing the access principle, these statutes could be used to remove or minimize participation barriers, such as language, to people of color through appropriate procedural innovations.

Finally, a "community preservation principle" is necessary to address the particular socioeconomic harm suffered by minority communities in proximity to environmental hazards. The documented reaction of people of color living in contaminated areas provides "bottom up" evidence of neighborhood disruption and psychological stress. Recognition of these injuries to community cohesion has traditionally been limited in American law, particularly at the federal level, due to narrow judicial interpretations of NEPA. State environmental jurisprudence, however, offers greater potential because many

---

[36] [Ed.] The pertinent portion of the Fifth Amendment is its mandate that no person shall "be deprived of life, liberty, or property, without due process of law." The Fourteenth Amendment declares that no state shall "deny to any person within its jurisdiction the equal protection of the laws."

SEPAs explicitly provide for the consideration of socioeconomic impacts before a project may obtain approval. As with the equality and access principles, the ideal of community preservation furnishes a basis for shielding minorities from disproportionate pollution risks.

Thus, a comprehensive theory of environmental race discrimination must include components dealing with equality, public access, and the preservation of communities. These principles are the jurisprudential means of addressing the major aspects of environmental racism: disparate siting of hazards, limited participation in planning, and harm to community cohesion. As will be seen, the theory may be far easier to implement at the state level than at the federal level due to more expansive state interpretations of equal protection, environmental decisionmaking procedure, and socioeconomic impacts.

Equality jurisprudence at the federal level is restricted by *Washington v. Davis*[37], the equal protection case in which the United States Supreme Court required discriminatory intent to trigger strict scrutiny of a facially race-neutral governmental action. Intent can be proven circumstantially as well as from direct evidence. In *Village of Arlington Heights v. Metropolitan Housing Development Corp.*[38], the Supreme Court set out the following five categories of circumstantial evidence from which discriminatory motive may be inferred: (1) An official action's effect on a particular race; (2) the decision's historical background; (3) the sequence of events immediately preceding the action; (4) any departures, substantive or procedural, from the ordinary decisionmaking process; and (5) the action's legislative or administrative history. Statistical proof of an "invidious" discriminatory pattern may also give rise to an inference of intent, but sufficiently stark patterns are hard to establish. The result of the *Davis* intent requirement is that equal protection claims based on disproportionate effects alone are extremely difficult to win, despite the many injuries of racial inequality that exist irrespective of motive.[39]

****

Bean v. Southwestern Waste Management Corporation, 482 F. Supp. 673 (S.D. Texas 1979), aff'd without op., 782 F.2d 1038 (5th Cir. 1986)

On October 26,1979, plaintiffs filed their complaint and Motion for Temporary Restraining Order and Preliminary Injunction contesting the decision by the Texas Department of Health to grant Permit No. 1193 to defendant Southwestern Waste Management

---

[37] 426 U.S. 229 (1976) (holding disproportionate black failure rate on police test not an equal protection violation in absence of discriminatory intent).

[38] 429 U.S. 252 (1977) (holding city's refusal to change tract's zoning classification from single-family to multi-family to permit racially integrated housing project not an equal protection violation; arguably greater effect on minorities held insufficient to raise an inference of discriminatory intent).

[39] [Ed.] A procedural obstacle was fatal to this type of claim in *Aiello v. Browning-Ferris, Inc.*, 1993 U.S. Dist. LEXIS 16104 (N.D. California, October 29, 1993). Plaintiffs alleged that the county government had made a racially discriminatory decision to locate and approve a landfill in an area of the county where a high proportion of the county's minority residents lived. This claim was found to be barred by a one year, state statute of limitations, which was held to be applicable since "Congress has not established a time limitation for a federal cause of action" of this type. *Id.* at *13.

to operate a Type I solid waste facility in the East Houston-Dyersdale Road area in Harris County. They contend that the decision was, at least in part, motivated by racial discrimination in violation of 42 U.S.C. § 1983[40] and seek an order revoking the permit. The defendants deny the allegations and have moved to dismiss this case on the grounds of abstention, laches, and the absence of state action.

There are four prerequisites to the granting of a preliminary injunction. The plaintiffs must establish: (1) a substantial likelihood of success on the merits, (2) a substantial threat of irreparable injury, "(3) that the threatened injury to the plaintiff[s] outweighs the threatened harm the injunction may do to defendant[s], and (4) that granting the preliminary injunction will not disserve the public interest."

The plaintiffs have adequately established that there is a substantial threat of irreparable injury. They complain that they are being deprived of their constitutional rights. That, in itself, may constitute irreparable injury, but more is present here. The opening of the facility will affect the entire nature of the community—its land values, its tax base, its aesthetics, the health and safety of its inhabitants, and the operation of Smiley High School, located only 1700 feet from the site. Damages cannot adequately compensate for these types of injuries. Similarly, if a substantial likelihood of success on the merits were shown, there is no doubt that the threatened injury to the plaintiffs would outweigh that to the defendants and that the public interest would not be disserved by granting the plaintiffs an injunction.

The problem is that the plaintiffs have not established a substantial likelihood of success on the merits. The burden on them is to prove discriminatory purpose. *Washington v. Davis*, 426 U.S. 229, 96 S.Ct. 2040, 48 L.Ed.2d 597 (1976); *Village of Arlington Heights v. Metropolitan Housing Development Corp.*, 429 U.S. 252, 97 S.Ct. 555, 50 L.Ed.2d 450 (1977). That is, the plaintiffs must show not just that the decision to grant the permit is objectionable or even wrong, but that it is attributable to an intent to discriminate on the basis of race. Statistical proof can rise to the level that it, alone, proves discriminatory intent, as in *Yick Wo v. Hopkins*, 118 U.S. 356, 6 S.Ct. 1064, 30 L.Ed. 220 (1886), and *Gomillion v. Lightfoot*, 364 U.S. 339, 81 S.Ct. 125, 5 L.Ed.2d 110 (1960), or, this Court would conclude, even in situations less extreme than in those two cases, but the data shown here does not rise to that level. Similarly, statistical proof can be sufficiently supplemented by the types of proof outlined in *Arlington Heights*, *supra*, to establish purposeful discrimination, but the supplemental proof offered here is not sufficient to do that.

---

[40] [Ed.] The pertinent portion of Section 1983 is as follows:

Every person who, under color of any statute, ordinance, regulation, custom, or usage, of any State or Territory or the District of Columbia, subjects, or causes to be subjected, any citizen of the United States, or other person within the jurisdiction thereof to the deprivation of rights, privileges or immunities secured by the Constitution and laws, shall be liable to the party injured in an action at law, suit in equity, or other proper proceeding for redress.

Two different theories of liability have been advanced in this case. The first is that TDH's approval of the permit was part of a pattern or practice by it of discriminating in the placement of solid waste sites. In order to test that theory, one must focus on the sites which TDH has approved and determine the minority population of the areas in which the sites were located on the day that the sites opened. The available statistical data, both city-wide and in the target area, fails to establish a pattern or practice of discrimination by TDH. Citywide, data was produced for the seventeen sites operating with TDH permits as of July 1, 1978. That data shows that 58.8% of the sites granted permits by TDH were located in census tracts with 25% or less minority population at the time of their opening and that 82.4% of the sites granted permits by TDH were located in census tracts with 50% or less minority population at the time of their opening. In the target area, an area which roughly conforms to the North Forest Independent School District and the newly-created City Council District B and is 70% minority in population, two sites were approved by TDH. One, the McCarty Road site, was in a census tract with less than 10% minority population at the time of its opening. The other, the site being challenged here, is in a census tract with close to 60% minority population. Even if we also consider the sites approved by TDWR in the target area, which, as discussed earlier, are not really relevant to TDH's intent to discriminate, no pattern or practice of discrimination is revealed. Of all the solid waste sites opened in the target area, 46.2 to 50% were located in census tracts with less than 25% minority population at the time they opened. It may be that more particularized data would show that even those sites approved in predominantly Anglo census tracts were actually located in minority neighborhoods, but the data available here does not show that. In addition, there was no supplemental evidence, such as that suggested by *Arlington Heights, supra,* which established a pattern or practice of discrimination on the part of TDH.

The plaintiffs' second theory of liability is that TDH's approval of the permit, in the context of the historical placement of solid waste sites and the events surrounding the application, constituted discrimination. Three sets of data were offered to support this theory. Each set, at first blush, looks compelling. On further analysis, however, each set breaks down. Each fails to approach the standard established by *Yick Wo, supra,* and *Gomillion, supra,* and, even when considered with supplementary proof, *Arlington Heights, supra,* fails to establish a likelihood of success in proving discriminatory intent.

The first set of data focuses on the two solid waste sites to be used by the City of Houston. Both of these sites are located in the target area. This proves discrimination, the plaintiffs argue, because "the target area has the dubious distinction of containing 100% of the type I municipal land fills that Houston utilizes or will utilize, although it contains only 6.9% of the entire population of Houston." There are two problems with this argument. First, there are only two sites involved here. That is not a statistically significant number. Second, an examination of the census tracts in the target area in which the sites are located reveals that the East Houston-Dyersdale Road proposed site is in a tract with a 58.4% minority population, but that the McCarty Road site is in a tract with only an 18.4% minority population. Thus, the evidence shows that, of the two sites to be used by the City of Houston, one is in a primarily Anglo census tract and one is in a primarily minority census tract. No inference of discrimination can be made from this data.

The second set of data focuses on the total number of solid waste sites located in the target area.[41] The statistical disparity which the plaintiffs point to is that the target area contains 15% of Houston's solid waste sites, but only 6.9% of its population. Since the target area has a 70% minority population, the plaintiffs argue, this statistical disparity must be attributable to race discrimination. To begin with, in the absence of the data on population by race, the statistical disparity is not all that shocking. One would expect solid waste sites to be placed near each other and away from concentrated population areas. Even considering the 70% minority population of the target area, when one looks at where in the target area these particular sites are located, the inference of racial discrimination dissolves. Half of the solid waste sites in the target area are in census tracts with more than 70% Anglo population. Without some proof that the sites affect an area much larger than the census tract in which they are in, it is very hard to conclude that the placing of a site in the target area evidences purposeful racial discrimination.

The third set of data offered by the plaintiffs focuses on the city as a whole. This data is the most compelling on its surface. It shows that only 17.1% of the city's solid waste sites are located in the southwest quadrant, where 53.3% of the Anglos live. Only 15.3% of the sites are located in the northwest quadrant, where 20.1% of the Anglos live. Thus, only 32.4% of the sites are located in the western half of the city, where 73.4% of the Anglos live. Furthermore, the plaintiffs argue, 67.6% of the sites are located in the eastern half of the city, where 61.6% of the minority population lives. This, according to the plaintiffs, shows racial discrimination.

The problem is that, once again, these statistics break down under closer scrutiny. To begin with, the inclusion of TDWR's sites skew[s] the data. A large number of TDWR sites are located around Houston's ship channel, which is in the eastern half of the city. But those sites, the Assistant Attorney General argues persuasively, are located in the eastern half of the city because that is where Houston's industry is, not because that is where Houston's minority population is. Furthermore, closer examination of the data shows that the city's solid waste sites are not so disparately located as they first appear. If we focus on census tracts, rather than on halves or quadrants of the city, we can see with more particularity where the solid waste sites are located. Houston's population is 39.3% minority and 60.7% Anglo. The plaintiffs argue, and this Court finds persuasive, a definition of "minority census tracts" as those with more than 39.3% minority population and Anglo census tracts as those with more than 60.7% Anglo population. Using those definitions, Houston consists of 42.5% minority tracts and

---

[41] It should be noted that there are some problems with the definition of the target area as selected and defined by the plaintiffs. There is some question as to whether the definition of the area was entirely scientific. Even so, the approach is a useful one and the target area data should be examined.

57.5% Anglo tracts. Again using those definitions, 42.3% of the solid waste sites in the City of Houston are located in minority tracts and 57.7% are located in Anglo tracts. In addition, if we look at tracts with one or more sites per tract, to account for the fact that some tracts contain more than one solid waste site, 42.2% are minority tracts and 57.8% are Anglo tracts. The difference between the racial composition of census tracts in general and the racial composition of census tracts with solid waste sites is, according to the statistics available to the Court, at best, only 0.3%. That is simply not a statistically significant difference. More surprisingly, from the plaintiffs' point of view, to the extent that it is viewed as significant, it tends to indicate that minority census tracts have a tiny bit smaller percentage of solid waste sites than one would proportionately expect.

In support of the proposition that there is a city-wide discrimination against minorities in the placement of solid waste sites, the plaintiffs also argue that the data reveals that, in 1975, eleven solid waste sites were located in census tracts with 100% minority population and none were located in census tracts with 100% Anglo population. There are problems with this argument, too, however. To begin with, the 1975 data is not entirely reliable. Compared with both the 1970 and the 1979 data, the 1975 data appears to overcount minority population. For example, of the eleven sites mentioned by the plaintiffs, only one had a 100% minority population in 1979. More importantly, there were, in fact, two sites located in 100% Anglo tracts in 1975. In addition, 18 other sites were located in tracts with a 90% or greater Anglo population in 1975. Thus, even according to the 1975 data, a large number of sites were located in census tracts with high Anglo populations.

Arlington Heights suggested various types of non-statistical proof which can be used to establish purposeful discrimination. The supplementary non-statistical evidence provided by the plaintiffs in the present case raises a number of questions as to why this permit was granted. To begin with, a site proposed for the almost identical location was denied a permit in 1971 by the County Commissioners, who were then responsible for the issuance of such permits. One wonders what happened since that time. The plaintiffs argue that Smiley High School has changed from an Anglo school to one whose student body is predominantly minority. Furthermore, the site is being placed within 1700 feet of Smiley High School, a predominantly black school with no air conditioning, and only somewhat farther from a residential neighborhood. Land use considerations alone would seem to militate against granting this permit. Such evidence seemingly did not dissuade TDH.

If this Court were TDH, it might very well have denied this permit. It simply does not make sense to put a solid waste site so close to a high school, particularly one with no air conditioning. Nor does it make sense to put the land site so close to a residential neighborhood. But I am not TDH and for all I know, TDH may regularly approve of solid waste sites located near schools and residential areas, as illogical as that may seem.

It is not my responsibility to decide whether to grant this site a permit. It is my responsibility to decide whether to grant the plaintiffs a preliminary injunction. From the evidence before me, I can say that the plaintiffs have established that the decision to grant the permit was both unfortunate and insensitive. I cannot say that the plaintiffs have established a substantial likelihood of proving that the decision to grant the permit was motivated by purposeful racial discrimination in violation of 42 U.S.C. § 1983. This Court is obligated, as all Courts are, to follow the precedent of the United States Supreme Court and the evidence adduced thus far does not meet the magnitude required by *Arlington Heights, supra.*

The failure of the plaintiffs to obtain a preliminary injunction does not, of course, mean that they are foreclosed from obtaining permanent relief. Because of the time pressures involved, extensive pre-trial discovery was impossible in this case. Assuming the case goes forward, discovery could lead to much more solid and persuasive evidence for either side. Ideally, it would resolve a number of the questions which the Court considers unanswered.

Where, for instance, are the solid waste sites located in each census tract? The plaintiffs produced evidence that in census tract 434, a predominantly Anglo tract, the site was located next to a black community named Riceville. If that was true of most sites in predominantly Anglo census tracts, the outcome of this case would be quite different.

How large an area does a solid waste site affect? If it affects an area a great deal smaller than that of a census tract, it becomes particularly important to know where in each census tract the site is located. If it affects an area larger than that of a census tract, then a target area analysis becomes much more persuasive.

How are solid waste site locations selected? It may be that private contractors consider a number of alternative locations and then select one in consultation with city or county officials. If that is so, it has tremendous implications for the search for discriminatory intent. It may be that a relatively limited number of areas can adequately serve as a Type I solid waste site. If that is so, the placement of sites in those areas becomes a lot less suspicious, even if large numbers of minorities live there. Either way, this is information which should be adduced. At this point, the Court still does not know how, why, and by whom the East Houston-Dyersdale Road location was selected.

What factors entered into TDH's decision to grant the permit? The proximity of the site to Smiley High School and a residential neighborhood and the lack of air conditioning facilities at the former were emphasized to the Court. It is still unknown how much, if any, consideration TDH gave to these factors. The racial composition of the neighborhood and the racial distribution of solid waste sites in Houston were primary concerns of the plaintiffs. It remains unclear to what degree TDH was informed of these concerns.

At this juncture, the decision of TDH seems to have been insensitive and illogical. Sitting as the hearing examiner for TDH, based upon the evidence adduced, this Court would have denied the permit. But this Court has a different role to play, and that is to determine whether the plaintiffs have established a substantial likelihood of proving that TDH's decision to issue the permit was motivated by purposeful discrimination in violation of 42 U.S.C. § 1983 as construed by superior courts. That being so, it is hereby ORDERED, ADJUDGED, and DECREED that the plaintiffs' Motion for a Preliminary Injunction be, and the same is, DENIED. For the reasons stated above, the defendants' Motions to Dismiss are also DENIED.

****

East Bibb Twiggs Neighborhood Association v. Macon-Bibb County Planning & Zoning Commission, 706 F. Supp. 880 (M.D. Georgia 1989), aff'd. 896 F.2d 1264 (11th Cir. 1989)

This case involves allegations that plaintiffs have been deprived of equal protection of the law by the Macon-Bibb County Planning & Zoning Commission ("Commission"). Specifically, plaintiffs allege that the Commission's decision to allow the creation of a private landfill in census tract No. 133.02 was motivated at least in part by considerations of race. Defendants vigorously contest that allegation. Following extensive discovery by the parties, this court conducted a nonjury trial on October 4-5, 1988. . . .

[T]his court is convinced that the Commission's decision to approve the conditional use in question was not motivated by the intent to discriminate against black persons. Regarding the discriminatory impact of the Commission's decision, the court observes the obvious – a decision to approve a landfill in any particular census tract impacts more heavily upon that census tract than upon any other. Since census tract No. 133.02 contains a majority black population equaling roughly 60% of the total population, the decision to approve the landfill in census tract No. 133.02 of necessity impacts greater upon that majority population.

However, the court notes that the only other Commission approved landfill is located within census tract No. 133.01, a census tract containing a majority white population of roughly 76% of the total population. This decision by the Commission and the existence of the landfill in a predominantly white census tract tend to undermine the development of a "clean pattern, unexplainable on grounds other than race . . . ." *Village of Arlington Heights*, 429 U.S. at 266.

Plaintiffs hasten to point out that both census tracts, Nos. 133.01 and 133.02, are located within County Commission District No. 1, a district whose black residents compose roughly 70% of the total population. Based upon the above facts, the court finds that while the Commission's decision to approve the landfill for location in census tract No. 133.02 does of necessity impact to a somewhat larger degree upon the majority population therein, that decision fails to establish a clear pattern of racially motivated decisions.[42]

---

[42] The court further finds it clear that the Commissioner's decision to approve petitioners' application is not a "single invidiously discriminatory act" which makes the establishment of a clear pattern unnecessary. *See Village of Arlington Heights*, 429 U S. at 266 n. 14.

Plaintiffs contend that the Commission's decision to locate the landfill in census tract No. 133.02 must be viewed against an historical background of locating undesirable land uses in black neighborhoods. First, the above discussion regarding the two Commission approved landfills rebuts any contention that such activities are always located in direct proximity to majority black areas. Further, the court notes that the Commission did not and indeed may not actively solicit this or any other landfill application. The Commission reacts to applications from private landowners for permission to use their property in a particular manner. The Commissioners observed during the course of these proceedings the necessity for a comprehensive scheme for the management of waste and for the location of landfills. In that such a scheme has yet to be introduced, the Commission is left to consider each request on its individual merits. In such a situation, this court finds it difficult to understand plaintiffs' contentions that this Commission's decision to approve a landowner's application for a private landfill is part of any pattern to place ''undesirable uses'' in black neighborhoods. Second, a considerable portion of plaintiffs' evidence focused upon governmental decisions made by agencies other than the planning and zoning commission, evidence which sheds little if any light upon the alleged discriminatory intent of the Commission.

Finally, regarding the historical background of the Commission's decision plaintiffs have submitted numerous exhibits consisting of newspaper articles reflecting various zoning decisions made by the Commission. The court has read each article, and it is unable to discern a series of official actions taken by the Commission for invidious purposes. Of the more recent articles, the court notes that in many instances matters under consideration by the Commission attracted widespread attention and vocal opposition. The Commission oft times was responsive to the opposition and refused to permit the particular development under consideration, while on other occasions the Commission permitted the development to proceed in the face of opposition. Neither the articles nor the evidence presented during trial provides factual support for a determination of the underlying motivations, if any, of the Commission in making the decisions. In short, plaintiffs' evidence does not establish a background of discrimination in the Commission's decisions. . . .

For all the foregoing reasons, this court determines that plaintiffs have not been deprived of equal protection of the law. Judgement, therefore, shall be entered for defendants.

****

R.I.S.E. v. Kay, Inc., 768 F. Supp. 1144, 1150 (E.D. Virginia 1991)

At worst, the [County] Supervisors appear to have been more concerned about the economic and legal plight of the County as a whole than the sentiments of residents who opposed the placement of the landfill in their neighborhood. However, the Equal Protection Clause does not impose an affirmative duty to equalize the impact of official decisions on different racial groups. Rather, it merely prohibits government officials from intentionally discriminating on the basis of race. The plaintiffs have not provided sufficient evidence to meet this legal standard.

****

Peter L. Reich, "Greening the Ghetto: A Theory of Environmental Race Discrimination," 41 *University of Kansas Law Review* 271, 291-95, 299, 301-02, 305, 311-12 (1992)

Given the Supreme Court's limited reading of the scope of equal protection, the negative results in the three reported environmental race discrimination cases that were brought with disparate impact evidence are not surprising.

The *Bean* court reached its conclusion despite its liberal construction of the *Arlington Heights* "historical background" factor, in which it admitted evidence of a nonparty agency's past siting decisions on the theory that a current permitting authority should not be allowed to "put its stamp of approval" on any previous discrimination. Significantly, the judge even conceded that plaintiffs had proven the permitting decision to be "insensitive" and "illogical," before stating that she was obligated to uphold it under the intent standard.

The *East Bibb* court read the *Arlington Heights* historical background factor more restrictively than *Bean*, holding that evidence of past decisions by agencies other than the county planning commission was irrelevant to the discrimination issue at hand. Although the court also stated in dicta that the landfill approval did "of necessity impact to a somewhat larger degree" upon the African-American majority in the census tract, this concession did not affect the holding, which was affirmed on appeal.

The most recent of the federal decisions, *R.I.S.E., Inc. v. Kay*, closely followed *Bean* and *East Bibb* in both reasoning and result. In *R.I.S.E.*, a neighborhood organization, Residents Involved in Saving the Environment (R.I.S.E.), opposed a landfill joint venture between a private corporation and a Virginia county. In 1990, the supervisors of King and Queen County, most of whom were white, rezoned a rural, traditionally African-American community for the landfill, which would receive waste from the entire region. The residents filed an equal protection lawsuit to invalidate the county's action, claiming that a racially discriminatory pattern existed because the population within a half-mile radius was sixty-four percent black, the county's three existing landfills were located in ninety to one hundred percent black areas, and the one waste site briefly operated in a white suburb had been shut down.

The federal district court denied relief after a bench trial, citing *Davis*, *Arlington Heights*, and *East Bibb* on the motive requirement. Applying the *Arlington Heights* background factor, the court admitted that the county's past placement of landfills "had a disproportionate impact on black residents." The historical siting pattern was only a "starting point," however, for determining whether an invidious purpose could be inferred; in authorizing the new landfill the county had not acted in an unusual or suspicious manner. The court concluded that there was insufficient evidence of intentional discrimination, and that equal protection did not "impose an affirmative duty to equalize the impact of official decisions on different racial groups."

In all three federal cases reviewed, disparate impact proof of environmental race discrimination has not been adequate to overcome the *Davis* motive requirement. No court has been willing to infer intent from a historical pattern under *Arlington Heights*, although at least two, *Bean* and *R.I.S.E.*, have liberally admitted such evidence. To varying extents, all three courts conceded that disproportionate effects were present, but relief was precluded in the absence of intentional discrimination. Disparate waste siting is a type of injury that, like other racial inequities discussed earlier, is not usually accompanied by evidence of motive. In order to apply the equality principle to the distribution of environmental hazards, an effects rather than an intent standard is necessary.

One possible alternative to constitutional equal protection would be a new federal statute specifically prohibiting racial discrimination in issuing environmental permits and incorporating a disparate impact concept. Such legislation could be patterned after Title VII of the 1964 Civil Rights Act, as amended by the 1991 Civil Rights Act,[43] which imposes an effects test for determining the existence of employment discrimination. The Fair Housing Act of 1968 (FHA),[44] which allows disparate impact proof of discrimination in the sale, rental, or financing of housing, is another potential model. A statute of this type might help plaintiffs in situations similar to those in *Bean*, *East Bibb*, and *R.I.S.E.*, where ample evidence of racially disproportionate environmental effects exists.

Equality guarantees contained in many state constitutions may provide opportunities to remedy environmental racism that are not available under federal equal protection. State constitutional provisions include bars against the denial of equal protection, enumerations of civil rights, prohibitions against special privileges, and guarantees of due process. Many of these provisions have been interpreted more broadly than their federal counterparts. For instance, some state courts apply strict judicial scrutiny to sex-based equal protection claims, while the United States Supreme Court applies intermediate scrutiny to these claims. Furthermore, some states allow an equal protection claim without the state action required by the Fourteenth Amendment. Significantly, a number of state courts have also held that disparate impact alone may be used to prove an equal protection violation. Such precedent offers a means of bypassing the discriminatory intent requirement that precluded relief in the federal environmental race discrimination cases.

The most consistent group of state disparate impact decisions have used equality provisions to invalidate educational financing systems heavily dependent on local property taxes, a structure which resulted in wide funding variations among school districts.

---

[43] 42 U.S.C.A. §§ 2000e-1 to 2000e-17.
[44] 42 U.S.C. §§ 3601-3619.

These courts have held that such spending schemes systematically denied equal education to children in "property-poor" districts, and thus no discriminatory intent was required to declare them unconstitutional.

c. *Title VI of the Civil Rights Act of 1964*

Richard J. Lazarus, "Pursuing 'Environmental Justice': The Distributional Effects of Environmental Protection," 87 Northwestern University Law Review 787, 827-29, 834-36, 839 (1993)

Litigation provides another medium for addressing the distributional issue. Two basic litigation strategies are available. First, an administrative or judicial complaint could be filed on behalf of a minority group for the purpose of preventing the siting of an unwanted facility in its community, and the basis of the lawsuit could be the facility's non-compliance with an applicable environmental statute. The possibility of distributional inequities would not be directly relevant to the substantive merits of the administrative challenge or lawsuit. It would simply be the reason why the lawsuit was necessary and why, for example, a minority community should be entitled to a greater share of enforcement resources. Alternatively, the distributional inequities could provide the substantive basis for the lawsuit by supporting a civil rights cause of action. In other words, the cause of action would itself derive from the fact that a distributional inequity exists.

To date, minority plaintiffs appear to have favored the civil rights approach. However, virtually none of those suits has been successful. This is largely because existing equal protection doctrine, which has been the focal point of most lawsuits has not proved hospitable to the kinds of arguments upon which environmental justice claims have depended. For this reason, federal and state environmental laws may offer the best opportunity for minority plaintiffs to ameliorate environmental inequities. Many of these statutes impose a panoply of procedural and substantive limitations on those wishing to site polluting facilities, and many confer private attorney general status on citizens aggrieved by actions that violate applicable statutory limitations. Plaintiff organizations with the necessary resources have consequently been quite successful in resisting environmentally undesirable facilities under these environmental statutes. To the extent that such legal and technical resources are made available to minority communities, those statutes could likewise provide a basis for considerable relief from distributional inequities.

There is nonetheless substantial reason for continued emphasis on civil rights litigation aimed at redressing distributional inequities in environmental protection. Burdens of proof are difficult to overcome under existing doctrine, but if litigation efforts were to receive additional resources, some isolated successes might be achievable. In addition, the cases brought so far have relied on only a few legal theories. Several promising theories have not yet been fully explored and warrant greater attention.

Perhaps more importantly, the real value of these lawsuits extends beyond their ability to obtain a favorable decision in a given case. Indeed, the symbolic value of filing the lawsuit is itself substantial. The mere filing of a formal complaint provides a very powerful and visible statement by minorities regarding their belief that distributional inequities exist in environmental protection. The publicity that frequently surrounds the complaint's filing enhances public awareness of these concerns and thereby serves an important educational function. Should, moreover, a victory on the merits be achieved, the benefits could be tremendous. For many within the minority community it is extremely important that a formal judicial decision be obtained confirming their belief that environmental protection presents its own unique civil rights issues.

One option not yet well explored by civil rights plaintiffs in the environmental context is Title VI of the Civil Rights Act of 1964. Title VI provides that: "No person in the United States shall, on the ground of race, color, or national origin, be excluded from participation in, be denied the benefits of, or be subjected to discrimination under any program or activity receiving Federal financial assistance."

The principal advantage of Title VI over equal protection is that courts have not required a showing of discriminatory intent in the Title VI context; disparate impact has been enough. Hence, in *Lau v. Nichols*[45], where non-English-speaking Chinese students had allegedly been deprived of equal educational opportunities, the Supreme Court concluded that Title VI had been violated because of the discriminatory effect of the challenged school policies "even though no purposeful design is present." Although the Court's subsequent ruling in *Regents of University of California v. Bakke*[46] casts some doubt on the continuing validity of this aspect of *Lau*, the Court later reaffirmed, in *Guardians Ass'n v. Civil Service Commission*[47], that discriminatory intent is not required under Title VI where that had been the view historically endorsed by applicable federal agency regulations implementing the statutory mandate. Notably, EPA's Title VI regulations embrace a discriminatory *effects* test.[48] It is also well settled that Title VI provides an implied private right of action on behalf of individuals who have suffered discrimination deemed unlawful by Title VI.

There are, however, two limitations to Title VI. Although each is significant, Title VI's reach in the environmental protection arena remains potentially great. The first limitation is that Title VI's nondiscrimination mandate applies only to "any program or activity receiving Federal financial assistance." Thus, while covering all federal agency activities, nonfederal actions are within Title VI's mandate only when a sufficient federal financial nexus can be established. Federal financial assistance for environmental protection is extensive, however, particularly assistance to state governments. Virtually

---

[45] 414 U.S. 563 (1974).
[46] 438 U.S. 265 (1978).
[47] 463 U.S. 582, 584 & n.2 (1983), *cert. denied*, 463 U.S. 1228 (1983).
[48] 40 C.F.R. sec. 7.35.

all federal environmental laws, including those dealing with hazardous waste, toxic substances, water pollution control, and clean air provide funding to state programs. These state programs make many of the decisions that, when not initiated by the federal government, effectively determine the distribution of benefits and burdens from environmental protection at the state and local level. In 1986, for example, federal grants to state governments made up forty-six, thirty-three, and forty percent of the state budgets for air, water, and hazardous waste programs, respectively. Given this significant federal financial assistance to state environmental programs, the potential reach of Title VI is correspondingly great.

The second Title VI limitation is remedial in nature. Until recently, it appeared fairly well settled that in the absence of a showing of discriminatory intent, equitable relief was the only remedy available to redress a Title VI violation. [H]owever, the U.S. Supreme court unanimously ruled, in *Franklin v. Gwinnett County Public Schools*,[49] that a damages remedy is available in implied private rights of actions brought under Title IX of the Education Act Amendments of 1972. Because the language of Title IX was expressly modeled after Title VI of the Civil Rights Act, and because the court has frequently relied on constructions of one in interpreting the other, it would seem fair to assume that a damages remedy is now generally available for Title VI violations, even absent a showing of discriminatory intent.

To date, however, there has been very little reliance on Title VI in any of the litigated cases. EPA has likewise not exploited its Title VI responsibilities as it could to redress distributional inequities.[50] There are a host of ways that EPA could implement Title VI's nondiscrimination mandate in the agency's disbursement of federal pollution control funds. A relatively modest measure would be for EPA to require the recipient of the funds to make a showing that the funds are being disbursed according to racially neutral criteria. A more aggressive approach would be to require a further showing that racial minority groups are proportionately represented among the ultimate beneficiaries of the federal funds. Such a showing could include proof that the "neutral" distribution of federal funds in no manner perpetuated the vestiges of past racial discrimination within the relevant community. For instance, in the case of a federally funded wastewater treatment facility, EPA would need to be satisfied that the community's sewage treatment program provides service to minority communities (e.g., connections to sewage treatment plants) equal to that provided to nonminority communities in the affected area.

Indeed, there is Title VI precedent virtually on point that has largely been ignored by those bringing environmental justice claims. These are cases where minority plaintiffs have invoked Title VI to redress distributional inequities associated with the availability of environmental amenities or quality resources, such as public parks and water quality

---

[49] 112 S. Ct. 1028 (1992).

[50] [Ed.] Consider whether the Executive Order presented in Chapter 7(D), *infra*, may put EPA in a more active role relative to Title VI.

treatment facilities. Courts have upheld Title VI challenges to these federally financed programs based on their racially disparate effects.[51]

In sum, Title VI provides a possible basis for civil rights litigation to redress environmental inequities and is an approach that warrants greater emphasis and attention. Most importantly, by using Title VI as a vehicle for these suits, the bugaboo of proving discriminatory intent can be avoided. And, while Title VI's federal financial assistance requirement is not insignificant, the fact that states receive so much of their environmental budgets from the federal government suggests that that limitation may not be much more practically significant than equal protection's threshold requirements that there be "state action." Finally, courts may be more willing to grant relief under Title VI than under equal protection because the focus of the lawsuit is, at least superficially, the provision of governmental benefits as opposed to the redistribution of environmental risks. To that extent, a Title VI lawsuit is more analogous to equal protection challenges concerning provision of municipal services (which have fared substantially better in federal courts) than to those suits which more overtly seek a judicial redistribution of "harmful" environmental risks.

****

Notes

1. On July 14, 1994 the Attorney General of the United States sent to all agencies that provide federal financial assistance a Memorandum concerning the "use of the disparate impact standard in administrative regulations under Title VI." She "reminded" agencies that their Title VI regulations "apply not only to intentional discrimination but also to policies and practices that have a discriminatory *effect*," and she emphasized the Clinton Administration's intention to enforce disparate impact provisions vigorously.[52] As the materials in the next part of this Chapter indicate, this same intention was earlier expressed with particular reference to federal financial assistance to environmental and health programs.

2. One of the first attempts to rely upon Title VI with respect to disproportionate environmental burdens of project siting was the complaint filed in March 1993 in *Clean Air Alternative Coalition, Inc. v. U.S. Department of Transportation* (Case No. C 93

---

[51] *See, e.g., Johnson v. City of Arcadia*, 450 F. Supp. 1363 (M.D. Fla. 1978) (black neighborhoods not being provided with same level of municipal services as white neighborhoods). [S]imilarly based equal protection claims have been successfully advanced.

[Ed.] *See also Ammons v. Dade City, Florida*, 783 F.2d 982 (11th Cir. 1986) (constitutional violation proven through intentional racial discrimination in provision of municipal services such as street paving and storm water drainage facilities).

[52] For further analysis of the Title VI approach, *see* James H. Colopy, "The Road Less Traveled: Pursuing Environmental Justice Through Title VI of the Civil Rights Act of 1964," 13 Stanford Environmental Law Journal 125 (1994); Alice L. Brown, "Environmental Justice: New Civil Rights Frontier," Trial, Volume 29, No. 7, at 48 (July 1993).

0721 VRW, N.D. California). The case, which ultimately was settled, concerned the rebuilding in Oakland, California of a freeway segment that had been destroyed during the 1989 Loma Prieta earthquake. Plaintiffs alleged that the proposed rebuilding route would run though a predominantly minority community, with disastrous consequences in terms of damage to residences and businesses, and demolition of historic properties and cultural landmarks. They also alleged that the project would "endanger the health of residents in this minority community, already at a high risk for a variety of health problems, by subjecting them to continuous exposure to freeway noise and emissions of carbon monoxide, particulates, benzene, and other toxins."

Although plaintiffs relied upon a variety of alleged environmental violations, their first cause of action was based upon Title VI and implementing regulations under the Federal Highway Act. The following allegations were included in Paragraphs 67 and 68 of the complaint:

The Proposed Project will have a racially disproportionate adverse impact on members of racial minority groups. The purported justifications for this discriminatory effect are inadequate. Alternative freeway alignments exist which will eliminate or sharply reduce negative impacts associated with the Proposed Project. These alternatives were identified and presented to defendants early in the planning process, but were rejected without adequate cause. These freeway alignments are less discriminatory alternatives.

In addition, federal and state defendants have treated the severely impacted West Oakland minority residents' neighborhood less favorably than other areas by failing to consider alternative freeway alignments, while deferring to opposition from the Port of Oakland and business entities located in the Port area. As a result, defendants have subjected minority residents to discrimination because of disparate treatment.

What types of evidence are suggested in these allegations as being necessary in order for plaintiffs to prevail on this civil rights claim? What other types of evidence would you advise plaintiffs to attempt to present as well? Would these Title VI plaintiffs have to offer the type of detailed demographic analysis of different neighborhoods presented in equal protection cases such as *Bean* and *East Bibb*?

D. Presidential and Congressional Responses

Executive Order 12898, "Federal Actions To Address Environmental Justice in Minority Populations and Low-Income Populations," February 11, 1994

By the authority vested in me as President by the Constitution and the laws of the United States of America, it is hereby ordered as follows:

Section 1-101. To the greatest extent practicable and permitted by law, and consistent with the principles set forth in the report on the National Performance Review, each

Federal agency shall make achieving environmental justice part of its mission by identifying and addressing, as appropriate, disproportionately high and adverse human health or environmental effects of its programs, policies, and activities on minority populations and low-income populations in the United States and its territories and possessions, the District of Columbia, the Commonwealth of Puerto Rico, and the Commonwealth of the Mariana Islands.

Section 1-102(a). Within 3 months of the date of this order, the Administrator of the Environmental Protection Agency or the Administrator's designee shall convene an interagency Federal Working Group on Environmental Justice ("Working Group").

Section 1-103(a). [E]ach Federal agency shall develop an agency-wide environmental justice strategy . . . that identifies and addresses disproportionately high and adverse human health or environmental effects of its programs, policies, and activities on minority populations and low-income populations. The environmental justice strategy shall list programs, policies, planning and public participation processes, enforcement, and/ or rulemakings related to human health or the environment that should be revised to, at a minimum: (1) promote enforcement of all health and environmental statutes in areas with minority populations and low-income populations; (2) ensure greater public participation; (3) improve research and data collection relating to the health of and environment of minority populations and low-income populations; and (4) identify differential patterns of consumption of natural resources among minority populations and low-income populations. *Section 1-103(e).* Within 12 months of the date of this order, each Federal agency shall finalize its environmental justice strategy and provide a copy and written description of its strategy to the Working Group.

Section 2-2. Each Federal agency shall conduct its programs, policies, and activities that substantially affect human health or the environment, in a manner that ensures that such programs, policies, and activities do not have the effect of excluding persons (including populations) from participation in, denying persons (including populations) the benefits of, or subjecting persons (including populations) to discrimination under, such programs, policies, and activities, because of their race, color, or national origin.

Section 3-301(a). Environmental human health research, whenever practicable and appropriate, shall include diverse segments of the population in epidemiological and clinical studies, including segments at high risk from environmental hazards, such as minority populations, low-income populations and workers who may be exposed to substantial environmental hazards.

Section 5-5(b). Each Federal agency may, whenever practicable and appropriate, translate crucial public documents, notices, and hearings relating to human health or the environment for limited English speaking populations.

Section 6-606. Each Federal agency responsibility set forth under this order shall apply equally to Native American programs. In addition, the Department of the Interior, in coordination with the Working Group, and, after consultation with tribal leaders, shall coordinate steps to be taken pursuant to this order that address Federally-recognized Indian Tribes.

Section 6-607. Unless otherwise provided by law, Federal agencies shall assume the financial costs of complying with this order.

****

President William J. Clinton, "Memorandum on Environmental Justice," February 11, 1994

Today I have issued an Executive Order on Federal Actions to Address Environmental Justice in Minority Populations and Low-Income Populations. That order is designed to focus Federal attention on the environmental and human health conditions in minority communities and low-income communities with the goal of achieving environmental justice. That order is also intended to promote nondiscrimination in Federal programs substantially affecting human health and the environment, and to provide minority communities and low-income communities access to public information on, and an opportunity for public participation in, matters relating to human health or the environment.

The purpose of this separate memorandum is to underscore certain provisions of existing law that can help ensure that all communities and persons across this Nation live in a safe and healthful environment. Environmental and civil rights statutes provide many opportunities to address environmental hazards in minority communities and low-income communities. Application of these existing statutory provisions is an important part of this Administration's efforts to prevent those minority communities and low-income communities from being subject to disproportionately high and adverse environmental effects.

I am therefore today directing that all department and agency heads take appropriate and necessary steps to ensure that the following specific directives are implemented immediately:

In accordance with Title VI of the Civil Rights Act of 1964, each Federal agency shall ensure that all programs or activities receiving Federal financial assistance that affect human health or the environment do not directly, or through contractual or other arrangements, use criteria, methods, or other arrangements that discriminate on the basis of race, color, or national origin.

Each Federal agency shall analyze the environmental effects, including human health, economic and social effects, of Federal actions, including effects on minority communities and low-income communities, when such analysis is required by the National Environmental Policy Act of 1969. Mitigation measures outlined or analyzed in an environmental assessment, environmental impact statement, or record of decision, whenever feasible, should address significant and adverse environmental effects of proposed Federal actions on minority communities and low-income communities.

Each Federal agency shall provide opportunities for community input in the NEPA process, including identifying potential effects and mitigation measures in consultation with affected communities and improving the accessibility of meetings, crucial documents, and notices.

The Environmental Protection Agency, when reviewing environmental effects of proposed action of other Federal agencies under section 309 of the Clean Air Act, 42 U.S.C. section 7609, shall ensure that the involved agency has fully analyzed environmental effects on minority communities and low-income communities, including human health, social, and economic effects.

Each Federal agency shall ensure that the public, including minority communities and low-income communities, has adequate access to public information relating to human health or environmental planning, regulations, and enforcement when required under the Freedom of Information Act, 5 U.S.C. section 552, the Sunshine Act, 5 U.S.C. section 552b, and the Emergency Planning and Community Right-to-Know Act, 42 U.S.C. section 11044.

This memorandum is intended only to improve the internal management of the Executive Branch and is not intended to nor does it create, any right, benefit, or trust responsibility, substantive or procedural, enforceable at law or equity by a party against the United States, its agencies, its officers, or any person.

****

David Schoenbrod, "Environmental 'Injustice' is About Politics, Not Racism," The Wall Street Journal, February 23, 1994, p. A21

In response to complaints that minority communities suffer disproportionately from environmental hazards, President Clinton has ordered the Environmental Protection Agency and other federal agencies to stop inflicting "environmental injustice." . . .

But the very existence of "environmental injustice" is far from clear. Although minority communities have a disproportionate share of environmental problems, research suggests that the cause is not necessarily racial discrimination. . . .

Against this complex reality, Mr. Clinton's command that agencies avoid "disproportionately high and adverse. . .effects on minority populations and low-income populations" is nothing but fluff.

Suppose that the EPA determines that XYZ Corp.'s proposed incinerator would produce a risk to health sufficiently low to meet generally applicable health standards. Under the executive order, people living near the proposed site could nonetheless object that they would suffer a disproportionate impact because other areas have lower air pollution levels. The order does not tell the agencies how to decide whether a pollution differential is large enough to be disproportionate. Nor does it make clear whether lower environmental quality in poor areas is disproportionate if caused by market forces, which are the chief source of such differentials.

Most people would oppose using income to determine who gets exposed to high risks, but not to low risks or aesthetic problems. After all, our market system allows the wealthy to buy healthier foods and nicer homes. Under modern environmental laws, agency actions typically do not cause high risks. So, to what extent must agencies, in gauging disproportionate impact under Mr. Clinton's order, chuck the market system that he, in other contexts, applauds? Does Mr. Clinton's order mean that nothing can be sited in areas that are not rich and white until every rich, white suburb gets a pro-rata equal share of environmental problems?

Whether an environmental risk is disproportionate is a question that cannot be answered by science or legal criteria and so must be answered by politics. Instead of addressing that question forthrightly, our political leaders once again try to shift the blame to agencies, raising expectations that are destined to be dashed. . . .

The point is that because charges of environmental injustice often originate in [regulatory] actions of legislators and the president, they are disingenuous in making agencies the scapegoat.

The procedures that political leaders use to shift the blame to the agencies may well do more harm than good. Every agency and department must within 12 months develop a strategy that makes environmental justice a part of its decision-making in every aspect of its operations. This applies not only to licensing, but also to federal grants, facilities, rule-making and enforcement. Examples include environmental impact statements under the National Environmental Policy Act and records of decision under the Superfund toxic cleanup program, to name just two. The race-conscious decision-making mandated by the order will open agencies to lawsuits under the Civil Rights Act, which the order interprets as applicable to them.

The red tape and litigation will significantly delay many environmental decisions and increase the cost to agencies of making them. The ultimate losers will be the corporations and state and local governments that seek federal decisions and the communities, especially the minority communities, that want agencies to speed up the cleanup of toxic wastes. The costs will be particularly heavy for the EPA, on which Congress and the president already have heaped duties far in excess of what it can accomplish with the resources they have appropriated. The fine print of Mr. Clinton's order says "Federal agencies shall assume the financial costs of complying with this order."

The costs and delay might be worthwhile if the executive order made environmental programs more just. But the order presents only the illusion of justice, which may well suffice to deflect the blame to the agencies at least until after the next presidential election.

****

Notes

1. If you were Administrator of the Environmental Protection Agency, what would be your response to Schoenbrod's criticism of the Executive Order? If you are prepared to admit that any of his objections are valid, what steps could you take, or urge other federal agencies to take, in order to respond to them?

2. As of August 1994, a working draft of the EPA's own "Outline of Proposed Environmental Justice Strategy" listed a range of general and specific projects to be

undertaken in response to the Executive Order.[53] Among other areas of activity, the draft addressed enforcement, inspections, and compliance as follows:

> EPA will give prominent attention to environmental justice issues through compliance analysis and targeted data analysis of communities exposed to multiple environmental risks, enforcement initiatives, Title VI implementation, and review and enforcement of other federal agencies' proposals under the National Environmental Policy Act and Section 309 of the Clean Air Act.

From the perspective of a potential target of EPA enforcement, and bearing in mind the considerations discussed in Chapter 4, *supra*, with respect to fairness in the selection of enforcement targets, what concerns might be raised by this new emphasis in Agency policy?

The draft also declares the EPA's intention to ''make sure environmental justice is part of all the Agency's programs, policies, and activities including those Agency programs authorized/delegated to the States.'' Presumably the Agency's efforts to give effect to this intention would have impacts on permitting and other siting-related functions of both EPA and the states under many of the federal environmental statutes, including the Clean Air Act and RCRA.

3. If the President were to ask you to fill in a notable gap in the Executive Order, the absence of any definition of ''environmental justice,'' what definition would you offer?[54]

4. As of the end of 1994, and despite the introduction of many environmental justice bills over the past few years,[55] Congress had not adopted any such legislation. What can you identify as some of the major legal and political obstacles to enactment of Congressional legislation to address siting inequities? Is the promulgation of the Presidential Executive Order a sufficient federal response to the concerns of the environmental justice movement regarding siting and enforcement policies, so that the need for Congressional action is now greatly diminished or eliminated?

5. If you were to attempt to draft the principal components of a federal law addressing environmental injustice in siting, what would they be? Some of the elements of recent legislative proposals may be worth considering for inclusion in your draft.[56] For example, the proposed Environmental Equal Rights Act (H.R. 1924, 103rd Congress, 1st

---

[53] The public availability of EPA's January 1995 Draft, and of other federal agencies' drafts, was announced by the Working Group at 60 Fed. Reg. 6710 (Feb. 3, 1995).

[54] For one EPA definition of the term, *see* 59 Fed. Reg. 50757 (Oct. 5, 1994) (''fair treatment of people of all races, cultures; and income with respect to . . . environmental laws, regulations, and policies. [N]o . . . group should bear a disproportionate share of . . . negative environmental consequences. . . .'')

[55] As of February 1994, one commentary noted ''at least nine bills before Congress'' with ''environmental-justice related provisions.'' Steven Keeva, ''A Breath of Justice,'' ABA Journal, Volume 80, February 1994, at 88.

[56] *See also* Vicki Been, ''Conceptions of Fairness in Proposals for Facility Siting,'' 5 Maryland Journal of Contemporary Legal Issues 13 (1993) (''Five major legislativestrategies for preventing discriminatory siting of various kinds of LULUs either have been adopted by state or local governments, or proposed for federal legislation.'').

Session) sought to identify "environmentally disadvantaged" communities and to disallow the permitting under RCRA of a waste facility in such an area if health or environmental quality in the community would be threatened.[57] The proposed Environmental Justice Act (H.R. 2105, 103rd Congress, 1st Session) would have prevented the permitting of "toxic chemical facilities," under a variety of federal statutes, in the 100 counties most seriously qualifying as "environmental high impact areas."[58] That bill also would have allowed under certain circumstances for the imposition of "a moratorium on the siting or permitting [in any EHIA] of any new toxic chemical facility . . . shown to emit toxic chemicals in quantities found to cause significant adverse impacts on human health."

In contrast, one commentator has emphasized that siting "is essentially a state and local government land use problem," although the NIMBY syndrome has become a pervasive, national problem. Orlando E. Delogu, "'NIMBY' is a National Environmental Problem," 35 South Dakota Law Review 198, 209 (1990). Professor Delogu suggests a more modest federal approach, i.e., "federal legislation that does not itself attempt to find sites or locate facilities, but unequivocally requires each state (and through the states, local levels of government) to fashion mechanisms that will provide needed sites, locational alternatives, for a carefully defined but fairly wide range of socially or environmentally necessary activities and facilities now caught in the NIMBY syndrome." His proposal also would incorporate requirements aimed at "the widest possible geographic distribution of NIMBY-type activities." *Id.* at 216.

****

---

[57] Professor Been analyzed this bill as adopting a corrective justice rationale for a progressive siting approach. Vicki Been, "What's Fairness Got To Do With It? Environmental Justice and the Siting of Locally Undesirable Land Uses," 78 Cornell Law Review 1001, 1084 (1993).

[58] "Rawls' 'difference principle,' . . . would allocate social goods so as to result in the greatest benefit (or least burden) to the least advantaged social classes. Recent legislation, such as the proposed Environmental Justice Act of 1992, also echoes this model of justice and Rawls' difference principle. That Act would limit further siting of toxic chemical facilities in environmental high impact areas if it is shown that adverse human health consequences have resulted from the level of toxic emissions in those areas as compared to other areas." Sheila Foster, "Race(ial) Matters: The Quest for Environmental Justice," 20 Ecology Law Quarterly 721, 747 (1993).